W9-DDO-890

Inspiring WOMEN

Pergamon Titles of Related Interest

McNaron THE SISTER BOND
Christian BLACK FEMINIST CRITICISM
Newman MEN'S IDEAS/WOMEN'S REALITIES

Related Journals

(Free sample copies available upon request)

WOMEN'S STUDIES INTERNATIONAL FORUM

---

the ATHENE series

General Editors
Gloria Bowles
Renate D. Klein

Consulting Editor
Dale Spender

The ATHENE series assumes that all those who are concerned with formulating explanations of the way the world works need to know and appreciate the significance of basic feminist principles.

The growth of feminist research has challenged almost all aspects of social organization in our culture. The ATHENE series focuses on the construction of knowledge and the exclusion of women from the process—both as theorists and subjects of study—and offers innovative studies that challenge established theories and research.

ON ATHENE—When Metis, goddess of wisdom who presided over all knowledge was pregnant with ATHENE, she was swallowed up by Zeus who then gave birth to ATHENE from his head. The original ATHENE is thus the parthenogenetic daughter of a strong mother and as the feminist myth goes, at the "third birth" of ATHENE she stops being Zeus' obedient mouthpiece and returns to her real source: the science and wisdom of womankind.

Inspiring Women

Reimagining the Muse

Mary K. DeShazer
Xavier University, Cincinnati

New York • Oxford • Beijing • Frankfurt
São Paulo • Sydney • Tokyo • Toronto

Pergamon Press Offices:

U.S.A.	Pergamon Press, Maxwell House, Fairview Park, Elmsford, New York 10523, U.S.A.
U.K.	Pergamon Press, Headington Hill Hall, Oxford OX3 0BW, England
PEOPLE'S REPUBLIC OF CHINA	Pergamon Press, Qianmen Hotel, Beijing, People's Republic of China
FEDERAL REPUBLIC OF GERMANY	Pergamon Press, Hammerweg 6, D-6242 Kronberg, Federal Republic of Germany
BRAZIL	Pergamon Editora, Rua Eça de Queiros, 346, CEP 04011, São Paulo, Brazil
AUSTRALIA	Pergamon Press (Aust.) Pty., P.O. Box 544, Potts Point, NSW 2011, Australia
JAPAN	Pergamon Press, 8th Floor, Matsuoka Central Building, 1-7-1 Nishishinjuku, Shinjuku-ku, Tokyo 160, Japan
CANADA	Pergamon Press Canada, Suite 104, 150 Consumers Road, Willowdale, Ontario M2J 1P9, Canada

---

First printing 1986

Library of Congress Cataloging in Publication Data

DeShazer, Mary K.
Inspiring women.

(The Athene series ;)
1. Women poets, American--20th century--Biography.
2. Creation (Literary, artistic, etc.) 3. American poetry--Women authors--History and criticism.
4. American poetry--20th century--History and criticism.
I. Title. II. Series.
PS151.D47 1986 811′.5′099287 86-15080
ISBN 0-08-034475-5
ISBN 0-08-034474-7 (pbk.)

Printed in the United States of America

For Marilyn, with gratitude

Contents

Foreword

The contemporary women's movement must be credited with creating an appetite and awakening hungers for information on women's status and contributions. The information unearthed so far has alerted us to the practical aspects of denial and prejudice: the disparity of salaries between the sexes, the paucity of job openings for women in the corporate upper echelon, and the horrific escalation of crimes against women. We have needed to have those dire facts and will want to have them elucidated time and again in order to eliminate injustice and take our fair share in the balanced human dream.

We have also needed, often without being aware of our need, an insight into our mysterious poetic selves. We have needed to enter into the realm of creativity/destruction where our goddess-muse selves dwell, into that queendom, sacred, and so sweet that we are often ignorant of its very existence.

This welcome book shines a bright beam on the landscape of women's poetic observations, analysis, and subsequent writing. There is a disquieting irony in the fact that with this illumination we are now able to see how drastically the landscape has been denuded.

With DeShazer's keen eye, we see the female poet personae, wrestling for years with issues formerly considered as masculine on the penile thrust of skyscrapers. She lifts the veiled entrance, beckoning us to follow her into caverns of the female-poet-self where we can search for identification, healing, and rejuvenation. Her choice of poets is inspired. We meet, through DeShazer's generous work and intelligence, the poetic courage of May Sarton, the transcendent poetry of H.D., the aesthetic conflicts of Louise Bogan, the conscious and unconscious poetic honesty of Adrienne Rich, the combustible and insouciant poetry of Audre Lorde.

DeShazer, by enlarging the entrance to the goddess shrine, increases every woman's possibility. At no time does she suggest that we should genuflect or humble ourselves to the muse goddess. Rather, this work frees us to stand even more erect, more confident, more divine, and more female.

Dr. Maya Angelou
May 1986

Preface

This book explores ways in which modern women writers have re-visioned creativity and the creative process. Rejecting the traditional male pattern of reliance on a classical female "Other" for imaginative sustenance, these women have struggled to define their artistic identities, their sources and resources of inspiration, on their own terms. Rather than invoking that passive inspirer whom Milton deems "Heav'nly Muse" and Robert Graves calls "sister of the mirage and echo," modern women claim as muses powerful, active women through whom they find voice. These inspirational figures may be goddesses or mythological forces; literary foremothers or feminist cocreators; women from their own lives—mothers, lovers, one or many sisters; aspects of their own psyches. Like the prepatriarchal goddess Athene, for whom this series is aptly named, writing women have refused to be obedient mouthpieces of male culture and literary convention. Instead, they have delved into what Adrienne Rich has called "the cratered night of female memory" to touch their true matrix: the wisdom of womankind.

It may seem strange in this postmodernist age to be speaking of the muse, that apparently antiquated notion, but as we shall see, modern poets, women and men, continue to write about "the muse" as a central part of their creative endeavors. For men, interaction with the muse often seems a straightforward business: she comes, she unleashes genius, she goes her way. For women seeking a strong artistic identity, however, naming a muse of their own can be problematic. At times, women view this female force with ambivalence: she may evoke anger or awe, be overpowering, even annihilating. But more often, creative women confront their ambivalent responses and ultimately celebrate the women who, literally or figuratively, nurture and sustain their art.

Chapter 1, therefore, examines the tradition of the muse in literature by men from the Greeks to the present, and analyzes modern women's diverse and potent ways of reimagining her. Why have women needed a muse? How do their sources of inspiration differ from the conventional models? Why do they seldom turn to a male inspirer, as several nineteenth-century poets—notably Emily Dickinson and Emily Brontë—sometimes tried to do? What patterns of invoking a female muse can we discern in modern women's poetry? My methodology, in this chapter and throughout, is both descriptive and theoretical: I rely extensively on the poets' own words—and glorious words they often are—as a means of exploring how and why women have undertaken this multifaceted project of creative re-vision.

The five poets discussed in the following chapters—Louise Bogan, H.D., May Sarton, Adrienne Rich, and Audre Lorde—are representative of the efforts of many writers, especially in modern America, to "bring women to writing" by naming and celebrating a powerful female muse, a mother-goddess-sister-self. Of these five, Bogan displays the strongest conflict in grappling with her roles as woman and artist, perhaps because she is neither lesbian nor what contemporary feminists call "woman-identified." Her search for poetic identity is fraught with ambivalence: she fears her creative power, deems herself inadequate, and dissociates herself from "female songbirds" of her time. Yet she also proclaims the efficacy of women's poetic legacy and vision—in her essay "The Heart and the Lyre" and in her poems invoking dream women, goddesses, and Furies. Her contemporary, H.D., displays some of Bogan's artistic insecurity, particularly in her literary and personal relationships to men writing in the modernist period: Richard Aldington, to whom she was married, Ezra Pound, and D. H. Lawrence. Yet she gleans power by reimagining a variety of mythological women in her early lyric poems: Eurydice, Artemis, Aphrodite, to name a few. In longer "epic" works, like *Trilogy* and *Helen in Egypt*, H.D. invokes a potent mother-muse as "Our Lady" from Christian mythology, Isis from Egyptian lore, or the "Sage Femme" who inspires the poet in her old age. Frequently she pays homage to the women in her life who sustained her: her mother, Helen Wolle Doolittle, and her lifetime companion, Bryher (Winifred Ellerman).

The three contemporary poets are vocal on the subject of female creative identity. May Sarton speaks often of the crucial relationship between woman poet and female muse—in *Mrs. Stevens Hears the Mermaids Singing*, in numerous interviews, and in poems that portray the muse as Medusa, Aphrodite, and Kali, among other goddesses. For Sarton, interaction with a female muse is central to the artistic woman's quest for wholeness. Adrienne Rich, in contrast, sees the word *muse* as a patriarchal construct to be rejected along with terms like *humanism* and *androgyny*. Yet she renounces the passive, idealized metaphor in order to re-vision her source of inspiration as "my self . . . my selves," the woman poet in lesbian-feminist communion and community with women too like her to be Other. Audre Lorde also invokes a communal female muse, as she speaks of and for those women who cannot find voice, and especially for women of color. In addition, she celebrates as muses African goddesses by whom all struggling women are empowered: the Dahomean queen Mawulisa; her counterpart Seboulisa, "the mother of us all"; her sister Amazons of Dan.

The last chapter assesses these five poets as inspiring women for one another, sisters woven in a complex web of creative reciprocity. Louise Bogan served as an often rigorous muse and mentor for May Sarton; H.D.'s woman-centered poems inspirited Adrienne Rich; Rich and Audre Lorde offer a feminist model of literary interdependence. Such affiliations give credence to Rich's assertion that writers today are exploring "a whole new psychic geography" of women's creativity, beyond the borders of patriarchal space.

Like most writers of books about women, I owe thanks to numerous muses and mentors of my own. I am especially grateful to Marilyn Farwell, whose keen understanding of feminist poetics and whose exemplary teaching and friendship have made possible my own work in women's poetry. I am also deeply indebted to my dear friend Anita Helle for "hearing me into speech" again and again; to my frequent travel companion, Susan Carlson, for rich desserts and dialogue; and to my spirit-sisters, Catherine Keller, Lynda Hart, and Leslie Thrope, for constant and loving encouragement.

For feminist friendship throughout this project, I want to express appreciation to Inzer Byers, Cynthia Caywood, Anne Leonard, Ozzie Mayers, Patti Patridge, Ellen Peel, Carol Rainey, and Judith White. For emotional and practical support over many years, I thank Roger Chickering and Alan and Sandra Bryant. Elaine Singleton has deepened my awareness of what it means to be woman-centered. And I am grateful to my parents, Marian and Henry DeShazer, and to other members of my family for their faith in me and their many gifts.

I also owe much to the universities and colleagues whose support has allowed this project to reach completion. I thank Dorothy and William McMahon of Western Kentucky University for helping me find delight in poetry. The English Department at the University of Oregon, especially then Chairman George Wickes, provided resources during the book's early stages. At Wake Forest University, the aid of Dean Thomas Mullen and Provost Edwin Wilson, as well as a Summer Faculty Grant awarded me by the Graduate Council, assisted significantly in manuscript preparation. For their loyalty and enthusiastic responses to my work, I am most grateful to my English Department colleagues at Wake Forest: Nancy Cotton, Andrew Ettin, Gillian Overing, Dolly McPherson, Elizabeth Phillips, and Robert Shorter. At Xavier University, I wish to thank Dean Charles Cusick and former Academic Vice President John Minahan for a Faculty Development Grant and other financial aid during my final stages of writing. And I greatly appreciate the collegiality and support of the members of Xavier's English Department, especially Ernest Fontana, who believed strongly enough in Women's Studies to hire me, and John Getz, who suggested the title of this book.

The work of other feminists—literary critics, writers, and editors—has been crucial to my own ideas and writing. The insights of Joanne Feit Diehl, Rachel Blau DuPlessis, Susan Stanford Friedman, Sandra M. Gilbert, Susan Gubar, Margaret Homans, Audre Lorde, Alicia Ostriker, and Adrienne Rich have inspired me; I cannot imagine my feminist theories finding articulation without the guiding spirit of theirs. For valuable readings of my book-in-progress,

I thank Gloria Bowles, Suzanne Comer, Diane Middlebrook, and Alicia Ostriker. May Sarton has been a kind friend and loyal supporter, and for her art and example I am grateful. I am also deeply indebted to Maya Angelou for her illuminating work and her generosity of spirit in offering to write the Foreword to this book.

Finally, I want to express gratitude to my manuscript typists, Connie Tekulve and Eunice Staples, and to my editors at Pergamon: Gloria Bowles and Renate Duelli-Klein, who coedit the Athene series, Sarah Biondello, and Lynn Rosen. To Gloria goes a special word of appreciation for her many efforts on my behalf.

All of these people have contributed to this book; none of them, of course, is responsible for its shortcomings. As for the "inspiring women" whose words inform these pages, I can hope only that my work brings to other women a bit of the energy their writings have given me.

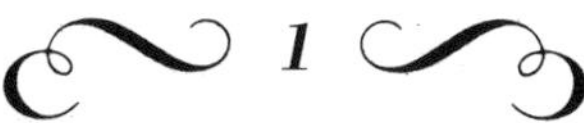

"A Whole New Psychic Geography": Women Poets and Creative Identity

All saints revile her, and all sober men
Ruled by the God Apollo's golden mean—
In scorn of which I sailed to find her
In distant regions likeliest to hold her
Whom I desired above all things to know,
Sister of the mirage and echo.

—Robert Graves, *The White Goddess*

If [women] continue to speak the same language to each other, we will reproduce the same story. Begin the same stories all over again. . . . If we continue to speak this sameness, if we speak to each other as men have spoken for centuries, as they taught us to speak, we will fail each other.

—Luce Irigaray, "When Our Lips Speak Together"

It's been said, we are of one mind.
It's been said, she is happy whom
we, of the muses, love.

Spiral Mountain: the cabin
full of our tools: guitar, tapedeck, video
every night

stars we can cast the dice by. We are
of one mind, tuning
our instruments to ourselves, by our triple light.

—Olga Broumas, "Triple Muse"[1]

For Robert Graves, the male poet's central quest is for the "white goddess," the quintessential source of poetry, the muse whom poets through the ages have invoked and by whose inspiration they have created their works of art. As the Jungian analyst Maud Bodkin suggests, the idea of the muse conjures a vision "of the poet who sings, not alone, but inspired by the song of another—a female figure for whose origin we must go far back in the history of the poetic imagination."[2] This female figure has been described as the male poet's "inspiring anima," who "in her character of shaman, sibyl, priestess, and wise woman, has influenced mankind"; as "a Power that inspires his song, or kindles his vision."[3] For the contemporary poet Gary Snyder she is "anything other that touches you and moves you . . . breaks through the ego-barrier. . . . Man in his sexual nature has found the clearest mirror to be his human lover."[4] This enigmatic female figure, whether wise sibyl or chosen lover, exists for the male poet as a series of opposites: he is subject, she is object; he is lover, she is beloved; he is begetter, she is begotten upon. As inspiration incarnate, this traditional muse has served male poets from Plato to Dante to Milton to Keats to Yeats. Socrates in Plato's *Ion* affirms her universality: "and every poet has some Muse from whom he is suspended, and by whom he is said to be possessed."[5] As divine inspirer, idealized woman, sexual and creative stimulus to the poet, the muse represents an important symbolic aspect of the male literary imagination.

These definitions of the muse as object identify her, and by extension woman, as "Other": that which is not the self and in contrast to which, therefore, man can best define himself subjectively. Simone de Beauvoir argues that this construct of the Other is essential to male self-definition: "once the subject seeks to assert himself, the Other, who limits and denies him, is none the less a necessity to him: he attains himself only through that reality which he is not, which is something other than himself."[6] For the male poet, the invocation of a female muse—his particular way of naming an Other—leads ultimately to a strong sense of poetic autonomy, an identity vital to his creativity. Although the poet is typically portrayed as possessed by his muse, in reality it is he who possesses, since the act of naming is by nature hierarchical. As Adam in the biblical tale of creation declared his own superiority over the animals by naming them, so the male poet asserts his power over his creative inspirer even as he invokes her. Adrienne Rich hypothesizes that the muse is an objectification of the male poet's own female side, with which he has difficulty coming to terms and therefore must subdue.[7] Whatever the psychological motivation, the male poet's invocation of his muse is an act of appropriation and control: to produce poems, he typically consumes the female muse, absorbing her creative energy into himself. The sexual implications of such a model for creativity are obvious; it is little wonder that the most common metaphor used to describe the poetic process is that of the sexual act. The poet's desire for his muse has been depicted through the ages as a sexual passion, and from his coitus with her, in reversal of natural biological functions, he, not she, begets their offspring, poetry.

This traditional poet-muse paradigm suffices as long as the poet is male. But what of the woman poet seeking creative identity? Although the struggle for poetic affirmation is difficult for any poet, it is intensified for the woman, since this tradition of the objectified muse has made it hard for her to transcend her Otherness and thus attain the subjectivity crucial to a strong poetic stance. To define herself as active creator rather than passive inspirer, the woman poet must invent her own metaphor for poetic inspiration; she must name a muse of her own. Yet who or what might this figure be? Our culture offers no language and no mythology for describing a woman poet's muse. As Columbia professor Carolyn Heilbrun explains, "Sidney's direction from his muse, 'Look into your heart and write,' is less simple for those who suspect, or know, that what they find in their hearts will not be sanctioned by the males in power."[8] Furthermore, as many feminist critics argue, the patriarchal tradition that dominates both Christianity and Western literature has dissociated woman not only from the active role of poet but also from language itself, and thereby from its power.[9] This dissociation, in turn, has made it difficult for the woman poet to conceive of such an Other, much less to name it. Thus one of her chief dilemmas has been how to appropriate a "masculinist" language and imagery for herself, how to forge her "logos" and "mythos" of creative inspiration.

It seems at first glance logical that the traditional paradigm of poet and muse would be reversible, that the woman poet would invoke a male muse. However, a survey of women poets writing in English from the Renaissance to the present indicates that this is rarely the case—perhaps because fecundity is the special province of woman or perhaps, as Rich suggests, because "it is man and man's world which makes it especially difficult for [the woman] as artist."[10] Several women poets, particularly in the nineteenth century, do pay homage to male sources of inspiration: Emily Dickinson, Emily Brontë, and Christina Rossetti, for example, sometimes personify their poetic power as a divine "he." In fact, as Rich notes in her essay on Dickinson, some poems by women traditionally read as works about possession by God or by some human lover may best be seen as poems about the muse, since often "a woman's poetry about her relationship to her daemon—her own active, creative power—has in patriarchal culture used the language of heterosexual love or patriarchal theology."[11] Imagining her inspirer as male—as one who enchants but may also overpower—raises for the woman poet the complex issue of "author-ity": will a patriarchal muse inspire or control, aid or appropriate her writing? Because she fears dependence on a "stronger" male figure, such a poet may write with extreme ambivalence, sabotage her own work, or opt, finally, for silence.[12] Despite occasional attempts to make the muse male, therefore, no woman poet has imagined a sustained masculine figure comparable to the traditional female muse. Does the woman poet, then, have a muse? If so, what are its sex and nature, and how does it differ from the "inspiring anima" of the male poet?

The poetry of twentieth-century women provides a useful locus from which to address these questions. Like the work of their female predecessors, much of this poetry reveals its creators' ambivalence toward their creativity: they question their "right to write," yet simultaneously affirm their imaginative potency.

Modern women poets continue to struggle with what the literary critic Suzanne Juhasz has called a "double bind": a quest for both personal and poetic identity within a society and a literary tradition that view "woman" and "poet" as mutually exclusive terms. Frequently, this struggle causes fragmentation; the woman poet asserts "I am" but follows her statement of identity with a question mark as often as an exclamation.[13] Another feminist critic, Catherine Smith, speculates as to why creative women may feel both powerful and powerless:

> Female imagination may work from biological patterning for emission of blood, babies, and milk, compounded with existence in a social context that ambivalently worships and fears precisely that expressivity and limits female range accordingly. If so, then it is not surprising that women's imaginative reality, including self-apotheosis, emerges from a fused core of felt capacity and restraint, of power and powerlessness, of peculiarly female wish and fear.[14]

Unlike writing women from earlier ages, however, modern women often challenge these limiting forces in an effort to define their own "imaginative reality." It is from a desire to come to terms with their "peculiarly female wish and fear," I would argue, that women poets have been compelled to re-mythologize the muse—or, in Luce Irigaray's words, to "begin the same stories all over again."

The Harvard psychologist Carol Gilligan offers a theory of women's psychological development that helps us understand the nature of and reasons for the woman poet's re-visioned muse. According to Gilligan, a woman's values posit the strength of interdependence, of sharing and exchanging resources; her psychological world, therefore, is a complex web of connectedness. Men, in contrast, typically view separation, autonomy, individuation, as ideal states for which to strive, as means of attaining power. Gilligan quotes from Virginia Woolf's *A Room of One's Own*: "It is obvious that the values of women differ very often from the values which have been made by the other sex"—yet "it is the masculine values that prevail." In contemporary society, Gilligan concludes, it is essential that we acknowledge and examine closely not just one ethical sphere, that of men, but two:

> As we have listened for centuries to the voices of men and the theories of development that their experience informs, so we have come more recently to notice not only the silence of women but the difficulty in hearing what they say when they speak. Yet in the different voice of women lies the truth of an ethic of care, the tie between relationship and responsibility, and the origins of aggression in the failure of connection. The failure to see the different reality of women's lives and to hear the differences in their voices stems in part from the assumption that there is a single mode of social experience and interpretation. By positing instead two different modes, we arrive at a more complex rendition of human experience which sees the truth of separation and attachment in the lives of women and men and recognizes how these truths are carried by different modes of language and thought.[15]

Male and female imaginative renderings of the muse illustrate such "different modes of language and thought." For most women poets, Graves' "sister of the mirage and echo" does not suffice. Rather than following the male model of invoking a passive Other, creative women have called forth strong female figures from their matriarchal and mythological heritage who serve as sources of power and sustenance. The work of such poets as H.D., Edna St. Vincent Millay, Louise Bogan, Sylvia Plath, Anne Sexton, Denise Levertov, Muriel Rukeyser, May Sarton, Audre Lorde, Olga Broumas, and Judy Grahn reveals a recurring imagery of goddesses and mythic women, especially in poems about creativity and the poetic process: women who function not merely as key images or dramatic personae but as muses. Ishtar, Isis, Aset, and Astarte from Eastern myths appear, as do Greek deities, such as Aphrodite, Artemis, Demeter, and Kore (Persephone). A striking number of women poets focus on mythological figures traditionally viewed as "demonic": Kali, Circe, Medusa, Helen, the Furies, the Amazons. Unable or unwilling to idealize their inspirational sources as passive, erotic manifestations of the opposite sex, these poets employ powerful goddesses as extensions of their creative selves. Such goddesses may be forceful role models, or Jungian "shadows" who express the dark side of the psyche, or nurturing inspirational figures. Whatever their guise, they are part of women's efforts to come to terms with their literary imaginations, to assert their "different voice."

Furthermore, many poets invoke as muses women from their own lives, who function as part of a broad feminine or, in some cases, feminist community in and by which they are sustained. For H.D., Lorde, Rich, Alice Walker, this search begins, as Walker says, in their "mothers' gardens." In H.D.'s words, "the mother is the Muse, the Creator." For some women—Sarton, Broumas, Lorde come to mind—the muse is a female lover: not one to be seduced and controlled or abandoned, however, but one with whom to speak and share, to love and work as an equal. At times the muse is an extraordinary woman whose accomplishments inspire—Rich's Marie Curie or the mountain climber Elvira Shatayev, for instance—or an ordinary woman, like Judy Grahn's waitress Ella, one who, in Rich's words, "reconstitutes the world." Or the muse may be plural, "our selves," the individual woman in intimate communion with other women through whom is found "after so long, this answer."[16]

Since the woman poet's muse differs radically from the male poet's passive, detached Other, the poems and circumstances in which she is invoked may also vary from the male norm–that is, they may be less obviously recognizable as poems about inspiration and poetry-making. The male poet's experience and gender credentials allow him to be single-minded in his poetic task, to invoke his muse in a ritualized way dictated by a tradition of which he considers himself an inheritor: "Sing, Heav'nly Muse!" The female poet, in contrast, typically views herself as outside of that tradition, and so her experience of making poems will differ from his. The dynamic between poet and muse often allows the woman metaphorically to *become* her own muse: not to be inspired by a distant female Other, but to share the inspirer's powers—to be *interdependent with* her muse rather than *dependent on* or *superior to* her, as the male paradigm has traditionally dictated. Not all strong female figures in poems by modern women are muses, certainly. But some poems not overtly about creative inspiration do ultimately address the poet-muse relationship.

A case in point is Alexandra Grilikhes' untitled prose poem from *On Women Artists*. Although the word *muse* is never mentioned, the poem captures the energy and fulfillment of an interdependent exchange between the woman poet and her female source of inspiration:

> Reading another woman's work, looking at her art; spirit and bread. Passion. It's what I live for, the beautiful alive, the reality that passes between us, something that makes me live, a kind of nurturing. The elements lie inert in me ready to burn on contact. A laval heat.

To "seek succor" in the art of other women, Grilikhes suggests, is not to compete with them but to cohabit, to embrace the self in the muse and the muse in the self.

> Their work moves into mine and so suggests to me that mine is available to me, somewhere in me.
>
> . . . .
>
> I dream of a whole word which contains the fragments of my self. It waits at the edge of language, always.[17]

Women poets, then, name their muses not by casting off or consuming or appropriating but by taking on, connecting, inheriting. Thus Yale critic Harold Bloom's paradigm of an "anxiety of influence"—the "strong" male poet's compulsion to undo, isolate, empty, even kill (all Bloomian verbs) his literary predecessors and control his whoring muse—manifests itself in the woman poet as an affirmation of influence.[18] This affirming impulse leads her to construct, complete, confront the self through the power of a female poetic construct, a revised and revitalized female muse. Not that such affirmation is always without anxiety: these sources of inspiration sometimes intimidate the woman poet with their dazzling brilliance, disturb her with their potent evocations of inner malignancies. She may, therefore, respond ambivalently to this flux of creative vitality, this "intoxicating" (empowering/annihilating) bond.[19] But in contrast to Bloom's male "ephebe," who undertakes a solipsistic quest for "discontinuity," the woman poet typically strives to establish continuity, to connect aesthetically with her foremothers, her contemporaries, her muses. Rather than searching for an Other against whom to define the self, creative women turn first inward for sustenance to the multiple selves of their own psyches, then outward to the doubles and shadows reflected in other powerful women: mothers, sisters, lovers, muses—alternate selves interwoven by the common thread of female imagination and experience. By invoking a newly envisioned female muse, women poets are fast becoming, in Olga Broumas' words, "of one mind, tuning / our instruments to ourselves, by our triple light."

To understand the woman poet's re-mythologizing of the muse, her invention of and reliance on a female creative principle, we must first examine the mythology that surrounds the traditional muse of the male poet. The concept of a divine inspirer to the poet, as we know it, originated with the ancient Greeks. "Sing, O Muse"; "Sing me, O Muse"; "Sing, Goddess"; "Sing, begin, tell me the story"—such are the opening words of most Greek hymns and poems.[20] Ovid describes the Muses as nine goddesses of arts and sciences, "gifted sisters" born of Zeus and Mnemosyne, who reside on Mt. Helicon and offer divine comfort and inspiration to the gods.[21] Although Ovid portrays the Muses as beneficent, virginal mountain nymphs, Robert Graves notes that this is a later patriarchal manifestation; these mountain goddesses, originally a triad, "are the Triple-Goddess in her orgiastic aspect. Zeus's claim to be their father is a late one; Hesiod calls them daughters of Mother Earth and Air."[22] The Muses' paradoxical link to both divinity and orgiastic passion is, of course, part of their attraction: the muse-possessed poet becomes a transfigured lover whose sexual desire evokes his poetic genius.

According to the *Oxford Classical Dictionary*, the Muses have few myths of their own; they served originally not as inspirational sources to individual poets but as a general metaphoric idea for poetic inspiration. Thus it was the abstract concept of the Muses rather than their individuality that was important to the classical male poet. Ovid mentions only two of them by name: Calliope, the goddess of epic poetry, the powerful eldest who often leads her sisters in song; and Urania, the goddess of astronomy, who becomes important in Milton's *Paradise Lost*. Also, despite their significance in Greek mythology, the Muses are not accorded the status of actual deities; instead, their male successor, Apollo, becomes the god of poetry and song to whom even the Muses must pay tribute. Graves asserts that this shift of emphasis from the Muses to Apollo as chief patron of poetry paralleled the switch from matriarchal to patriarchal consciousness and hence was part of an effort to suppress the cult of the Great Goddess, the Lunar Mother, in favor of the more rational Greek pantheon of predominantly male deities. Whatever the reason, Graves explains, Apollo "brought the Muses down from their home on Mt. Helicon to Delphi, tamed their wild frenzy, and led them in formal and decorous dances."[23] Yet despite his rational powers, Apollo could not totally tame the Muses, nor could he supplant them as both sexual and divine inspirers to the male poet.

The other male successor of the Muses is Orpheus, son of Calliope, so renowned for the power and beauty of his music that a good lyrical poet today is often said to have an Orphic voice. The myth of Orpheus and Eurydice, as recounted by Ovid, partially explains the Muses' symbolic transformation from active singers to passive inspirers. As poet and musician of Thrace, Orpheus reaches his full poetic potential upon the death of his bride, Eurydice, pierced by a snake's bite on the morning of her wedding. In *The Metamorphoses*, Ovid describes the lyrical mourning of the bereaved husband:

> Her bridegroom, Orpheus, poet of the hour,
> And pride of the Rhapsode, sang loud his loss
> To everyone on earth. When this was done,
> His wailing voice, his lyre, and himself
> Came weaving through the tall gates of Taenarus
> Down to the world of Death and flowing Darkness
> To tell the story of his grief again.[24]

The Orphic saga is familiar: since neither Queen Persephone nor the King of Darkness "could resist / The charms of Orpheus and his matchless lyre," they agreed to let Eurydice return to earth on the condition that Orpheus not look back at her until their ascent from Hell was completed. But, Ovid tells us, Orpheus did not keep his vow:

> . . . as they neared the surface of the Earth,
> The poet, fearful that she'd lost her way,
> Glanced backward with a look that spoke his love—
> Then saw her gliding into deeper darkness,
> As he reached out to hold her, she was gone;
> He had embraced a world of emptiness.[25]

As a result of this second loss, Orpheus went "melancholy-mad" yet became more powerfully musical, his song so enchanting that it stilled nature, seduced goddesses and nymphs. Such seductions led to Orpheus' downfall, since he incurred the wrath of the vengeful maenads, who ultimately tore him asunder. Yet his dismembered head and dead tongue continued to sing. Not even the power of the impassioned Furies could silence him.

The legend of Orpheus serves as a metaphor for the male poet/female muse relationship as depicted from Plato to the present. The male is singer-creator whose potent song moves the gods of Hades, the mountain nymphs and goddesses, nature herself. The reason behind his song, on the other hand, is a woman, Eurydice, who in the myth becomes universal Woman: that distant, detached love object whom the poet longs to possess, but who remains unattainable. Traditionally, then, woman serves the male poet as an objectified muse, a catalyst stimulating male creativity. As such, she, like Eurydice, is often overlooked.

The Orphic saga also contains the seeds of three major "categories" of imagery in which the muse through the ages has been portrayed: the sexual category, seen in Orpheus' desire to possess Eurydice yet his inability or unwillingness to curb his passion, even at the risk of losing her; the spiritual category, symbolized by Orpheus' journey to and from Hades, his negotiations with the gods, and Eurydice's transformation from mortal to divine woman; and the natural category, seen in Orpheus' ability to quiet "all beasts, all birds, all stones" with the spell of his mesmerizing song—music whose power stems from the poet's lament for a muselike woman closely associated with nature. Although these three categories overlap, each is more clearly reflected in a particular poetic tradition. The muse as an erotic objectification of woman is best seen in the courtly tradition, which began with the eleventh-century troubadours of Provence and reached its pinnacle with the Elizabethan love sonnet. The view of woman as divine muse, the bridge through whom man can attain spiritual unity with God, has as its central figure Dante's Beatrice; but its seeds are sown in Dante's Italian predecessors and in medieval celebrations of the Virgin, and the metaphor is expanded in Milton's invocations of the "Heav'nly Muse" in *Paradise Lost*. And woman as human muse linking the poet to the natural world appears in the English Romantic poets of the early nineteenth century. An examination of this tradition will help us understand the muse as she has been conceived and brought to fruition by male poets.

The sexual implications of the poet-muse relationship are first suggested by Plato, who describes this interaction in terms of seduction and possession. In the *Phaedrus*, for example, Socrates speaks specifically of the muse-possessed poet as a madman: "the third kind is the madness of those who are possessed by the Muses; which taking hold of a delicate and virgin soul, and there inspiring frenzy, awakens lyrical and all other numbers; with these adorning the myriad actions of ancient heroes for the instruction of posterity."[26] The Muses' haunting song transforms the otherwise rational poet into a frenzied being who is nonetheless awakened into creativity. Socrates also describes to the rhapsode Ion a chain of inspiration: "the Muse first of all inspires men herself; and from these inspired persons a chain of other persons is suspended, who take the inspiration. For all good poets, epic as well as lyric, compose their beautiful poems not by art, but because they are inspired or possessed."[27]

Yet the Muses are not altogether a positive influence, since they lead poets from the realm of the rational. For this reason, Plato suggests in the *Republic*, one must be wary of the Muses' effect upon the state. Their powers may suspend reason in the poets they seduce, and the poets, in turn, might threaten the principles of order on which a productive society must be based: "for if you go beyond this and allow the Honeyed Muse to enter, either in epic or lyric verse, not law and the reason of mankind, which by common consent have ever been deemed best, but pleasure and pain will be the rulers of our state."[28] At the heart of the ancient conceptualization of the Muses, then, lies a paradox: they evoke beautiful poetic lyrics, yet they upset order and disband reason. For Plato, the classical Muses ultimately represent passion, irrationality, disorder.

One might assume that muses generally function as formidable, active forces, since they transform the otherwise rational male poet into a "possessed" madman. However, muses have typically been portrayed as passive catalysts who stimulate lyricism in the active male poet, helping him "give birth" to a new entity. Only at the seduction stage does a muse hold the power; once a "union" between poet and muse has been consummated, this power is transferred to the male as active creator. Such a view conforms to the prevailing biological theories of ancient times regarding male and female roles at the moment of conception. Aristotle was first to insist that the male provides the homunculus, the spiritual "matter" of conception, while the female serves as receptacle, a material nurturing locus for the new being.[29] This belief held well into the Middle Ages, as St. Thomas Aquinas' argument indicates: "the active power in the male seed tends to the production of a perfect likeness according to the masculine sex." Woman, on the other hand, was viewed by Aquinas as "a misbegotten male, an inferior form of humanity, a mill-second, so to speak, in the biological process."[30] This biological theory parallels the poet-muse relationship: the muse "receives" the male creative seed, responsible for the production of the offspring; hence the active male engenders his poetry upon the body of a passive female muse.

Furthermore, woman is sometimes made a tertiary figure in the creative process by being identified as the male poet's very creation: poetry itself is often anthropomorphized as a benign female force, a "she." In the *Republic*, for example, Plato portrays poetry as a woman whose lovers must defend both her virtue and her utility: "and we may further grant to those of her defenders who are lovers of poetry and yet not poets the permission to speak in prose on her behalf: let them show not only that she is pleasant but also useful to states and to human life, and we will listen in a kindly spirit."[31] In discussing why woman is often objectified as poetry, Simone de Beauvoir suggests that "poetry is supposed to catch what exists beyond the prose of every day; and woman is an eminently poetic reality since man projects into her all that he does not resolve to be." In her role as muse, poetry feminized, Beauvoir continues, woman bridges the gap between man and nature, man and self. "A muse creates nothing by herself; she is a calm, wise Sibyl, putting herself with docility at the service of a master."[32] Although the image of the muse-possessed madman is a common one, then, such a poet is no passive victim. Instead, he is an active master-possessor who invokes his female muse, appropriates her generative capacities, and claims her power—and her—for himself.

The muse as sexual stimulus and creative inspirer whose powers the male poet must appropriate is best reflected in the literary tradition of courtly love. This phenomenon began in eleventh-century Provence, culminated once with the *canzoniere* of Petrarch in the fourteenth century, reached yet another zenith with the sonneteers of Elizabethan England, and still displays vestiges of its power in many modern lyric poems. This literary code of lovemaking was affected by the socioeconomic environment of feudalism, by Ovid's sensual romances, and by the Christian veneration of the Virgin Mary. The main goal of such poetry was the exaltation of the beloved. According to the Renaissance scholar Lu Emily Pearson, "one reads how the lover came to regard his mistress partly with the adoration which he lavished upon the Virgin, partly with the loyalty due his lord, and partly with the jealous devotion of the male."[33] Thus, the chief influences on the poet's devotional behavior were feudal, religious, and sexual.

This courtly tradition began with Guillaume IX of Provence, known for eleven extant songs dating from the early twelfth century. For Guillaume and successive troubadours, love's misery and love's object—woman—served as inspiration. According to the literary critic Maurice Valency,

> the lady's image was impressed upon the poet's soul, and it was in the unswerving contemplation of this image and under its constant influence that the song was fashioned. In the "finding" of the song, the poet was, accordingly, in a sense a passive recipient of inspiration. Through love the song came to his mind; the closer he came to love, the better he heard love's dictation.[34]

But "love's dictation" often differed little from one Provençal poet to the next. These two prose translations of poems by Piere Rogier and Bernart de Ventadorn illustrate the stock emotions of courtly song:

> For love of her I live, and if I should die so that it should be said that I died loving, Love would have done me so great an honour, that I know and believe she never did greater to any lover. . . . From you I find all ills benefit, damage adventure, folly sense, wrongs justice and right.
>
> Those who think I am here do not know how my spirit is private and at home in her, even if the body is distant: know the best message that I have from her is my thought, which recalls to me her beautiful appearance.[35]

Although each troubadour pays homage to his *midon*, or lady, he also asserts himself as a forceful "I," an active singer to whom others must listen. His lady, in contrast, is often designated *res*, "thing."[36] The paradox of the poet as passive lover yet active creator lies at the heart of the courtly tradition.

This tradition spread rapidly from France to Italy, where it was popularized in the Italian love song, or *canzone*, and in the writings of one particular courtier-poet: Petrarch. The divine Laura is paramount in Petrarch's poetry; he celebrates her eyes, her hair, her bosom with all the lush, lustful exuberance manifested by earlier troubadours, but with a greater technical and imaginative proficiency:

> How well I call to mind,
> When from those boughs the wind
> Shook down upon her bosom flower on flower;
> And there she sat, meek-eyed,
> In midst of all that pride,
> Sprinkled and blushing through an amorous shower,
> Some to her hair paid dower,
> And seem'd to dress the curls,
> Queenlike, with gold and pearls;
> Some, snowing, on her drapery stopp'd,
> Some on the earth, some on the water dropp'd;
> While other, fluttering from above,
> Seem'd wheeling round in pomp, and saying
> "Here reigns Love."[37]

The more the poet lauds Laura's physical charms, however, the more distressed he is by her apparent coldness, her refusal to return or even recognize his abject love. A lover of Cicero and himself a great rhetorician, Petrarch often employs grand rhetorical flourishes, castigating the beloved for her Medusa-like glances, her stony heart. Such doleful complaints are as much at the heart of the Petrarchan tradition as is the lyrical fascination with the mistress's beauty.

Although Petrarch's sonnets at first appear to focus on Laura, the central character of this love saga is not the beloved but the lover himself. Lu Emily Pearson argues that narcissism makes Petrarch's poetry philosophical rather than passionate in nature: "his dominant subjectivity made it impossible for him to picture her [Laura] as she was in body and soul, however, for she was always as he saw her. His conception of intellectual and moral self-culture determined his ideal, and became actually an absorbing egotism. His love, thus centered on himself, could never become a passion."[38] Yet narcissism does not preclude passion: the poet's passion is merely self-directed; the poet himself, not Laura, is at the poem's center. Take, for example, Sonnet CIV:

> I find no peace and bear no arms for war,
> I fear, I hope; I burn yet shake with chill;
> I fly the Heavens, huddle to earth's floor,
> Embrace the world yet all I grasp is nil.
> Love opens not nor shuts my prison's door
> Nor claims me his nor leaves me to my will.

Laura serves as stimulus to the poet's passion, as object rather than subject of the poem: "My Lady, thus I am because of you."[39] Such narcissism is nothing new, for medieval literature frequently treats the theme of self-love: the Dreamer in Guillaume de Lorris' *Roman de la Rose* (1240), for instance, first sees the object of his desire in the pool of Narcissus. But Petrarch goes further than other troubadours in his egocentric celebration of self under the guise of an exaltation of Laura.

The love code of the Renaissance sonneteers also celebrates woman's physical charms as a means of self-reflection. The central figure in initiating this tradition was Thomas Wyatt, whose trips to Italy during the 1530s and 1540s on matters of state may well have altered the history of the English lyric. Sixteenth-century England was ripe for the *canzone*, and with the influence of Castiglione's *Courtier*, circulated in 1516, and the later publication of translations of Petrarch's sonnets by Wyatt and by the Earl of Surrey (Henry Howard) in Tottel's *Miscellany* (1557), Petrarch's *canzoniere* became popular in schools and at court. Both Wyatt and Surrey were attracted not only to the Petrarchan convention of exalting the mistress but also to the expression of personal emotion. Indeed, though Wyatt's early sonnets imitate Petrarch, both he and Surrey go beyond him in exploring both the sensual and the psychological sides of love. Wyatt burns and freezes, hopes and despairs in Petrarchan fashion, yet he is a more spirited lover; when rebuffed, he is indignant and self-laudatory:

Tangled I was in love's snare,
Oppressed with pain, torment with care,
Of grief right sure, of joy full bare,
Clean in despair by cruelty—
But ha! ha! ha! full well is me,
For I am now at liberty.[40]

Wyatt thumbs his nose at despair, rejecting the lover-muse who "assigned" him "feigned words which were but wind." Once "fed" by woman, he now will feed himself.

This ambivalence toward woman as muse is also seen in Sidney's *Astrophel and Stella* and Spenser's *Amoretti*. As Petrarch's Laura was supposedly modeled upon an actual woman, Sidney's Stella was thought to be Penelope Devereaux, Lady Rich, unattainable because she was married. Like Petrarch, Sidney celebrates his beloved as "perfection's heire":

For let me but name her whom I do love,
So sweet sounds straight mine care and heart do hit,
That I will find no eloquence like it.[41]

At other times, however, Stella makes him angry, and writing becomes his means of escape, a cathartic outpouring: "as good to write as for to lie and grone."[42] Spenser's *Amoretti*, the second major Renaissance sonnet sequence, further expands Petrarch's themes yet anticipates Shakespeare's anti-Petrarchan impulse. Influenced by Castiglione's realistic portrayal of woman's virtues as well as by a strong sense of morality, Spenser concentrates primarily on his lady's human worth and his own capacity for spiritual growth:

Deepe in the closet of my parts entyre,
her worth is written with a golden quill:
that me with heauenly fury doth inspire,
and my glad mouth with her sweet prayses fill,
Which when as fame in her shrill trump shal thunder
let the world chose to enuy or to wonder.[43]

Yet despite his attempts to idealize the lady, Spenser often falls prey to her physical charms:

Her goodly bosome lyke a Strawberry bed,
her neck lyke to a bounch of Cullambynes;
her brest lyke lillyes, ere theyr leaues be shed,
her nipples lyke yong blossomd Iessemynes.[44]

Both sexual and idealized love, then, inform Spenser's invocation of the muse.

With Shakespeare, the courtly tradition of exalting the lady begins to be reversed and parodied. The poet's view of the excesses of courtly love can be seen in Berowne's scornful comments in *Love's Labour's Lost*:

This is the liver-vein, which makes flesh a deity,
A green goose a goddess; pure, pure idolatry.
God amend us, God amend! We are much out o' the way.[45]

Shakespeare's sonnets also defy the conventions of idealized love. Most are directed to a young man, offering advice on "love rational," while the remainder depict a "dark lady," Laura's opposite, wanton and alluring. Shakespeare's choice of male friendship as a key motif is unusual, given that heterosexual courtship lay at the center of the sonnet tradition; perhaps the best explanation, in addition to the poet's obvious distaste for the increasingly clichéd Petrarchan conventions, is that the friend represents an aspect of the poet himself. It is also possible that the male "friend" is a lover. At times Shakespeare actually equates the friend with the muse, as in Sonnet 78: "So oft have I invoked thee for my Muse / And found such fair assistance in my verse / As every alien pen hath got my use / And under thee their poesy disperse."[46] At other times, however, the poet invokes the aid of a traditional female muse in paying homage to his friend. In Sonnet 100, for example, the poet chides his negligent muse: "Where art thou, Muse, that thou forget'st so long / To speak of that which gives thee all thy might?"[47] Although he again scolds his "truant muse" in Sonnet 101, the poet is also confident of her ability to help him immortalize the friend in verse: "Then do thy office, Muse: I teach thee how / To make him seem long hence as he shows now."[48]

More significant to this study, however, is Shakespeare's choice of the dark lady as anti-muse. Although some critics suggest that he is anti-Petrarchan sham and not anti-mistress, it is often hard to tell where one response begins and the other ends. The most famous dark lady sonnet, 130 ("My mistress' eyes are nothing like the sun"), is anti-Petrarchan satire. But Shakespeare's lady's "blackness" does not stop at her eyes; she also lacks virtue: "in nothing art thou black save in thy deeds, / And hence this slander, as I think, proceeds."[49] The poet has a perverse bond with this mistress-muse; though aware that she is false, he pretends to believe her every word and so deliberately deceives and is deceived. "Therefore I lie with her, and she with me, / And in our faults by lies we flattered be."[50] The pun here is obvious; the sexual act both facilitates the deception and is the reason behind it. Shakespeare's dark lady dispenses favors indiscriminately, the poet implies, but in her sexuality lies her attraction.

A contrasting yet equally pervasive view of the muse is that of woman spiritualized, the earthly manifestation of heavenly powers. In addition to sexual frenzy, Plato also admits to a frenzy inspired by heaven, a "divine delirium"—for the Greeks, *enthusiasm*, possession by a god. Such possession often is effected with the aid of a female liaison. In her beneficent wisdom, for example, the lady Diotima of the *Symposium* teaches Socrates that Eros in its purest form can lead him to divine wisdom, the highest good. In her role as enlightened educator, woman serves the poet as spiritual muse, a divine mediator between man and God.[51]

Woman has always had mystical associations with divinity. For the Druids she was divine Eros in the guise of woman; to the Cathars and the Gnostics she was Sophia Maria, the feminine principle of divinity; to Arab mystical sects she was "the Lady of Thoughts," the "Veiled Idea," representing the spiritual part of man.[52] Throughout the Middle Ages especially, the female body possessed powers as holy as those of the Grail. The most pervasive Western symbol of the "Eternal Feminine," of course, was the Virgin Mary. In thirteenth-century France, Maryolatry took the form of religious love songs like the *Planctus Mariae*, similar in tone to troubadour poetry. But homage to the Virgin also provides a major theme of medieval English religious lyrics. "I Sing of a Maiden," for example, visualizes the mystery of the Virgin birth as analogous to the falling of dew; the Corpus Christi carol, on the other hand, personifies the Virgin as a maiden lamenting the wounds of Christ her "knight."

But it was in Italy that the poetic tradition of woman as spiritual mediator reached fruition, as the Florentine school of the *dolce stil nova* took form in the latter half of the thirteenth century. Dante's most famous predecessor, Guido Cavalcanti, viewed woman as a means by which the poet could know love as an inaccessible divine ideal. With Dante, the lady is further spiritualized: she is beautiful because her soul is beautiful, and through her the poet can know the world of pure spirit. In the *Vita Nuova*, Beatrice first appears as a human lover rather than a spiritual force. Her gradual shift from earthly beloved to spiritual muse begins with the poet's premonition of her death, a fear that leads him to associate her with divine rather than physical love. This spiritualization of Beatrice culminates in the *Paradiso*, where she reveals to the poet the way to God. By the final chapters she has come to represent for Dante not a human lover but Philosophy, Wisdom, Holy Science—the Divine Revelation of Paradise and its mysteries.

As the Dante scholar Marianne Shapiro has pointed out, Beatrice is not the only female muse whom Dante invokes:

> Dante has recognized the generative and nourishing power of the illuminating aspect of the feminine character in the prose commentary of the *Vita Nuova* and praised it in the Lady Philosophy of the *Convivio*. In the *Comedy* this power is accorded to and shared by a variety of feminine representations. Dante endows his Muses with qualities eminently compatible with Christian virtues. They are to him the *Sacrosante Vergini* to whom he as poet offered the appropriate sacrifices of hunger, cold, and long vigils. . . . Their purity incarnates his ideal of poetry mirroring vision. . . . They are the singing, dancing, and prophetic forces to whom in time of need the poet turns for wisdom.[53]

Yet Beatrice best reveals Dante's belief in the capacity of woman to act as liaison between man and God. In Shapiro's words, "when the poet is actively aware of the discrepancy between man's creative potential and the miraculous nature of the things to which he must apply it, he has recourse to one of the hallowed feminine sources of inspiration."[54] Certainly Beatrice is Dante's most frequently invoked and most hallowed inspirational source.

Dante's English successor in transforming the muse from the earthly to the heavenly sphere was Milton in *Paradise Lost*. In tracing parallels between Dante and Milton, the critic Irene Samuel notes that both follow an elaborate and conscious plan yet at the same time attribute dictation of their verse to an inspiring female power.[55] Dante in the *Purgatorio* assigns to love the role of muse, to whom the poet is "careful to give ear and but so writes as he dictates within"; and Milton in *Paradise Lost* likewise pays homage to a

> . . . celestial patroness, who deigns
> Her nightly visitation unimplored
> And dictates to me slumbering, or inspires
> Easy my unpremeditated verse.[56]

Furthermore, both poets vary the source of their power, calling the muse by different names as their themes heighten. In the *Inferno*, for instance, Dante calls upon the classical Muses, along with Genius and Memory, to guide him; and at the beginning of the *Purgatorio* he appeals to dead Poesy, to the *sante muse*, and especially to Calliope. Later he invokes the *sacrosante Vergini*, as well as Urania, and at the start of the *Paradiso* he calls upon first Apollo, then the "goddess Pegasian," and finally the *luce eterna*, the ultimate source of inspiration. Likewise, Milton relies upon an entire catalog of muse-figures, from the "Heav'nly Muse" and "Spirit" of the first invocation, to "Holy Light" at the beginning of Book III. His quest culminates in the rejection of Calliope in Book VII in favor of Urania, whose otherworldly associations make her a more fitting inspirational source. Clearly Milton wants to cut off ties to the pagan by dedicating himself to the sanctifying muse. In fact, as one of the nine Greek Muses, even Urania has more secular associations than the poet wishes; hence he asserts that it is "the meaning, not the Name I call."

This cluster of muse terms in Milton is a controversial and unresolved aspect of *Paradise Lost*. Traditional Milton scholars often debate whether the "Heav'nly Muse" is God the Father or the Son, and the literary critic Christopher Grose notes that the identification of Urania has "challenged Milton's exegetes . . . fiercely." Furthermore, there is evidence for viewing Milton's source of inspiration as androgynous: the "Heav'nly Muse" and Urania are often cross-listed as synonymous figures; and the critic Joan Webber notes "the ambiguous sex of Milton's muse, which some scholars have identified with the Son" but asserts that "the traditionally feminine source of inspiration is not a woman on a pedestal but a creative drive that incorporates and transcends both sexes." However, Milton's "patroness" of the invocations in Books VII and IX is clearly a female figure, one who pays calls to him "nightly" when he is otherwise "alone," who comes "unimplored." And the brood / impregnate image of creation in Book I (lines 21–22), which is joined to the poet's request that he be inspired (breathed into), also suggests a female metaphor at work. One other possible reading is to view the spirit of God as a feminine inspirational source, in which case the mystical interaction between poet and divine inspirer may assume a sexual dimension. The Milton scholar John T. Shawcross elaborates this point:

> As I read *Paradise Lost* . . . I am struck by the metaphor of inspiration with its sexual overtones: the poem itself is the creation of God and the poet; it simulates an act of generation through the psychological motif, subject matter, strategically placed proems, and rhythm; it deals with creation which is bodily, conceptual, and physical; and it suggests constant generation through impregnation of its readers with its "message."[57]

Milton's muses, however, remain essentially spiritual forces. Indeed, both Dante and Milton create a hierarchical doctrine of heavenly grace that parallels Plato's stairway of love in the *Symposium*. Only with Beatrice's divine guidance can Dante realize a union with God; likewise, Milton can know the divine only through a visionary "companion," the "Heav'nly Muse."

The third category through which the female muse has traditionally been depicted, woman as a link to nature, is especially evident in the Romantic movement of the early nineteenth century. The typical Romantic persona is that of the masculine philosopher-seer or poet-prophet, a representative voice of a certain age and sensibility granted what Wordsworth calls "an internal brightness . . . shared by none." The central thematic concern of the Romantic poets, the autonomy and primacy of the imagination, is closely related to this focus on the poet's identity. What he sees and feels and imagines is an integral part of what he is, and anything he is becomes fit subject matter for his art.

This view of the masculine poetic self directly informs the Romantic poet's view of the feminine Other: the source of his creative inspiration. Among the Romantics, the muse often reveals herself through nature as the universe itself, feminized. As Mother Nature's "son," the poet is the inheritor of her vast powers: by appropriating his mother's strength, the poet can "give birth" to his poems. The Romantic poet most responsible for articulating this metaphor is Wordsworth, who believed that through nature the male poet could attain "visionary power." A direct successor of Milton, Wordsworth adopts a bardic voice appropriate to one who viewed himself as a poet-prophet of his age. At the beginning of the "Prospectus" to *The Recluse*, for instance, the poet preempts Urania, Milton's muse, in favor of a still more powerful one:

> . . . Urania, I shall need
> Thy guidance, or a greater muse, if such
> Descend to earth or dwell in highest heaven!
> For I must tread on shadowy ground, must sink
> Deep—and, aloft ascending, breathe in worlds
> To which the heaven of heavens is but a veil.[58]

A spiritual intermediary, the poet suggests, will not suffice for exploring the shadowy expanse he wishes to investigate—"Our minds . . . the Mind of

Man— / My haunt, and the main region of my song." Unlike Milton's depiction of man's fall and redemption, Wordsworth's landscape is the more immediate internal region of the poet's psyche.

Who or what, then, replaces Urania as muse? Although there is no single answer, for Wordsworth or for other Romantic poets, nature often serves as a feminized inspirational power to activate the male poet's imagination. As the feminist critic Margaret Homans points out, nature represents for Wordsworth everything he is not: a maternal force with whom the poet was once united but from whom he is now separated; a spiritual force linked to the lost paradise, God's gift to humanity; and a sexual force, a desirable and desired feminine Other whom the poet must love and fear.[59] To overcome his fear and consummate his love for nature, the male poet must "tame" her by subsuming her into himself, by internalizing her as part of an androgynous whole, so that the dominant male principle can reap the rewards of a female creative power. For Wordsworth and others, the frequent poetic symbol of such a union is marriage: the merging of two opposing yet complementary forces, the male intellect and the feminized universe, into a state of conjugal bliss. This rejuvenating marriage between man and nature—a prominent metaphor also in Blake's *Jerusalem*, Coleridge's *Dejection Ode*, and Shelley's *Prometheus Unbound*—serves as a central image in Wordsworth's "Prospectus" to *The Recluse*. The poet's description of the marriage reveals his function as a maker of "spousal verse":

> . . . Paradise, and groves
> Elysian, Fortunate Fields—like those of old
> Sought in the Atlantic Main—why should they be
> A history only of departed things,
> Or a mere fiction of what never was?
> For the discerning intellect of Man,
> When wedded to this goodly universe
> In love and holy passion, shall find these
> A simple produce of the common day.
> —I, long before the blissful hour arrives,
> Would chant, in lonely peace, the spousal verse
> Of this great consummation.[60]

As bardic voice and representative of a new age, the poet has both intimacy and distance. As universal man, he is attached to nature as lover, husband, and—when Nature wears her maternal guise—son; while as individual man, the poet, he can become a detached observer, a free agent whose task it is to command song, not to be overwhelmed by it.

Whether individual or universal man, however, the poet retains his power and autonomy, while the female muse is objectified, rendered powerless. In fact, in Wordsworth's "Lucy" poems, she must die for the poet to come into his own. In "She dwelt among the untrodden ways," for example, Lucy is identified with nature as "a violet by a mossy stone / . . . Fair as a star." Yet this extraordinary woman "lived unknown" to all but him whom she inspires: "But she is in her grave, and, oh, / The difference to me!" This theme of the male poet who writes at the bequest of his dead but still revelatory muse is also found in "Three years she grew in sun and shower." Here the poet's rival, Nature, claims Lucy as "a Lady of my own, / . . . sportive as the fawn," yet one to be restrained, silenced by "an overseeing power":

> And hers shall be the breathing balm,
> And hers the silence and the calm
> Of mute, insensate things.

The poet cannot compete directly with Nature, cannot return life to his Lucy; indeed, it is to his advantage to have her "mute, insensate." Like Nature, he then can claim her as his source of inspiration, the "tool" of his trade.

> Thus Nature spake—the work was done—
> How soon my Lucy's race was run!
> She died, and left to me
> This heath, this calm, and quiet scene;
> The memory of what has been,
> And never more will be.[61]

Woman appears again as a source of inspiration for Wordsworth in "The Solitary Reaper." By seeing and hearing "Yon solitary Highland Lass," a symbol of beneficent "feminine" nature, the poet can ultimately appropriate her powers of creativity:

> Whate'er the theme, the Maiden sang
> As if her song could have no ending;
> I saw her singing at her work,
> And o'er the sickle bending—
> I listened, motionless and still;
> And, as I mounted up the hill,
> The music in my heart I bore,
> Long after it was heard no more.[62]

Her song does not end, the poet implies, because it has become *his* music.

For other Romantic poets, too, the mythmaking faculty is overseen by a female force, sometimes spiritual, sometimes sexual, often linked to the natural world. Although Shelley's "Hymn to Intellectual Beauty" does not explicitly name as female the "unseen Power" to which he prays, the poet's language implies the feminine: his muse is the "Spirit of Beauty," "thou messenger of Sympathies," "awful Loveliness," "Spirit fair." Furthermore, the poet's love for Emilia, the Beatrice of the "Epipsychidion," reveals both sexual and spiritual devotion to a female inspirer:

> Sweet Spirit! Sister of that orphan one,
> Whose empire is the name thou weepest on,
> In my heart's temple I suspend to thee
> These votive wreaths of withered memory.[63]

Still more Beatrician is Moneta in Keats' "The Fall of Hyperion: A Dream," whom the poet deems "Holy Power" and "High Prophetess." Early in the poem Keats beseeches Moneta to "purge off / Benign, if so it please thee, my mind's film," to corroborate his view of the poet as "a sage; / A humanist, physician to all men." To attain spiritual and creative insights, the speaker must learn from Moneta, who is closely identified with the mother of the classical Muses, Mnemosyne:

> . . . "Shade of Memory!"
> Cried I, with act adorant at her feet,
> "By all the gloom hung round thy fallen house,
> By this last temple, by the golden age,
> By great Apollo, thy dear Foster Child,
> And by thyself, forlorn divinity,
> The pale Omega of a wither'd race,
> Let me behold, according as thou saidst,
> What in thy brain so ferments to and fro."

Clearly Moneta/Mnemosyne is of a matriarchal age no longer glorious; one wonders why the poet/persona needs her intercession. Nevertheless, Moneta is willing to reveal all, and in language a mere mortal can comprehend: "Mortal, that thou may'st understand aright, / I humanize my sayings to thine ear." Gifted through her revelation, the poet is able finally to stand "in clear light . . . / Reliev'd from the dusk vale," while his goddess-muse becomes a mere reflection, pure but remote in "her priestess-garments."[64]

Modern male poets have inherited this tradition of a passive female muse, although some have rebelled against it. For Whitman, the muse emanates from himself: "Walt Whitman, a kosmos, of Manhattan the son"; his inspirational source is thus "my own voice, orotund, sweeping and final."[65] But Whitman's muse is also female: recall the maternal sea of "Out of the Cradle Endlessly Rocking," the "old crone" who at last, the poet tells us, "whisper'd me."[66] For Emerson, the poet is also an isolated figure, "the plain old Adam . . . the simple, genuine self against the whole world." Yet "plain old Adam" is often exalted; Emerson describes him in "The Poet" as "the Namer or Language-Maker," "the man without impediment, who sees and handles that which others dream of, traverses the whole scale of experience, and is representative of man, in virtue of being the largest power to receive and to impart."[67] From what or whom the poet "receives," Emerson does not explicitly reveal, yet he rejects the "courtly muses of Europe" for the homespun inspiration of a feminized America.

Most of the significant male modernists—Pound, Williams, Eliot, Auden, Stevens, Yeats—also invoke female muses, in traditional or nontraditional ways. Particularly in their early poems, both Ezra Pound and William Carlos Williams rely heavily on the conventional poet-muse interaction. Pound's "Praise of Ysolt," for example, resembles troubadour poetry in its homage to a woman of transcendent powers, yet it is Wordsworthian in its appropriation of the song of a solitary reaper:

> But my soul sent a woman, a woman of the wonderfolk,
> A woman as fire upon the pine woods
>   crying "Song, a song,"
> As the flame crieth unto the sap.
> My song was ablaze with her and she went from me
> As flame leaveth the embers so went she unto new
>   forests
> And the words were with me
>   crying ever "Song, a song."[68]

Another early poem, "The Summons," is, according to Pound scholar Louis L. Martz, "addressed to a lady who seems to be an image of poetic inspiration," probably in fact the poet H.D., to whom Pound was briefly engaged during the time of his earliest Imagist explorations.[69] "I cannot bow to woo thee / with honey words and flower kisses / . . . Of broidered days foredone," protests the poet to his muse. Yet this modern Beatrice is essential, for she leads him "upward / To the centre of all truth":

> So must I bear thee with me
> Rapt into this great involving flame,
> Calling ever from the midst thereof,
>   "Follow! Follow!"
> And in the glory of our meeting
> Shall the power be reborn.[70]

In "The Wanderer: A Rococo Study," Williams calls forth a muse imaged first as a female crow who "sprang from the nest" to guide him, then as a crone who gives him insight. The poem's first of seven sections, "Advent," reveals the poet's ambivalence toward his inspirational force: while he glories in the way she "showed me / Her mind, reaching out to the horizon," he also feels frustrated by her insistence: "I had been wearying many questions / Which she had put on to try me: / How shall I be a mirror to this modernity?" When the crow gives way to the crone in section three, "Broadway," the poet initially "falls back sickened!" Yet he is compelled to listen to this "marvelous old queen," "horrible old woman," "mighty, crafty prowler"; in fact, he implores her: "Great Queen, bless me with thy tatters!" And so the crone-muse blesses him, taking him "Abroad" to see nature at its loveliest and bleakest, himself both young and old. The section entitled "Soothsay" reveals a particularly interesting poetic epiphany, as the crone offers the poet the gift of foresight and the voice of the wind, both explicitly male powers:

"You are the wind coming that stills birds,
Shakes the leaves in booming polyphony—
Slow winning high way amid the knocking
Of boughs, evenly crescendo,
The din and bellow of the male wind!"

Interestingly, the male's task is to subdue a "female chorus":

"Leap then from forest into foam!
Lash about from low into high flames
Tipping sound, the female chorus—
Linking all lions, all twitterings
To make them nothing! Behold yourself old!"

In the final section of "The Wanderer," the poet is "heavy of heart," aware that "the novitiate was ended / The ecstasy was over, the life begun." When the crone-muse takes the "young soul" of the poet to the river god as an offering, the poet is powerless to stop himself from "being borne off under the water." But this death leads to rebirth. Despite a final ironic admonition from the crone to "Be mostly silent!", the poet inherits her legacy of words. At the end of the poem the crone and her river lover celebrate their son, this "new wanderer," the "child I have brought you in the late years."[71]

As poets inclined to "make it new," both Pound and Williams invoke the landscape of the city as a female muse, using the metaphor of sexual liaison. In "Und Drang," for instance, Pound attempts "to imitate and then to disengage his muse from nineteenth-century trappings and move into his own world."[72] This effort is also apparent in "N.Y.":

My City, my beloved,
Thou art a maid with no breasts,
Thou are slender as a silver reed.
Listen to me, attend me!
And I will breathe into thee a soul,
And thou shalt live for ever.[73]

Williams' cityscape in *Paterson* is an equally passive muse-figure, the subject of the poet's lust as well as his pen:

The scene's the Park
upon the rock,
female to the city
—upon whose body Paterson instructs his thoughts
(concretely).[74]

Another interesting variant on the traditional female muse appears in "The Library," the last section of *Paterson*, as "Beautiful thing, / my dove," that "something" that brings the speaker "back to his own / mind." Tempted to "give up the shilly- / shally of art," the poet experiences an apocalyptic vision in which books from the "wadded library" are engulfed by a "dark flame." As the poet meditates on the flame's beauty, "a defiance of authority," his muse merges with the fire, cleansing him and allowing him to name himself:

> . . . Beautiful thing
>
> —intertwined with the fire. An identity
> surmounting the world, its core—from which
> we shrink squirting little hoses of
> objection—and
> I along with the rest, squirting
> at the fire
>
> Poet.

Near the poem's end, the speaker pays tribute to his source of inspiration: "Dear heart / It's all for you, my dove, my / changeling."[75]

For T. S. Eliot and W. H. Auden the muse sometimes acts as an antiquated rhetorical device, a crutch to be acknowledged ironically. The epigraph to Eliot's *The Waste Land*, for example, is spoken by the sibyl of Cumae from Petronius' *Satyricon*, a prophetess linked traditionally to solemn religious rituals but here undercut by the narrator's implicit scorn of her weak, corrupted powers. Likewise, in part two of *The Waste Land* the Lady Belladonna, hardly sexually alluring, is granted none of the muse's traditional powers of supernal beauty or insight; and in the "Fire Sermon," a trio of muselike "Thames sisters" sing of meaninglessness.[76] Similarly, Auden in "Homage to Clio" invokes the muse of history only after seeing her picture "in the papers." Despite her vulgarization, however, Auden does restore to the muse some vestige of her traditional role; he deifies her as "Madonna of silences," the possessor of insights the poet wishes to obtain:

> When we have lost control, your eyes, Clio, into which
> We look for recognition after
> We have been found out.

Muse figures in other Auden poems are also treated with irony. The fertility goddess of "Dame Kind," for instance, is but a shadow of her former glory: "She mayn't be all / She might be but / She *is* our Mum."[77] These poets wish to defy the convention of invoking a muse, it would seem, even as they rely on it.

Yet despite some resistance to the traditional muse, she appears to flourish among modern poems by men. In "Ash Wednesday," for example, Eliot's religious conversion leads him to a latter-day Beatrice who guides him both creatively and spiritually:

> Because of the goodness of this Lady
> And because of her loveliness, and because
> She honours the Virgin in meditation,
> We shine with brightness.

Though she is named "Lady of silences," this muse helps the poet to find words appropriate for his new vision:

> Blessed sister, holy mother, spirit of the fountain, spirit of the garden,
> Suffer us not to mock ourselves with falsehood
> Teach us to care and not to care
> Teach us to sit still
> Even among these rocks,
> Our peace in His will
> And even among these rocks
> Sister, mother
> And spirit of the river, spirit of the sea,
> Suffer me not to be separated
>
> And let my cry come unto Thee.[78]

For Wallace Stevens, "death is the mother of beauty; hence from her, / Alone, shall come fulfillment to our dreams / And our desires."[79] And like Pound and Williams, Stevens in "The Idea of Order at Key West" celebrates woman as singer—"she was the maker of the song she sang." The muse's voice moves the poet, inspiring him to respond in "Words of the fragrant portals, dimly-starved, / And of ourselves and of our origins . . ."[80] Hart Crane's Pocahontas qualifies as a modern-day muse, an earth goddess who rejuvenates both the land and the poet in *The Bridge*. Yeats' Maud Gonne is his "phoenix," his "sweet-heart from another life" whose "Ledean body" inspired his work for many decades. The traditional female muse, such examples prove, is far from obsolete in modern poetry.

Works by five contemporary male poets reveal the muse's current status and variations. She is invoked in most traditional terms in Robert Creeley's "Air: 'The Love of a Woman' ":

> The love of a woman
> is the possibility which
> surrounds her as hair
> her head, as the love of her
>
> follows and describes
> her. But what if
> they die, then there is
> still the aura
>
> left, left sadly, but
> hovers in the air, surely,
> where this had taken place?
> Then sing, of her, of whom
>
> it will be said, he
> sang of her, it was the
> song he made which made her
> happy, so she lived.[81]

Again, the poet is the powerful singer, the new-age Orpheus; his lady, or her "aura," is a passive figure "made happy" by his song—indeed, at the end of the poem, restored to life by and in this song.

A similar portrayal of the poet-muse dynamic occurs in James Merrill's "From the Cupola," in which the poet "submits" to the goddess Psyche's poetic powers, yet speaks on behalf of his "love," whom he is compelled to "defend" from the onslaught of any creative imaginings of her own:

> Help me when the christenings shall start
> O my love
> to defend your sleep from them
> and see according to our lights.

"Our lights" are ultimately male-defined, however, as the poet names himself as creator and the "light" as an interpretive but secondary Other:

> . . . My hands move. An intense,
> Slow-paced, erratic dance goes on below.
> I have received from whom I do not know
> These letters. Show me, light, if they make sense.[82]

In "Kaddish" Allen Ginsberg claims as muse his dead mother, Naomi Ginsberg: "Now I've got to cut through—to talk to you as I didn't / when you had a mouth."[83] Mourning his mother's loss yet assured of her conspiratorial silence, the poet credits her as the source of his creativity:

> O glorious muse that bore me from the womb, gave suck first mystic
> life & taught me talk and music, from whose pained head I first took
> Vision—[84]

Driven to come to terms with her absence, the speaker asserts his own presence, ending his lament with an agonized cry of tribute: "Blessed be Thee Naomi in Death!"[85]

A different sort of mother-muse is Anne Bradstreet, a source of inspiration for John Berryman, who identifies his modern world and quest with her colonial milieu. "We are on each other's hands / who care," the poet asserts, addressing his Puritan predecessor: "both of our worlds unhanded us." This bond between poets of different sexes and ages also has sexual overtones. "Lie stark," bids the male poet-lover, "thy eyes look to me mild. Out of maize & air / your body's made, and moves. I summon, see, / from the centuries it." Fearing desertion by his muse ("I think you won't stay"), Berryman in section four of *Homage to Mistress Bradstreet* adopts the female poet's voice; the rest of the work is predominantly "herstory," or at least the male writer's fantasy of her story.[86]

Finally, Irving Feldman invokes three variations on the traditional female muse in the title poem of his recent volume *Teach Me, Dear Sister*: "Teacher, muse, sibyl. / Three times in three guises / She appeared to him." Although Feldman's categories overlap, they parallel roughly those formulated by Petrarch, Dante, and Wordsworth, though not in historical order. The first inspirer, an older "sister," manifests her powers by virtue of her age—"her great eight to his five importunate years." As the poet's sibling-self, the muse resembles Wordsworth's sister, Dorothy; she moves her "brother" to speech by her presence and her eyes, "dark and kind." The second muse figure, the erotic manifestation, attracts the poet during a visit to an art museum: "What brought him to the bronze head / was the girl eye to eye, even nose to nose, with it," whose eyes swept up at him "like someone at the starting point / who asks both blessing and direction." Clearly, the poet concludes, "she was waiting for him to speak." The third muse, a sort of anti-Beatrice, is a woman dirty, barefoot, and bereft on city streets. This "weird sister," this modern sibyl, transfixes the poet by "the perfect blankness of her gaze":

> *Wake up, dear sister*, he was trying to say
> to the sibyl in her trance, but the woman
> would not respond, so deep the charm that held her.
> And the spell she was under was the end of the world.[87]

In all three of the muse's guises, her eyes are a prominent feature, spellbinding the poet yet moving him to sing her praises.

As this history of the male poet's muse has shown, a diverse lot of female Others inhabit poetry from the twelfth through twentieth centuries. These muses are linked by their objectified status, by their roles as vehicles, catalysts, emblems, against and through whom the active male poet asserts his imaginative power. The persistent authority of this masculinist tradition helps to explain the difficulties women poets have faced in naming themselves subjects rather than objects, active creators rather than passive inspirers. According to Adrienne Rich, when a woman seeks a poetic voice and stance,

> she meets the image of Woman in books written by men. She finds a terror and a dream, she finds a beautiful pale face, she finds La Belle Dame Sans Merci, she finds Juliet or Tess or Salomé, but precisely what she does not find is that absorbed, drudging, puzzled, sometimes inspired creature, herself, who sits at a desk trying to put words together.[88]

Neither does she find, Rich might have added, a muse of her own. Yet she needs such a muse, as a source and means of "parler femme," to use Irigaray's term—of "speaking female," creating her own myths and metaphors for poetic identity and inspiration. In so doing, she rejects the annihilating concept of woman as a secondary figure in the creative enterprise, as muse but not poet.

Denise Levertov challenges woman's traditional role as muse in *Relearning the Alphabet*:

In childhood dream-play I was always
the knight or squire, not
the lady:
quester, petitioner, win or lose, not
she who was sought.
The initial of quest or question
branded itself long since on the flank
of my Pegasus.[89]

In naming themselves questers, however, many women poets reject altogether the "I/thou" separation that Levertov's poem depicts. Instead, they redefine and embrace also her "who was sought," eschewing male-defined binary oppositions (subject/object, active/passive) in favor of a fluid, nonhierarchical construct—a female creative continuum. In Carol Gilligan's terms, they view the poet-muse relationship as one of interdependence instead of separation and/or control. Luce Irigaray claims that patriarchal discourse has neither "taught nor allowed [women] to say our multiplicity."[90] In challenging this discourse, therefore, women poets typically begin at the beginning: they reimagine in all her multiplicity the most emotionally pervasive and historically persistent image of creative inspiration, the female muse.

Such reimaginings, however, do not always come easy. One tactic of the woman poet has been to evade the problem of the muse altogether, to insist on writing poetry without invoking any superior or exterior force. In "To Mr. F., now Earl of W.," by the eighteenth-century poet Anne Finch, the speaker, Ardelia, remains undaunted when the traditional muses refuse to aid her because of her sex. Instead of relying on "foreign aid," Ardelia will "dictate from the heart," writing sonnets for "her Flavio alone."[91] A somewhat different response comes from the colonial poet Anne Bradstreet, herself entitled (ironically) "the Tenth Muse lately sprung up in America": an apposition that, the feminist critic Catharine Stimpson argues, "controls as it flatters."[92] Unlike Finch, Bradstreet seems overwhelmed by male-defined metaphors of inspiration; she apologizes for "my foolish, broken, blemished Muse," who appears inadequate to her awesome task. However, Bradstreet may denigrate her muse as an act of subversive and ironic rebellion against male constructs of woman, for later in the "Prologue" she complains that the ancient Greeks were more sympathetic to the creative female than are her male contemporaries:

But sure the antique Greeks were far more mild
Else of our sex, why feigned they those nine

And poesy made Calliope's own child;
So 'mongst the rest they placed the arts divine.[93]

In the nineteenth century, furthermore, Margaret Fuller advised that woman forego the role of muse to the male poet and instead serve as Minerva, goddess of wisdom, for herself.[94] Modern women poets as well have critiqued the traditional muse: Susan Griffin calls her "a cop-out," and Adrienne Rich considers the male-defined muse "uninteresting."[95] As their work indicates, however, both Griffin and Rich are vitally concerned with the woman writer's relationship to her own creativity; it is the objectified muse with her patriarchal trappings that they reject.

A number of feminist critics have explored the nineteenth-century woman poet's troubled attempts to invoke a male muse, a supernatural visitant or a father-lover-God image. Examining the "composite father" in the poems of Emily Dickinson, Elizabeth Barrett Browning, and Christina Rossetti, Joanne Feit Diehl argues that these three poets "present distinctly similar psychological patterns in dealing with tradition [sic] they face": each envisions "a father/lover that surpasses individuals."[96] Diehl's approach is Freudian, similar to Harold Bloom's application of Freud to his theory of male poetics, but her analysis also recalls Jung's definition of the woman's animus. The female poet's male muse functions as both a projection of her own male side and a composite figure of the male precursors whose tradition she is attempting to enter.

The work of Emily Dickinson best illustrates this perverse absorption with a male muse-figure, an Other whom the poet both desires and fears. In poems such as "Come slowly—Eden," "We shun it ere it comes," and "I am afraid to own a Body—," Dickinson reveals her ambivalent attitude toward her muse and her art. As these lines suggest, one part of the poet dreads the intrusion of this awesome force, which can give or withhold from her the impetus to write. Her extreme ambivalence toward this "he" reflects her mixed view of her own poetic powers and of language itself, which simultaneously "enchants" and "infects" her. As Diehl notes, Dickinson's relationship to her muse lacks the key advantage of the male poet: while he asserts his authority over the muse by naming and subordinating her, the woman poet may feel overpowered and violated by her "authoritative" masculine muse. As a "postromantic woman" for whom "the roles of muse and poet have shifted," Dickinson "wavers between feeling that she must wait to receive her Master/ muse and radical rejection of his presence."[97]

Adrienne Rich, in contrast, argues that Dickinson's muse is finally herself. Citing such poems as "He fumbles at your Soul," "He put the Belt around my life—," and "My life had stood—a Loaded Gun," Rich explores Dickinson's use of the masculine pronoun for depicting her muse. Traditionally, critics have hypothesized that this male figure refers either to God or to some human lover, but as Rich notes, such critical assessments are reductionistic. Many poems in which a "he" figures centrally are more likely poems

> about possession by the daemon, about the dangers and risks of such possession if you are a woman, about the knowledge that power in a woman can seem destructive, and that you cannot live without the daemon once it has possessed you. The archetype of the daemon as masculine is beginning to change, but it has been real for women up until now.[98]

In a Judeo-Christian and patriarchal society, Rich continues, the primary image of power available to woman has been the male metaphor; thus it is logical that Dickinson "would assign a masculine gender to that in herself which did not fit in with the conventional ideology of womanliness"—that is, to her own poetic powers and vision.[99]

Other feminist critics support Rich's view that Dickinson's muse is ultimately female. In a critique of Diehl's analysis, Lillian Faderman argues that Susan Gilbert, the woman who later became Dickinson's sister-in-law, served as the young poet's muse; lines such as "frigid and sweet Her panting face" indicate the strength of this bond. Elizabeth Barrett Browning also inspired Dickinson, as the poem "I think I was enchanted" reveals. Louise Bernikow argues convincingly that in this poem Dickinson invokes a "transforming female power" through the image of the witch: a deviant woman who "speaks in tongues, is visionary and reviled, threatens both the world and the poet, possesses secret knowledge, and is in touch with nature and the body." Thus Dickinson celebrates Elizabeth Barrett Browning's magic, her "witch's brew," even as she fears it:

'Twas a Divine Insanity—
The Danger to be Sane
Should I again experience—
'Tis Antidote to turn—
To Tomes of solid Witchcraft—
Magicians be asleep—
But Magic—hath an Element
Like Deity—to keep—[100]

The female muse may be "dangerous" for Dickinson, but she finally intrigues the poet more than she threatens her.

The poetry of Emily Brontë also illustrates the nineteenth-century woman poet's ambivalence when she feels compelled to invoke a paternal or a demonic inspirer. Margaret Homans has analyzed the masculine muse in Brontë's work, agreeing with Diehl that terror of this threatening male force causes the woman poet great internal conflict.[101] Although Brontë tries to see the male muse as nonhierarchical—as "comrade, slave, and king"—it is the muse as "king," or even "god," who takes precedence. This force she must resist, even as she invokes him: "Speak, God of Visions, plead for me / And tell why I have chosen thee!"[102] Like Dickinson, however, Brontë sometimes envisions the muse as female, and this muse, too, can be threatening. In her Gondal poems, for instance, she calls forth a demonic force in the person of A.G.A., the fiendish-angelic monarch of a complex imaginary world. This cold, willful queen serves as a shadow figure, a potent alternate self to whom Brontë gives birth and yet, paradoxically, through whom she herself as an artist is born. Adopting the voices of A.G.A.'s rejected lovers, Brontë presents a regal despot who acts as a catalyst for the poet's melodramatic outpouring:

There stands Sidonia's deity,
In all her glory, all her pride!
And truly like a god she seems:
Some god of wild enthusiast's dreams.[103]

These lines have particular significance when we recall that for the Greeks an "enthusiast" was a person possessed by the muse, a "madman." Like the troubadour obsessed by his distant female lover, Brontë pays reluctant homage to the woman who has captured her imagination but also set it free:

Do I not see thee now? Thy black, resplendant hair;
Thy glory-beaming brow, and smile, how heavenly fair!
Thine eyes are turned away—those eyes I would not see;
Their dark, their deadly ray, would more than madden me.[104]

The only muse toward whom Brontë does not feel some hostility, through whom she approaches her art unambivalently, is herself—her own feminized nature and inspiration. She often celebrates the power she wields as a creator, and she is willing to risk the censure of others to maintain her poetic authority. In "To Imagination," for example, Brontë pays tribute to her creativity, her muse, and her self as sovereign forces:

So hopeless is the world without,
The world within I doubly prize;
The world where guile and hate and doubt
And cold suspicion never rise;
Where thou and I and Liberty
Have undisputed sovereignty.[105]

The poet goes on to deify this "voice divine," the "benignant power" that emanates from herself. "No coward soul is mine," the poet insists in another poem; she is steadfast in her quest for poetic autonomy. Like her hero-muse A.G.A., under no circumstances and for no one's sake is Brontë willing to repudiate her creative powers: "I'll walk where my own nature would be leading: / It vexes me to choose another guide."[106]

Why this ambivalence toward any muse not directly linked to the female self? Rich offers a probable answer: "It seems likely that the nineteenth-century woman poet, especially, felt the medium of poetry as dangerous, in ways that the woman novelist did not feel the medium of fiction to be."[107] She felt endangered partly because society attributed the role of poet to men only, because in assuming the masculine privilege of creation she risked losing her "womanliness." Yet the solution to this dilemma for some women poets of the age, invocation of a male muse, also contributed to a sense of danger. The main problem with reversing the traditional paradigm is that the woman poet has difficulty separating the male muse from other intimidating and debilitating male forces, those that limit rather than expand her female identity. A "father lover," claims Carolyn Heilbrun, is "not a bad image of a muse, sexes reversed, except that the man, in turning to the muse, turned to what seduces, and the woman turns to what rapes."[108]

There is, however, a lengthy and impressive history of Western women poets, from the Renaissance to the present, who redefine the muse as a potent female force with whom to share the creative enterprise. Such poets are not totally devoid of ambivalence toward their same-sex inspirers, but their impulse is primarily celebratory. Two seventeenth-century women who invoke female muses as inspirers and equals are Katherine Philips and Anne Killigrew. In her poetic sequence to her friend Lucasia, Philips creates "dawning of the soul" poems conventional in their reliance on the metaphysical tradition, but unconventional in their celebration of woman-to-woman sustenance. Here, for example, the "Matchless Orinda" calls forth a nurturant muse as beloved guide and comrade:

> But never had Orinda found
>   A soul till she found thine;
>
> Which now inspires, cures and supplies,
>   And guides my darkened breast:
> For thou art all that I can prize,
>   My joy, my life, my rest.[109]

Anne Killigrew pays homage to a "Queen of Verse" more deified than Philips' Lucasia but equally personal and pleasing. In "Upon the Saying That My Verses Were Made by Another," Killigrew takes issue with her detractors by invoking a "sacred Muse" who, she claims, has never failed her:

> Next Heaven, my vows to thee, O sacred Muse!
> I offered up, nor didst thou them refuse.
>
>   O Queen of Verse, said I, if thou'lt inspire,
> And warm my soul with thy poetic fire,
> No love of gold shall share with thee my heart,
> Or yet ambition in my breast have part,
> More rich, more noble I will ever hold
> The Muse's laurel, than a crown of gold.
> An undivided sacrifice I'll lay
> Upon thine altar, soul and body pay;
> Thou shalt my pleasure, my employment be,
> My all I'll make a holocaust to thee.[110]

Like Philips' Lucasia, Killigrew's muse provides the nectar that the writer-supplicant sips, the "laurel" that she dons.

Modern women vary in the kinds of muses they invoke, but their inspirational sources are consistently female. The Soviet poet Anna Akhmatova, for instance, describes a Dantesque muse who provides the poet with both solace and legitimacy:

When at night I wait for her to come,
Life, it seems, hangs by a single strand.
What are glory, youth, freedom, in comparison
With the dear welcome guest, a flute in hand?

She enters now. Pushing her veil aside,
She stares through me with her attentiveness.
I question her: "And were you Dante's guide,
Dictating the Inferno?" She answers: "Yes."[111]

For Olga Broumas, in contrast, Dante's divine guide holds little attraction; she prefers a "triple muse" of her own invention and celebration, "our instruments / cared for, our bodies dark." These muses confront their male-determined past only to reject it, preferring instead the "pith" of self-defined and mutual knowledge:

False things
we've made seem true, by charm, by music. Faked
any trick when it pleased us

and laughed, faked
too when it didn't. The audience couldn't tell, invoking
us absently, stroking their fragile beards, waiting

for inspiration
served up like dinner, or sex. Past. Here
each of us knows, herself, the mineral-bright pith.[112]

The muse called forth by the modern woman poet is not always conducive to healing; sometimes the appearance of such an awesome presence makes reconciliation of one's personal and poetic selves difficult. In Sylvia Plath's "The Disquieting Muses," for example, the wary and troubled speaker accuses her mother of forcing upon her these "dismal-headed / Godmothers," the three muses who hover "mouthless, eyeless, with stitched bald head." Rather than enhancing the poet's creativity, these "traveling companions" are rigid, sterile forces who limit or perhaps destroy her imaginative vision:

Day now, night now, at head, side, feet
They stand their vigil in gowns of stone,
Faces blank as the day I was born,
Their shadows long in the setting sun
That never brightens or goes down.
And this is the kingdom you bore me to,
Mother, mother. But no frown of mine
Will betray the company I keep.[113]

The poet cannot or will not deny these muses, but both they and she are frozen, devoid of expression. In addition to her "matrophobia," Plath also illustrates dramatically the female poet's fear of inspiration, its potential as a source of entrapment and denial.

Sometimes the woman poet's reaction to her muse is not fear of her presence but frustration at her absence. In "Muteness," the contemporary Soviet poet Bella Akhmadulina laments the silence of the "black wound" where once her voice lay: "I shout but muteness, / like vapor, leaves my mouth and curls around my lips." Inspiration is "the mute soul's quick / uninterrupted breath," the poet insists; "another breath won't save it; / only the words I say." The muse in the self remains obstinately silent. When the stark March landscape consistently fails to release the poet's words, however, she determines to invoke a muse outside the self—yet one who is incarnated only at the poet's own anxious bidding:

To ease my overflowing pulse
any way I can, even accidentally,
I'll incarnate all I am
eager to sing about.

And because I am so mute,
and love the sounds of all words,
and am tired suddenly, as if dead,
sing, sing me.[114]

Most often, however, the modern woman poet envisions her muse as a sustaining force, part of a lost or buried female tradition long in need of unearthing. Such a source is the subject of Carolyn Kizer's "A Muse of Water":

We who must act as handmaidens
To our own goddess, turn too fast,
Trip on our hems, to glimpse the muse
Gliding below her lake or sea,
Are left, long-staring after her,
Narcissists by necessity;

Or water-carriers of our young
Till waters burst, and white streams flow
Artesian, from the lifted breast:
Cup-bearers then, to tiny gods,
Imperious table-pounders, who
Are final arbiters of thirst.

The imagery here relies on an analogy frequently employed by the modern woman poet in describing her muse, that of woman's artistic creativity and her physical powers. As woman gives birth to and nourishes her young, with "white streams" from the "lifted breast," so must she look to herself for creative nurture. She must go beyond her role as inspirer of man—"poultice for his flesh . . . water for his fire"—and instead bring forth her own long-buried music, that "lost murmur! Subterranean moan!" The invocation of such a voice, Kizer recognizes, is necessary for woman's poetic survival.[115]

Denise Levertov also imagines the female muse as water carrier in "The Well." Here the image cluster reveals interconnections among the silent, mysterious muse; her source of water, a deep and clear spring; the papyrus reeds that populate the spring; and the poet-recipient, who waits and watches on a nearby bridge.

> The Muse
>   in her dark habit,
> trim-waisted,
>   wades into deep water.
>
> The spring where she
>   will fill her pitcher to the brim
> wells out
>   below the lake's surface, among
> papyrus, where a stream
>   enters the lake and is crossed
> by the bridge on which I stand.

The poet is reminded of *The Miracle Worker*, a play in which Helen Keller's teacher, Annie Sullivan, spells the word "water" into the blind girl's palm, "opening / the doors of the world." The speaker, too, is without sight and voice until the goddess-muse delivers her gift from the sacred river:

> . . . I know
>
> no interpretation of these mysteries
>   although I know she is the Muse
> and that humble
>   tributary of Roding is
> one with Alpheus, the god who as a river
> flowed through the salt sea to his love's well
>
> so that my heart leaps
>   in wonder.
> Cold, fresh, deep, I feel the word "water"
>   spelled in my left palm.[116]

Archetypal theory helps to explain why women poets often image their muses as goddesses or potent alternate selves. For both sexes, the Jungian analyst M. L. von Franz asserts, the most powerful symbol of human totality and integration is the authentic self, an undivided essence that emerges only when an individual has wrestled sufficiently with the Others that constitute his or her psychic makeup: the anima, the animus, the shadow, a same-sex figure who acts as a demonic double. According to Franz, man in his dreams usually represents this integrated self as a masculine guardian of some sort, a guru or wise man. But "in the dreams of a woman this center is usually personified as a superior female figure—a priestess, sorceress, earth mother, or goddess of nature or love." As Franz further explains, such goddesses often appear as wise old women or supernaturally gifted young girls.[117] This description of women's dream imagery applies also to the poetic imagery of women seeking affirmation through their art. They, too, may envision their muse as a goddess, often an old, potent witch-woman or a mystical young girl.

Consider, for instance, Levertov's "In Mind":

> There's in my mind a woman
> of innocence, unadorned but
>
> fair-featured, and smelling of
> apples or grass. She wears
>
> a utopian smock or shift, her hair
> is light brown and smooth, and she
>
> is kind and very clean without
> ostentation—
> but she has
> no imagination.
> And there's a
> turbulent moon-ridden girl
> or old woman, or both,
> dressed in opals and rags, feathers
>
> and torn taffeta,
> who knows strange songs—
>
> but she is not kind.[118]

In this poem the innocent woman is that unimaginative, passive creature often idealized: the "feminine" woman, virginal and attuned to nature, kind. The "turbulent moon-ridden girl" and the old woman, in contrast, suggest woman's nontraditional role as poet, one who sings "strange songs" and eschews one of femininity's requisite attributes: kindness. To succeed as an artist, Levertov implies, woman strives to reconcile these disparate forces within. She does not completely renounce the virtue of kindness, yet neither does she cut herself off from poetic turbulence. She accepts her shadow as a vital muse and thus begins to heal the split between her private and public selves.

Often, then, the modern woman poet invokes as a muse a dual-faceted goddess, one to whom the poet attributes both beneficent and demonic qualities. Erich Neumann argues that most goddesses from both Eastern and Western mythologies are projections of the ancient Great Mothers; Sophia, for example, reflects the "Good Mother," Medusa the "Terrible Mother," while Isis combines the features of both. Neumann's schematic diagram illustrates the complexity and circularity of this female deity: one extreme is represented by divine virgins, traditional muse figures, and goddesses, such as Artemis, Athene, Demeter, Kore, and Sophia; its opposite pole consists of traditionally malevolent forces—Kali, Medusa, Hecate, Ishtar, and Isis and Artemis in their negative phases.[119] Aware that the creative woman has traditionally been considered "unfeminine," even demonic, many women rebel against this stereotype by turning to malevolent goddesses as symbols of their creativity. As the individual seeking wholeness struggles with a shadow figure, so the poet confronts these projections of the "Terrible Mother," transforming them from negative, demonic forces to positive, balanced figures. The result of such reimaginings are poems like Bogan's "Medusa," Sarton's "The Invocation to Kali," as well as other works by modern women addressing and invoking Circe, Medea, Isis, Helen, Hecate, Hera, the Sphinx, the Furies, witches and sorceresses.[120]

Sarton's "The Muse as Medusa" illustrates this transformation of the debilitating Gorgon into a sustaining muse. One on one with Medusa, the poet is determined to transcend the myth and confront her directly:

> I saw you once, Medusa; we were alone.
> I looked you straight in the cold eye, cold.
> I was not punished, was not turned to stone—
> How to believe the legends I am told?

Sarton goes on to claim the Gorgon's powers as her own. Rather than turning the poet into stone, this interaction with Medusa allows her to find a voice heretofore untapped, one born of pain, anger, and, paradoxically, stony silence. When the poet examines Medusa's "frozen rage," she recognizes her own "secret, self-enclosed, and ravaged place" and thanks the goddess for her "gift."[121] This confrontation and identification with a traditionally malevolent figure is for the woman poet a means of assuming creative power.

For many women, celebrating their creativity demands that they challenge the myth that established man as powerful singer and woman as object of the song: the myth of Orpheus and Eurydice. The poem that best illustrates this effort is Muriel Rukeyser's "The Poem as Mask." Earlier, Orpheus had been a source of inspiration for Rukeyser, who wished to claim his orgiastic song as her own. But here she rejects an Orphic mask and voice:

> When I wrote of the women in their dances and wildness, it
> was a mask,
> on their mountain, gold-hunting, singing, in orgy,
> it was a mask; when I wrote of the god,
> fragmented, exiled from himself, his life, the love gone down
> with song,
> it was myself, split open, unable to speak, in exile from myself.
>
> . . . .
>
> No more masks! No more mythologies!
>
> Now, for the first time, the god lifts his hand,
> the fragments join in me with their own music.[122]

As Rukeyser's poem suggests, the rejection of the Orphic myth is fraught with difficulty, even though such rejection finally reunites the pieces of the self. Literary critic Elizabeth Sewell comments on the efficacy of the Orpheus legend: "Poetry is a form of power. It fell to early thought to make that power visible and human, and the story of Orpheus is that vision and that mortality."[123] Sewell further describes poetry as the only "real science" and Orpheus as its central voice, and she turns in support of this thesis to great male thinkers of all ages—Bacon, Shakespeare, Milton, Hooke, Swedenborg, Goethe, Wordsworth, Coleridge, Shelley, Emerson, Hugo, Mallarmé, and Rilke—each of whom views himself as an Orphic "visionary." It is this pervasive tradition from which the woman poet is omitted. Where, then, does she find her Orphic voice?

Some poets invoke as an alternate self Eurydice, the silent woman behind the song. In such poems Eurydice becomes a muse figure called forth by the woman poet to sing with and for her. H.D., for instance, bitterly renounces Orpheus from the viewpoint of Eurydice:

> so for your arrogance
> and your ruthlessness
> I am swept back
> where dead lichens drip
> dead cinders upon moss of ash;
>
> so for your arrogance
> I am broken at last.[124]

Despite her efforts at self-affirmation, H.D.'s Eurydice emerges as a desperate voice rather than a confident singer; she tries to assert her own music, to be her own muse, but finds only lyrics of defiance. For the contemporary poet alta, in contrast, Eurydice offers a voice from which to claim the full power of self-inspiration:

> all the male poets write of orpheus
> as if they look back & expect
> to find me walking patiently
> behind them. they claim i fell into hell.
> damn them, i say.
> i stand in my own pain
> & sing my own song.[125]

Similarly, Rachel Blau DuPlessis' Eurydice refuses to accompany Orpheus, preferring instead to explore her own creative matrix:

> He wants me to retrace the steps of my journey.
> No.
> I am turning.
> I am going deeper
> into the living cave.
>
> In the cave
> I am a rope held out to myself
> silver and gleaming in the labyrinth.
> I know the center of the cave.

Ultimately, the poet explains, Eurydice will give birth to a complex female self; she will become her own mother, her own muse:

> She will brood and be born
> girl of her own mother
> mother of the labyrinth
> daughter
> pushing
> the child herself outward
>
> great head, the cave large inside it
> great limbs of a giant woman
> great cunt, fragrant, opening
> seeds of Eurydice.[126]

As DuPlessis' poem suggests, women poets frequently look within for their lost roots, that matriarchal and mythological heritage from which their creative energy emanates. This quest, in turn, leads them to motherhood as a metaphor for their poetic creativity, as they link their imaginative capacities to their physiological ones. One myth that reflects this connection between motherhood and female creativity is that of Demeter and Kore. It is interesting that Carol Gilligan uses this myth to illustrate women's psychological attitude toward power. Citing the psychologist David McClelland, Gilligan explains that for most women, power is based on "the strengths of interdependence, building up resources and giving." The legend of Demeter and Kore thus speaks to and for women, for it shows that "narcissism leads to death, that the fertility of the earth is in some mysterious way tied to the continuation of the mother-daughter relationship."[127]

The female poet/female muse relationship closely parallels this mother-daughter bond. If any one figure replaces Orpheus for the woman poet, it is Demeter, whose legend reveals metaphorically the woman's quest for an "interdependent" poetic voice, her symbolic finding again of that which is most crucial to her. The Demeter-Kore model connotes woman's efforts to articulate a female creative principle; it acknowledges the important link between poetic and biological creativity in the woman; it recognizes woman's key role as nourisher and inspirer to other women; and it symbolizes the poet's rejuvenation through her "journey," the transforming of female experience into art. Carl Kérenyi asserts that to identify symbolically with Demeter means "to be pursued, to be robbed, raped, to fail to understand, to rage and grieve, but then to get everything back and be born again."[128] This description aptly parallels the modern woman poet's struggle to attain poetic identity and to name a female muse.

As Adrienne Rich notes, the "cathexis between mother and daughter—essential, distorted, misused—is the great unwritten story."[129] As such, it provides the modern woman poet with a potent metaphor for creative identity. This cathexis is represented mythologically by the story of Demeter, who will not rest until she rescues from Hades her beloved daughter. Because of the passion and complexity of this myth and of the Eleusinian mysteries that emerged from it, some women invoke Demeter as a re-visioned muse. In "Demeter in Sicily," for instance, Dorothy Wellesley claims this "mother" as a source of inspiration, one who has persisted despite patriarchal efforts to undermine her authority: "Grain-mother, thou art still our mother: now / These men thy servants / Push between stones the small and wooden plough." In paying tribute to Demeter, Wellesley identifies with the goddess's maternal anguish:

Hearken, my mother! In this early morn
I kneel to thee among narcissus flower,
For thy child Persephone at edge of dawn
Stole these to star the dark of Hades' bower,
To star the shadowy beauty of a kiss
Within the dear and dreadful arms of Dis.

For these things were we born.[130]

As an English aristocrat (wife of the Duke of Wellington), Wellesley nonetheless struggled to have her art accepted, to find voice. "If I were a man," she claimed in a letter to W. B. Yeats, "and had a wife to take practical life off my shoulders, I might start the inner life again."[131] Significantly, the poet's "inner life" is made possible here through her identification with this earth mother.

The goddess in H.D.'s "Demeter," in contrast, lacks the vitality of Wellesley's, for she has been relegated to a "mighty plinth." No longer a "living" deity, she is instead a statue whose words are "cut deep on the marble surface." But she is also a rebel. Other gods may overshadow her, Demeter declares, but those who would understand "inner mysteries" must seek her out. Furthermore, since Demeter's captors are "those men," it is clear that her supplicants, and those to whom her words are primarily addressed, are women:

Sleep on the stones of Delphi—
dare the ledges of Pallas
but keep me foremost,
. . . .

I am greatest and least.[132]

An interesting variation on the Demeter-Kore theme occurs in Robin Morgan's "Network of the Imaginary Mother," in which the mother-daughter bond parallels the poet's relationship with her "sister," who helps the poet get in touch with her creative self. If their childhood had differed, Morgan explains, perhaps she could have begun early to sing rather than to whisper.

Instead, the ancient tragedy of women closed around us,
our version identical with every other, unique
only in minute details of Eleusinian translation

reenacted, even as my arms reached to close round you
—the daughter I thought I'd found,
the mother I thought I'd lost,
Oh Demeter, oh Kore—
then something rose and walked again in me
and would not let me rest until
I could stand scrying for you worlds
of what no one could stop you from becoming,
until you were my miracle, my lever, the shuttle
of my loom, you not even minding that,
not suffocating in it, yet.

When did you begin to sense my power?

At the end of the poem, Morgan begins to "learn" from the power of the goddesses she invokes and the sister she re-members, to give birth to herself:

The passageway is cramped and blind
I am learning
though Kali dances through it, past
where Demeter still seeks Persephone,
where Isis searches for the fragments of Osiris. . . .
There is nothing I have not been,
and I am come into my power.

There is nothing I cannot be.[133]

For many modern poets, women from their own lives replace goddesses as primary inspirers. Such "familial" muses hold particular reverence for women of color. "Image making is very important for every human being," Maya Angelou explains.

> It is especially important for black American women in that we are, by being black, a minority in the United States and by being female, the less powerful of the genders. . . . We need to see our mothers, aunts, our sisters, and grandmothers. We need to see Frances Harper, Sojourner Truth, Fannie Lou Hamer, women of our heritage. We need to have these women preserved.[134]

Foremost among these women to be preserved is the biological mother, who may serve her daughter as a source either of nourishment or of ambivalence. For Alice Walker, her mother's emotions and stories offer quite literal inspiration:

> Just as you have certain physical characteristics of your mother's—her laughter or her toes or her grade of hair—you also internalize certain emotional characteristics that are like hers. That is part of your legacy. They are internalized, merged with your own, transformed through the stories. When you're compelled to write her stories, it's because you recognize and prize those qualities of her in yourself.[135]

The mother also provides energy for Cherríe Moraga, "*a white girl gone brown to the blood color of my mother / speaking for her through the unnamed part of the mouth / the wide-arched muzzle of brown women.*"[136] Another American woman of color, Nellie Wong, pays overdue homage to the mother whose inspiration she once denied:

> Well, I'm not ashamed of you anymore, Momma.
> My heart, once bent and cracked, once
> ashamed of your China ways.
> Ma, hear me now, tell me your story
> again and again.[137]

For other women, however, the mother-muse evokes pain and anxiety. In *The Woman Warrior*, Maxine Hong Kingston names her mother "shaman" and revels in her wisdom, yet she also suffers from the "talk-stories" forced upon her: "My mother has given me pictures to dream. . . . I push the deformed into my dreams, which are in Chinese, the language of impossible stories. Before we can leave our parents, they stuff our heads like the suitcases which they jam-pack with homemade underwear."[138] For Sylvia Plath, the mother is "Medusa," from whom she would unwrap herself: "Off, off, eely tentacle! / There is nothing between us."[139] May Sarton speaks also of the mother's "monstrous" properties: "My mother still remains the great devouring enigma . . . the Muse, you see."[140] But the mother who devours may also sustain. In *Yin*, Carolyn Kizer bemoans her fate as the creative daughter of a pushy mother: "Why was I chosen to live the life she wanted . . . ?" Yet when her mother dies, the poet recognizes the extent of her debt to this maternal muse, whose "hot breath of . . . expectations" nurtured her. "I wrote the poems for her, I still do."[141] As Rich points out in *Of Woman Born*, creative women must grapple with their ambivalence toward the mother if they are to understand themselves. Thus many women poets image in their work both the literal mother, who often lacks creative or other power, and the mothers they themselves are, or are becoming, to their art. As this fragment from Margaret Fuller's diary indicates, literal and figurative motherhood are often vitally interrelated for the woman writer:

> I have no child and the woman in me has so craved this experience, that it seems the want of it must paralyze me. But now as I look on these lovely children of a human birth, what slow and neutralizing cares they bring with them to the mother! The children of the muse come quicker, with less pain and disgust, rest more lightly on the bosom![142]

Other modern women celebrate the muse as female lover, one whose eroticism energizes the poet, making her work possible and meaningful; they affirm the words of Anne Sexton that "a woman / who loves a woman / is forever young."[143] As Audre Lorde proclaims in "Recreation," "it is easier to work after our bodies meet," for the lesbian lovers mirror and re-create each other: "my body / writes into your flesh / the poem / you make of me."[144] For Olga Broumas, too, the lover's complex physicality offers a potent source of speech:

I lie
between your sapling thighs, my tongue
flat on your double-lips, giving
voice, giving
voice.[145]

Adrienne Rich's "Twenty-one Love Poems" offers perhaps the fullest treatment of women lovers as muses for one another. "No one has imagined us," the poet tells her lover early in this sequence. "We're out in a country that has no language / no laws," singing "old songs / with new words." Rich's goal is to describe "with new meaning" the complexity and power of "two lovers of one gender, / . . . two women of one generation," nurturing each other "outside the law." Thus she challenges both patriarchal edict and masculinist literature, calling into question the courtly tradition of the objectified, passive lover-muse:

Tristan und Isolde is scarcely the story,
women at least should know the difference
between love and death. No poison cup,
no penance.

Instead of rehashing male-defined myths of love and creativity, Rich continues, women who love women must realize that "the story of our lives becomes our lives":

two women together is a work
nothing in civilization has made simple.
two people together is a work
heroic in its ordinariness,
the slow-picked, halting traverse of a pitch
where the fiercest attention becomes routine
—look at the faces of those who have chosen it.[146]

The phrase "heroic in its ordinariness" suggests another aspect of the poet-muse dialectic important to Rich and other women poets. "With whom do you believe your lot is cast?" Rich asks in "The Spirit of Place," posing a question she herself had already answered in "Natural Resources":

I choose to cast my lot
with those who, age after age,
perversely, with no extraordinary power,
reconstitute the world.[147]

"Extraordinary/ordinary" women often appear as muses to their creative sisters. Alice Walker's "Women," for example, celebrates those of "my mamma's generation / Husky of voice—Stout of / Step," who fought for their daughters' educations and hence their survival. The poet's final question/statement reverberates:

How they knew what we
Must know
Without knowing a page
of it
themselves.[148]

For Lucille Clifton, the "ordinary" woman is epitomized by "Miss Rosie," once "the best looking gal in Georgia," now "wrapped up like garbage / sitting, surrounded by the smell / of too old potato peels." As the poet watches Miss Rosie, she is moved to assert her own voice and power: "I stand up / through your destruction / I stand up."[149]

Finding creative identity through ordinary women is also the subject of Sandra Gilbert's "For the Muses." Her treatment differs from Clifton's or Walker's, however, in that Gilbert challenges directly the patriarchal restrictions on women's right to write:

They said I couldn't find you.
They said because I'm a *she*,
because the *s* in my name blurs my features,
a hiss around my face like uncombed hair,
you wouldn't be interested.

But the muses do embrace the emerging poet, largely because they, too, are nontraditional, domestic. "You were the immigrant aunts I visited / in the suburbs of my childhood. . . ." Gilbert goes on to invoke each inspirer by name and traits: Aunt Rose, whose black hair "grew in wings from your / forehead," Aunt Lil, whose white hair "circled your skull like a shawl"—givers of a *female* creative legacy transmitted via closets and kitchens.

You spoke to me there, you told me the stories.
I was yours as much as any boy.
Or more: for the notion of my breasts was yours,
You planned them, you designed them.

These maternal muses gave sustenance to the poet-niece, fashioned her breasts like their own. From a "rosewood wardrobe," Gilbert concludes, they offered her the gift of light, which

. . . came spilling out
and wrapped itself around my arms, my thighs, my shoulders
like a bolt of old satin.

"A mantle, not a shroud," you said.[150]

For other poets—Nellie Wong, for instance—the muse is a complex multiplicity of selves in communion with others:

> You are fueled by the clarity of your own sight, heated by your own energy to assert yourselves as a human being, a writer, a woman, an Asian American, a feminist, a clerical worker, a student, a teacher, not in loneliness and isolation, but in a community of freedom fighters.[151]

As Wong's words suggest, the re-visioned muse, fueled from within but not isolated, is a far cry from the passive inspirer of Graves and his peers. Instead, she is an activist, a revolutionary aspect of the poet's female and feminist consciousness. Both poet and muse find their endeavors difficult, feminist poets acknowledge, but they are necessary to transform literature and society.

For the modern woman poet, it would seem, the re-mythologized female muse offers an important metaphorical source of imaginative energy. In a "tribute" to woman's inspirational powers, Goethe declared at the end of *Faust* that "the Eternal Feminine leads us away." Twentieth-century women writers typically challenge the notion of an "Eternal Feminine" and reconstruct their creative journeys as voyages "within" and "toward," explorations that affirm their female voices and interdependent identities. Sandra M. Gilbert and Susan Gubar have asserted that in order to achieve literary autonomy, the woman writer must "come to terms with . . . those mythic masks male artists have fastened over her human face both to lessen their dread of her 'inconsistency' and—by identifying her with the 'eternal types' they themselves have invented—to possess her more thoroughly."[152] One such "eternal type" is the traditional female muse, a figure central to the oldest extant myths used to explain men's relationships to their art. If woman is to transcend her role as muse and assume that of poet, of powerful yet interdependent creator, she must revise these male myths, substituting for them stories and metaphors true to her female experience. By invoking a potent female muse, the modern woman poet relates her creativity to complex and original mythic structures. She defines a whole new psychic geography of women's literary imagination.

2

"My Scourge, My Sister": *The Elusive Muse of Louise Bogan**

"What makes a writer?" Louise Bogan asked in a lecture given at New York University during the 1960s. Rejecting the purist notion of a passionate love for the act of writing in itself, she explored such contributing factors as intellectual power, talent, and in particular, "gift":

> It is as a gift that I prefer to think of it. The ancients personified the giver of the gift as the Muse—or the Muses: the Daughters of Memory. The French use the word *souffle* figuratively for what passes between the Muse and the artist or writer—*le souffle du génie*—the breath of inspiration; and any writer worth his salt has felt this breath. It comes and goes; it cannot be forced and it can very rarely be summoned up by the conscious will.[1]

This passage reflects the importance for Bogan of the muse as a metaphor for poetic creativity, a concern she shares with many other modern women poets. Furthermore, the language of the quotation suggests that peculiar brand of creative ambivalence, the problem of reconciling one's poetic identity with one's gender, which often permeates the woman poet's struggle for her own voice. Traditionally the writer, especially the poet, has been assumed to be male: a prophet, a priest, an Orphic bard who sings eloquently and forcefully to and for those less gifted. The muse, on the other hand, has typically been personified as female, an inspiring Other imaged as the male poet's beneficent maternal helpmate, his seductive, elusive beloved, or a combination of the two. For Bogan, as for other women poets, this paradigm does not hold, yet she finds that tradition offers no alternative. Unable or unwilling here to speak directly from her frame of reference as a woman poet—to say, that is, "any writer worth *her* salt"—she is equally hesitant to attribute a specific sex to the muse. The

*An earlier version of this chapter was published in *Coming to Light: American Women Poets in the Twentieth Century*, ed. Diane Middlebrook and Marilyn Yalom. Ann Arbor: The University of Michigan Press, 1985. Used with permission.

poetic gift is "the breath of inspiration," "it," and the issue of who or what may be the source of this gift is not directly addressed.

Yet Bogan is aware of the problematic nature of the relationship between woman poet and muse. Despite the improved status of women effected by the modern feminist movement, she asserts,

> the problem of the woman artist remains unchanged. Henry James, in *The Tragic Muse*, speaks of "that oddest of animals, the writer who happens to be born a woman." Robert Graves has more recently said that women poets have a distinctly difficult problem, since they must be their own Muse.[2]

Bogan does not discuss the implications of these remarks, choosing instead to analyze the various powers and terrors attributed through the ages to woman in her roles as goddess, mother, wife, and lover; thus the questions she raises here remain unanswered. Who or what does Bogan perceive as her inspirational source? And is Graves' assertion that the woman poet must be her own muse applicable to Louise Bogan?

Like other women poets, from Anne Killigrew to Emily Dickinson to Adrienne Rich, Bogan invokes a muse very different from that of her male counterparts. For Bogan, the muse often emerges as a female figure whom she re-visions and re-mythologizes as an active rather than a passive inspirational force, a powerful alternate self rather than an externalized, objectified Other. At times Bogan images the muse as a demonic force with whom she must wrestle and yet through whom her own powers of creativity are given rise, to take shape in a perverse but potent language and voice. This fascination with a demonic muse, along with a struggle to redefine the "monster" within as a source of creative nurture and sustenance, reflects a problem inherent in Bogan's poetry and poetics: an intense conflict over her own artistic powers, a male-defined concept of the woman artist, and yet a keen desire for poetic subjectivity and strength.

For Bogan, then, this issue of the poet-muse relationship is an extremely complex matter closely connected to her ambivalence toward both her womanhood and her art—or her "craft," as Bogan, with her emphasis on technique and poetic process, might prefer. "Craft" suggests this poet's preoccupation with the formal and linguistic elements of poetry, as well as her "crafty" aesthetic strategy of employing female personae as distancing or masking devices. Through a process of dissociation she creates guises and images that let her conceal her central poetic concerns at the same time she reveals them, thereby producing what she describes in one poem as "terrible, dissembling music."[3] In a letter to *Poetry* editor Morton Zabel, Bogan claims that the poet must opt for "reticence" but not "guardedness," but the difference to which she alludes is often difficult to distinguish in her own work.[4] Like many women poets, Bogan experiences the conflict of the double bind: how to function successfully as both woman and poet in a culture that considers the two a contradiction in terms.[5] Her poems are filled with images of fragmentation, division, things "riven," to use a favorite Bogan adjective. Her strategies for coping with this conflict are suggested in an imagery of rage, solitude, and, finally, silence—an isolation fraught with despair and anger, which culminates in her prevalent metaphor of the silent voice. Yet from this silent voice emerges a paradoxically powerful speech, one informed by an inspirational source born of the poet's own female experience and creative energies. Ultimately it is from a female perspective that Bogan creates her "aesthetic of silence," and it is as a female force both demonic and benevolent that she perceives and personifies the giver of her gift, the muse: "my scourge, my sister."[6]

To understand the connection between Bogan's poetic strategies and her relationship to her muse, we must examine her perceptions of herself as woman and poet, her view of her female creativity. Much of the difficulty she confronts in attempting to move beyond the double bind stems from her ambivalent perception of herself as a poet with a "masculine" mind trapped in a woman's body and encumbered by a woman's emotions—her partial adherence, at least, to the prevailing biological and psychological views of her time, which attributed to woman certain innate physical and mental limitations. For example, in "The Heart and the Lyre," an essay essentially complimentary to women in its assessment of their visionary capacities, Bogan offers this generalization: women "are not good at abstractions and their sense of structure is not large; but they often have the direct courage to be themselves."[7] Yet what most women poets cannot do, Bogan states elsewhere, she feels compelled to do. "I am a woman, and 'fundamental brainwork,' the building of logical structures, the abstractions, the condensations, the comparisons, the reasonings, *are not expected of me*. But it is only when I am making at least an imitation of such a structure that I am really happy."[8] The conflict and the assumptions operating here are obvious. Bogan is "really happy" only when she is behaving as a rational creature capable of abstract thinking and logical action—behaving "like a man," some would have it—or, by extension, when as a poet she is appropriating "male" formal structures and techniques. Yet she is a woman, and she senses that such strategies are not altogether appropriate for her. Still, she chooses a highly compressed, chiseled verse quite different from the traditional "feminine" lyrical mode of a nineteenth-century "poetess," such as, say, Lydia Sigourney, whom Bogan calls "pious and lachrymose."[9] Defying categorization and stereotype, Bogan clearly wishes to make her mark as a *poet*, not as a *woman poet*. After all, she claims in an essay on Anne Sexton and May Swenson, it is "highly unfeminist" to "separate the work of women writers from the work of men."[10]

Bogan's desire to dissociate herself from the stereotypically "feminine" is also revealed in her attitude toward other women poets of her time. As feminist critic Gloria Bowles notes, Bogan fears that to ally herself with such poets would be to sacrifice her objectivity as a literary critic and her reputation as a "formal" poet.[11] Bogan once headed a "hate list" with "other women poets (jealousy!)," and although she apparently was joking and also listed "other men poets," the remark is revealing.[12] In her first few years as a critic she refused to review women poets at all, and in 1931, having reconsidered and written several such reviews, she regretted her change of heart: "I have found from bitter experience that one woman poet is at a disadvantage in reviewing another, if the review be not laudatory."[13] A few years later, in 1935, when asked to edit an anthology of poetry by women, she rejected the offer in misogynistic terms: "As you might have expected, I turned this pretty job down; the thought of corresponding with a lot of female songbirds made me acutely ill. It is hard enough to bear with my own lyric side."[14] Bowles argues that "lyric" here connotes that "sentimental and sappy" verse so often associated with early American women poets, but Bogan's vitriolic comment suggests a deep-seated fear of and resentment toward her own penchant for lyric poetry, her perverse wish both to "say herself," as she calls it, and *not* to say herself.[15]

A similar ambivalence informs her advice to women poets in "The Heart and the Lyre," as an older poet reflects on her own and her colleagues' goals and tasks. On the one hand, she urges women to "throw off the more superficial fashions of . . . society" in their poetry, apparently an appeal for a more "male-centered" art. Yet in the next breath she criticizes women who imitate "male verbalizers and poetic logicians" and offers an eloquent appraisal of women's vital role as "natural singers":

> For women to abandon their contact with and their expression of deep and powerful emotional streams, because of contemporary pressures or mistaken self-consciousness, would result in an impoverishment not only of their own inner resources but of mankind's at large. Certainly it is not a regression to romanticism to remember that women are capable of perfect and poignant song; and that when this song comes through in its high and rare form, the result has always been regarded not only with delight but with a kind of awe.[16]

Despite her eschewal of a "feminine" lyrical mode, Bogan apparently believes that women can and should provide a unique type of poetic song: "the intensity of their emotions is the key to the treasures of their spirit."[17] Yet how to handle intense emotions is a key source of conflict for Bogan in her own work.

This tendency to dissociate herself from the stereotypically feminine is also obvious in Bogan's poetry. In "Women," for instance, she explores the female role of provider, a passive rather than an active stance:

> Women have no wilderness in them,
> They are provident instead,
> Content in the tight hot cell of their hearts
> To eat dusty bread.

At first glance this stanza would appear to be a scathing indictment of female passivity and a dissociation of the poet herself from such feminine weakness, but Bogan's words and images here are double-edged. "Wilderness" means "wildness," uncharted and uncultivated territory, but it can also refer to an area designated to preserve natural resources, a haven or refuge. Thus the implications here are paradoxical: women typically lack wilderness and the freedom that accompanies such a state, but neither do they have an unlimited capacity to set aside the self as, the poet suggests, has long been expected of them. The same mixed associations accompany the adjective *provident*, which generally means "prudent" or "frugal" but is also a variant of *providential*, which can mean "potent" or "godsent." Furthermore, there is obvious irony in the poet's juxtaposition of "content" and "tight hot cell," a phrase that evokes anything but contentment. Women's hearts, tight in their oppression, resist the strictures of their prison cells. Hence the question of just how content they really are with their allotted fare, "dusty bread," is at best debatable. Does Bogan, then, describe women as satisfied and complacent, or are they churning behind their physical and psychological bars? And from whose viewpoint is this assessment being offered?

At first glance the rest of the poem suggests that Bogan herself, or a voice closely aligned to the poet's, is condemning the female sex for their unthinking acceptance of their lot. She refers to women as "they," not "we," and from this position of detachment offers a catalog of female failures. Women "do not see," "do not hear," "wait, when they should turn to journeys," "stiffen, when they should bend." Women are out of balance, these stanzas assert, their primary refuge a dangerous extreme: "their love is an eager meaninglessness / Too tense, or too lax." Yet the poem's language and tone belie such a simple reading. After all, women do possess "that benevolence / To which no man is friend," even if they do "use [it] against themselves." Furthermore, in the last stanza the speaker seems to sympathize and identify with the plight of women, forced to become defensive in order to create their own vision of reality:

> They hear in every whisper that speaks to them
> A shout and a cry.
> As like as not, when they take life over their door-sills
> They should let it go by.[18]

Until the end the poem's language is definitive and assertive, but the phrase "as like as not" introduces an element of uncertainty that undercuts the apparent denunciation of women that precedes it. In fact, given the shift of tone in this last stanza, it seems likely that the ironic speaker has been describing women's weaknesses from a traditional patriarchal perspective, not necessarily from the poet's own point of view. This last stanza reflects Bogan's recognition of women's difficult position, as well as her strategy for coping with such limitations.

Bogan also suffers from an internal conflict over that implacable force, her creativity. Toward her art as toward her gender, she is ambivalent; her poetic talent is both a boon and an encumbrance, a blessing and a curse. "Oh God," the young poet despairs in a letter to the classicist and translator Rolfe Humphries, "why were women born with ambition! I wish I could sit and tat, instead of wanting to go and write THE poem, or lie and kiss the ground."[19] But she also considers poetry "the life-saving process," that impetus without which she could not survive.[20] As is true for many women poets, Bogan sees her art as a demon-angel, at once a gift offered to the privileged few and a severe psychological struggle. "The practice of lyric poetry—the most intense, the most condensed, the most purified form of language—must be centered in a genuine gift," Bogan asserts early in her career. Again, however, paradox abounds. "It's silly to suggest the writing of poetry is something ethereal, a sort of soul-crashing, devastating emotional experience that wrings you. I have no fancy ideas about poetry. . . . It doesn't come to you on the wings of a dove. It's something you have to work hard at."[21] Yet Bogan knows that the hard work of poetry *is* often "soul-crashing, devastating," and she admits elsewhere that the lyric poet often experiences both doubt and terror and would rather do anything than write. This particular type of writer's block is especially intense for the woman, who has long been expected to "sit and tat" rather than to "work hard" as a writer. "The poem is always the last resort," Bogan asserts.[22]

Poetry for Bogan, then, is an odd combination of repression and release. "The poet," she explains, "represses the outright narrative of his life. He absorbs it, along with life itself. The repressed becomes the poem."[23] Yet that fusion of emotion and experience that explodes poetically is always tempered for Bogan by a large measure of restraint, a heavy suit of protective armor. Significantly, the woman poet she most admires is Marianne Moore, that master guardswoman whose measured verse Bogan praises precisely because it is unencumbered by excessive emotion. "Neither wistfulness nor that self-pity which often attacks women writers when they let down their guard has invaded these self-possessed poems."[24] Bogan fears that temptation to let down one's guard, to lose control or lapse into self-pity; yet she also recognizes the need to "say herself," to reveal those intense emotions so crucial to the female lyricist's art. Despite her resistance to self-revelation ("It has been so hard for me to 'make a full breast'"), her poetry reveals much about Bogan the woman; but it does so in a fragmented, enigmatic way.[25] The poet recognized this. "It is too late," she claimed near the end of her life, "either to pour it out or to reconstruct it, bit by bit. What mattered got into the poems. . . with the self-pity left out."[26] Poetry for Bogan ultimately "becomes a difficult *task*. And one that must be dissembled."[27]

An early, unpublished poem that explores the woman poet's "difficult task" is "Portrait of the Artist as a Young Woman." Here Bogan describes a young writer living abroad, as she herself did:

> Sitting on the bed's edge, in the cold lodgings, she wrote it
> out on her knee
> In terror and panic—but with the moment's courage,
> summoned up from God knows where.
> Without recourse to saints or angels: a Bohemian, thinking
> herself free—
> A young thin girl without sense, living (she thought) on
> passion and air.

The youthful poet's conflict is apparent. Frightened and solitary, she seizes "the moment's courage" and turns to her art, which relieves her "terror and panic" but exacerbates her sense of isolation. The poem's detached speaker analyzes the girl's situation: all she has, even though she lacks the "sense" to realize it, is the cathartic and life-preserving act of writing, an almost religious ritual "summoned up from God knows where."

In the stanzas that follow, Bogan describes the young poet's lonely life, over which she has little control. Winds blew her to this foreign place, we are told; the girl is compelled by some vague and nameless grief to remain alone in a room inhabited by ominous artifacts: an armoire that "broods," a bed that "engulfs." Silence and alienation are the pervading images of this part of the poem. The girl's "only refuge" is the "provincial stair," yet her neighbors are voiceless, "people without palates" who "try to utter"; only the library books seem human in their generosity toward the "silly young creature." Her desperation increases; as she returns to her room, "the trap seems to close," there seems no "way through." Finally, however, inspiration rises from within:

> But at last, asking to serve, seeking to earn its keep, about and
> about,
> At the hour between the dog and the wolf, is it her heart that
> speaks?
> She sits on the bed with the pad on her knees, and writes it
> out.[28]

This recurring image of the girl on the bed, persistently writing, marks a subtle shift of tone between the first and last stanzas. The portrait in the first stanza is etched with apparent objectivity by an older and presumably wiser voice, whose attitude toward the girl is condescending; obviously, we are led to believe, the silly young creature lacks the mature woman's insights. The speaker's use of the past tense in the initial description—"she wrote," "she thought"—adds to the distance between persona and girl. As the poem progresses, however, the speaker becomes less an observer and more a participant. The verbs shift to present tense, and the detached description of the first stanza gives way to a painful, tentative recounting of a very personal experience. The scene virtually re-creates itself: like the girl's poem, it writes itself out. Although the speaker never actually uses the first-person pronoun, her final tone is far less detached than that of the disdainful, patronizing voice in stanza one. The girl's concerns seem finally those of the older poet, the youthful heart her heart, the process of "writing it out" likewise the mature poet's means of halting, tentative affirmation.

Bogan never published this poem, perhaps because she believed that it would reveal more about the young woman of the poem than she wished. Self-revelation for Bogan is always accompanied by editorial discretion; like Emily Dickinson, she often tells the truth but tells it "slant." This tendency is illustrated in several other poems that explore the creative process. In "Homunculus," for example, the poet calls her creation "a delicate precious ruse," and she assumes godlike powers slightly subverted by a demonic tone:

O see what I have made!
A delicate precious ruse
By which death is betrayed
And all time given use.

The speaker's guise is that of a proud and clever trickster, Satan plotting the overthrow of an omnipotent God, perhaps, or the power-hungry Victor Frankenstein attempting to breathe life into his perverse creature. The thing created is paradoxical—slight but strong, young but wise—and the speaker goes on to assert great hope for the linguistic powers of her "ruse":

See this fine body, joined
More cleanly than a thorn.
What man, though lusty-loined,
What woman from woman born,

Shaped a slight thing, so strong,
Or a wise thing, so young?
This mouth will yet know song
And words move on this tongue.

Significantly, it is by giving the creature speech that the creator will bring it to consciousness.

It lacks but life: some scent
Some kernel of hot endeavor,
Some dust of dead content
Will make it live forever.[29]

The life-giving power of the gods is the poet's end, her art the means. Bogan celebrates here the power of language to transform silence into oracular speech, art into life; she invokes from within an inspirational force, the "kernel of hot endeavor," which gives birth to the work of art.

The resistant poet confronts another demanding muse-self in "The Daemon":

Must I tell again
In the words I know
For the ears of men
The flesh, the blow?

Must I show outright
The bruise in the side,
The halt in the night,
And how death cried?

Must I speak to the lot
Who little bore?
It said *Why not?*
It said *Once more.*[30]

In a letter to May Sarton, Bogan discusses this poem in the context of religious revolt: " 'The Daemon' . . . was written (given!) one afternoon almost between one curb of a street and another. *Why not?* is always a great help. God presses us so hard often that we rebel—and we should. Auden once told me that we should *talk back* to God; that this is a kind of prayer."[31] Bogan connects the daemon-muse to God, poetry to prayer, and the poet to a rebellious novice; moreover, the language and imagery of the poem evoke a Christ-like figure who continually must reenact a torturous crucifixion in order that "the lot / Who little bore" might at last hear.

As prominent as the poem's religious overtones, however, are its images of woman's sexual and literary vulnerability. Possession by the muse, the poet implies, is tantamount to rape; the painful recollection of "the flesh, the blow" and the subsequent bruise, halt, and death knell imply an act of sexual violence that the speaker-victim would prefer not to dwell upon. But withholding is not her option: the words must come, the story be told, regardless of how vulnerable such a revelation might make her. Bogan takes refuge in a sex-neutral pronoun, "it," but this aggressive force is most readily seen as male. Yet her male daemon clearly emerges from within her female self. The daemon's responses to the poet's resistance suggest two opposing facets of Bogan's attitude toward her art. The first response—"*Why not?*"—is ambiguous: ironical, flippant, whimsical on the one hand, matter-of-fact and logical on the other. The question format of this reply is significant, since the traditional oracular voice often speaks in a circular, riddling manner. However, the daemon's second reply—"*Once more*"—is emphatic, insistent. Despite her unwillingness, the poet *must* "tell again" and "show outright" that which she would prefer to conceal. The language and imagery of this poem reveal an ironic duality and tension between poet and muse. The poet is associated with divinity and prophecy, traditionally a male role, yet her sex and speech make her vulnerable—hence the association with female victimization. The daemon as well is two-sided, questioning yet definitive, mocking yet encouraging. Like Dickinson and Brontë before her, Bogan here imagines her daemon as male but claims as its source herself.

Bogan often attributes to her poetry a power stronger than her own, an energy both beyond her control yet paradoxically bound to her own creative vitality. In "Single Sonnet," for example, she addresses her poem as a rival talent with which she wrestles for control of their relationship:

> Now, you great stanza, you heroic mould,
> Bend to my will, for I must give you love:
> The weight in the heart that breathes, but cannot move,
> Which to endure flesh only makes so bold.
>
> Take up, take up, as it were lead or gold
> The burden: test the dreadful mass thereof,
> No stone, slate, metal under or above
> Earth is so ponderous, so dull, so cold.
>
> Too long as ocean bed bears up the ocean,
> As earth's core bears the earth, have I borne this;
> Too long have lovers, bending for their kiss,
> Felt bitter force cohering without motion.
>
> Staunch meter, great song, it is yours, at length,
> To prove how stronger you are than my strength.[32]

Here the poet personifies her sonnet as a lover, a potent erotic force that she hopes will relieve her of the "weight in the heart," the "burden," the "dreadful mass" under which she suffers. The analogy between poet/poem and lover/beloved extends into the third stanza, which depicts the stasis that results when passion goes awry: "Too long have lovers, bending for their kiss, / Felt bitter force cohering without motion." Likewise, Bogan asserts, the once dynamic tension between poet and sonnet can become static and oppressive.

In this poem Bogan complains of the sonnet's fetters and struggles with its power to test the poet's art and artifice. Yet she also exults in her own mastery over both the sonnet's content and its form. As poets through the ages have written sonnets about love, so will she "give . . . love," but to the form itself rather than to a human lover. Bogan admires the sonnet form, but she also believes that women poets in particular have often fallen victim to its debilitating aspects. "The sonnet *as such* is never discursive," she writes to May Sarton. "It is dramatic: the dramatic lyric framework." Yet many women poets make it discursive, she asserts, and she goes on to decry the reliance of poets like Wylie and Millay on what she considers the "sentimental" sonnet sequence, which she thinks can no longer be written "with any hope of effectiveness."[33] While Bogan would hardly eschew the powerful sonnet form, she sets out to expand its traditional parameters, to "bend" this "heroic mould" to her own "will." She wants to be free from the oppressive weight of the traditional love sonnet: "too long . . . have I borne this." Thus she adds a new dimension to the sonnet convention and affirms her own poetic potency. As her stalwart creation asserts its voice, it also reveals its creator's power: "Staunch meter, great song, it is yours, at length, / To prove how stronger you are than my strength."

The sonnet is not the only poetic form that causes Bogan conflict; she also resists her occasional impulse to stray from a tightly crafted mode to a looser, longer line, which she perceives as self-indulgent and therefore dangerous. "Short Summary," for instance, begins,

> Listen but once to the words written out by my hand
> In the long line fit only for giving ease
> To the tiresome heart.[34]

The poet is attracted to yet put off by the "long line," which she views as too cathartic an impulse. As in "Single Sonnet," she struggles here with her art as a competitor. This same theme appears in "Poem in Prose":

> I turned from side to side, from image to image, to put you down,
> All to no purpose; for you the rhymes would not ring—
> Not for you, beautiful and ridiculous, as are always the true inheritors of love,
> The bearers; their strong hair moulded to their forehead as though by the pressure of hands.
> It is you that must sound in me secretly for the little time before my mind, schooled in desperate esteem, forgets you—
> And it is my virtue that I cannot give you out,
> That you are absorbed into my strength, my mettle,
> That in me you are matched, and that it is silence which comes from us.[35]

In this poem, as in "Short Summary" and "Single Sonnet," Bogan's formal struggle is poignantly rendered but ultimately resolved. After the initial complaint, again couched in the language of love, the poet quickly resumes control: "It is *you* that must sound in *me*" (my italics). Although her mind, "schooled in desperate esteem," resists this kind of self-expression, she ultimately revels in the flexible rhyme scheme and rhythm pattern that allow her to explore her own power. In so doing, she realizes that artist and artifact are essentially inseparable, that each is a match for the other because each *is* the other. In all three of these poems, therefore, Bogan struggles with a dual conflict peculiar to the woman poet: as an artist she wrestles for mastery of different but equally complex verse forms, and as a woman she strives for legitimacy and poetic power within the masculine literary tradition.

The final image of "Poem in Prose"—"it is silence which comes from us"—deserves special consideration because it helps us understand how Bogan uses silence as a metaphor for the female artistic quest. This understanding, in turn, sheds light on her views of her own creativity and her muse. Many of Bogan's poems about the creative process contain at least one central image of silence or thwarted speech:

People without palates trying to utter, and the trap seems to close.

Must I tell again / In the words I know . . . ?

This mouth will yet know song / And words move on this tongue.

A smothered sound . . . long lost within lost deeps.

Still it is good to strive . . . to echo the shout and the stammer.

Hearing at one time . . . / that checked breath bound to the mouth and caught / Back to the mouth, closing its mocking speech . . .

And it is my virtue . . . that it is silence which comes from us.

Similar lines appear in other poems, and an imagery of silence or aborted speech frequently informs the poet-muse interaction. Why does Bogan insist upon this perverse imagery that asserts even as it denies her poetic power?

Silence is hardly a new poetic image; indeed, textual silence—the absence of dialogue, the presence of elliptical, cacophonous speech—is a frequent metaphor in modern literature. In his discussion of silence as a central mode of expression, if not a *raison d'être*, in modern and postmodern works, contemporary critic Ihab Hassan asserts that a "sense of outrage" induces literary silence, "a metaphysical revolt and at the same time metaphysical surrender, which is the desire for nothingness." Hassan views this tendency toward negation as a paradoxically healthy sign, "a new attitude that literature has chosen to adopt toward itself" as a means of challenging traditional assumptions, and he argues that the metaphor of poetic silence parallels and extends the myth of Orpheus in a context applicable to the modern poet. Faced with existential despair and the possibility of annihilation, Hassan asserts, the modern poet *must* speak from a severed head; only by directly confronting his own fragmentation and the volatile nature of his world can he continue to sing.[36] I use the generic "he" deliberately, for although Hassan's analysis does not specifically exclude women writers, his focus is primarily on male writers, his assumptions about the artist's sex and nature those of traditional patriarchal literature and scholarship.

Feminist writer Tillie Olsen offers a different perspective on the significance of silence for the woman writer, for whom it has traditionally been an obstacle to overcome, "the unnatural thwarting of what struggles to come into being, but cannot."[37] Olsen is especially interested in Louise Bogan, and although she does not analyze Bogan's use of an imagery of silence, she does speculate about why this "consummate poet" wrote so little. Olsen views Bogan's passion for perfection as a compensatory mania that, she believes, often consumes women writers, who feel stigmatized by their gender and thus make excessive demands of themselves. Citing a letter in which Bogan describes her own critical bent as "the knife of the perfectionist attitude in art and life," Olsen concludes that this poet represents "one of our most grievous 'hidden silences.'"[38]

Both Hassan's and Olsen's analyses are relevant to the issue of silence as a prominent metaphor in Bogan's poetry, but neither accounts completely for the use of silence as a strategy in women's art. Like many other writers, Bogan uses silence as a means of transforming the liabilities of isolation and fragmentation into assets. But, as Olsen suggests, Bogan's search for voice is not merely that of the typical modern poet confronting the existential void, but rather that of the modern *woman* poet experiencing the predicament of gender alienation as well. Remote from the enterprise of poetry because of her sex and her time, she frequently responds to this isolation by setting inordinately high artistic standards and writing little, thus isolating herself still further by her self-imposed demands for perfection. Furthermore, she cannot deny her womanhood; thus her fear that her voice will be viewed by others as less "universal" than that of her male counterparts causes her to become her own harshest critic. She not only "consents to [her own] dismemberment," she actively participates in it.[39] This is not to suggest a masochism at work, however, for the woman writer typically dismembers in order to reconstruct. Once the old stance is broken down, she starts to "re-member" on her own terms, and by her own means. For Louise Bogan, one such means of re-membering is a perverse and stony silence that, ironically, provides a strong voice from which to speak. This silence is neither Hassan's "desire for nothingness" nor Olsen's "atrophy," but rather a singular response to the woman poet's quest for autonomous expression, a means by which she can both reveal and conceal her powerful poetic voice.

Bogan is not alone among women poets in adopting this strategy of the silent voice. In "The Art of Silence and the Forms of Women's Poetry," the feminist critic Jeanne Kammer discusses the tendency among a number of women poets—notably Emily Dickinson, H.D., and Marianne Moore—to use silence as a means of both expressing and denying their gender-related frustrations. Chief among the characteristics of "expression-suppression" is what Kammer, borrowing the term from the literary critic Philip Wheelwright, calls "diaphoric" metaphor: a type of linguistic and imagistic compression characterized by paradox, ellipsis, syntactic inversion, complex sentence embeddings, and ironic juxtaposition of two or more concrete images.[40] Although Kammer notes that diaphor is a trait of much modern poetry, she argues that the source of this aesthetic choice is unique for the woman poet. Her feeling of cultural powerlessness, her realization that the bardic "epiphoric" voice is not hers, leads her to diaphor.

Silence for Bogan is an aesthetic strategy functioning within the framework of the diaphoric mode. As a method of confrontation with world, art, and self, silence becomes a potent and dynamic strategy of subversion for her and ultimately a central tenet of her art. Silence is necessary for self-apotheosis for Bogan, and the metaphor of the silent voice reflects her creative ambivalence and her demonic and benevolent sides. This use of silence is particularly well illustrated in poems about the female muse, those that celebrate the goddess as a source of poetic energy. The line "it is silence which comes from us," then, reveals Bogan's view of the source of her inspiration, the "us" within, and suggests a key image by which she depicts that inspirational force. For Bogan, "the loud sound and pure silence fall as one."[41]

As her poetry about the creative process and her "aesthetic of silence" indicate, Bogan both fears and thrives on her creative strength. Female figures serve as muses in her poems, alternate selves at once sources and manifestations of the poet's struggle *with* herself *for* herself. These female figures provide artistic nourishment and sustenance that help Bogan come to terms with "that crafty demon and that loud beast," the demonic side of herself.[42] Bogan's muses are sometimes powerful women of the poet's own invention and sometimes mythological women, goddesses of vengeance and power; in either case, they represent her efforts to depict her internal conflict and her relationship to her creativity within the framework of a female-centered mythology.

Often the poems in this group have two female protagonists: a potent, dynamic force who may be either the muse or the poet, depending on the context; and a second woman, either curiously absent from the central action or, when present, passive and frightened. In "The Crossed Apple," for example, Bogan uses a fairy-tale motif to dramatize the plight of one suffering from psychic fragmentation, unable to reconcile body and mind, passion and reason. Although the sex of the speaker here is not specifically identified, the voice recalls both that of Satan goading Eve to taste the forbidden fruit and that of the stepmother-witch-temptress of such fairy tales as *Snow White*. If Bogan is following folk rather than religious lore, which seems likely given the casual narrative tone and singsong rhythm of the poem, the speaker is best envisioned as a female crone, envious yet solicitous. The younger woman remains significantly silent. "The Crossed Apple" begins with the speaker inviting the maiden to sample her prized fruit:

> I've come to give you fruit from out my orchard,
> Of wide report.
> I have trees there that bear me many apples
> Of every sort:
>
> Clear, streakèd; red and russet; green and golden;
> Sour and sweet.

Like the temptress of folklore, the speaker tries to enchant the maid with a special, magical fruit, half "red without a dapple," and half "clear and snowy":

> Oh, this is a good apple for a maid,
> It is a cross,
>
> Fine on the finer, so the flesh is tight,
> And grained like silk.
> Sweet Burning gave the red side, and the white
> Is Meadow Milk.

The sexual implications here are obvious, and the speaker delights in describing the tight, silky flesh of the crossed apple, ripe for the taking. The witch-woman further tempts the maiden by insisting that if she partakes of this apple, she will know the secrets of the universe:

> Eat it; and you will taste more than the fruit:
> The blossom, too,
> The sun, the air, the darkness at the root,
> The rain, the dew,
>
> The earth we came to, and the time we flee,
> The fire and the breast.

In this description are several images that appear throughout Bogan's poetry: the darkness faced by the struggling soul, the flight from time, the fires of passion and transformation. To these she adds another, the nurturing and pure "Meadow Milk," linked to the female breast and probably a symbol for female creativity. The speaker finally claims the white part of the fruit: "maiden, that's for me. / You take the rest."[43]

As with all good fairy tales, this one can be read a number of ways, but this fable seems to depict the division between woman and artist. The maiden and the crone represent two sides of a single psyche that, when combined, present a balanced version of innocence and experience, youth and old age, weakness and strength: Demeter and Kore, mother and daughter, fused and whole. As Bogan realizes, however, such a balanced state is difficult to attain; savoring the entire apple, after all, is simply not an option for either speaker or maiden. Significantly, the "I" of the poem rejects the "Sweet Burning" side of the apple in favor of the enriching "Meadow Milk," the substance on which the female artist is sustained. Bogan uses female imagery within a fairy-tale motif to describe the sexual ambivalence of the woman and the creative ambivalence of the poet.

Another poem that features two contrasting female forces is "The Dream," which also offers a "nightmare" account of Bogan's struggles as woman and poet:

> O God, in the dream the terrible horse began
> To paw at the air, and make for me with his blows.
> Fear kept for thirty-five years poured through his mane,
> And retribution equally old, or nearly, breathed through
> his nose.
>
> Coward complete, I lay and wept on the ground
> When some strong creature appeared, and leapt for the
> rein.
> Another woman, as I lay half in a swound,
> Leapt in the air, and clutched at the leather and chain.

Give him, she said, something of yours as a charm.
Throw him, she said, some poor thing you alone claim.
No, no, I cried, he hates me; he's out for harm,
And whether I yield or not, it is all the same.

But like a lion in a legend, when I flung the glove
Pulled from my sweating, my cold right hand,
The terrible beast, that no one may understand,
Came to my side, and put down his head in love.[44]

In a letter to May Sarton, Bogan describes "The Dream" as "a poem of victory and of release. The terrible power, which may v. well be the psychic demon, is tamed and placated but NOT destroyed; the halter and the bit were already there, and something was done about *control* and *understanding*."[45] Significantly, the person who ensures that "control and understanding" are attained is not the vulnerable "I" but a "strong creature," "another woman." This potent alternate self insists that the weaker woman renounce her fears and take action to charm the "terrible beast." She must tame and transform this "psychic demon" but not eliminate it altogether, for it serves a useful function. It is no accident that the demon is imaged as a wild male horse, an awesome creature that feeds on fear and retribution. This poem depicts what is most threatening to Bogan: the "masculine" side of her ambitious self, her "pathological pride," and an irrational, "feminine" fear, for which she castigates herself and which she would like to exorcise.[46]

Another letter by Bogan about "The Dream" supports this notion of "fright and horror" transformed into a vital, positive force:

> "The Dream" is a later poem, written in my late thirties, after a complete change in my way of living, and in my general point of view about life (and the universe at large!). It is the actual transcript of "a nightmare," but there is reconciliation involved with the fright and horror. It is through the possibility of such reconciliations that we, I believe, manage to live.[47]

The resolution and transformation of terror, then, is the subject of "The Dream" and indeed one of Bogan's chief poetic concerns. In her most powerful poems, those in which she struggles intensely for psychic control and artistic autonomy, she often portrays her persona as a passive or awestricken "coward complete," compelled by a superior force to push beyond her self-imposed limitations. By taking action, the persona learns to recognize the fallacy inherent in her assumption that "whether I yield or not, it is all the same." Significantly, this lesson can be taught only by a female Other who is at the same time an aspect of the self, a creative force emerging from within. Only with the assistance of this leaping, clutching, demanding female muse is the poet able to assume control over herself and her art.

In addition to the muses Bogan invents, she also turns to women from mythology, whose strength she must take on in order to release her own hidden powers. That Bogan recognizes the strong symbolic link between the woman poet and goddesses of antiquity is indicated in "What the Women Said," an essay in which she explores their beneficent and demonic nature:

> At first their manifestation is double: they cherish and they terrify. Cybele, mother of all the gods, with her crown of towers, brought over by the Greeks from the Asian continent, and to be treasured by the Romans; Isis, in the dark backward of Egyptian time, corn goddess, mother of earth and of heaven, sister and wife to Osiris; the Hindu Kali, wife of Siva, goddess, according to one definition, of "feminine energy," with her necklace of skulls. And it was a woman who, at Delphi, the center of the Greek world, uttered the words of the god. It was a woman (Socrates'—or was it Plato's?) Diotima, who, in the manner of all good female teachers down the ages, told the philosopher to follow his daemon; it was a female goddess [sic] who gave Athens its name. And, in the opinion of a modern Cambridge Hellenist, it was Spartan women who led the fullest, happiest, best adjusted lives of any women in history. This opinion is rather a blow to the female artist, since Spartan women produced no art of any kind; Sappho was an Eastern Greek from an island off Asia Minor.[48]

With characteristic irony, Bogan slaps the hands of the scholar who equates women's fulfillment with traditional female roles. For artistic sustenance, she suggests, the woman poet must draw upon her deific female predecessors.

Despite this celebration of mythological women as both "vocal and visible," however, Bogan often portrays her gift from these inspirational forces not as a bardic song but as a sphinxlike silence, a voice befitting the passive-aggressive female whom she envisions. As I suggested earlier, Bogan's silent voice is a poetic device by which she attains power and yet acknowledges her conflict. In this regard she anticipates contemporary French theorists who regard silence as one of the woman writer's most revolutionary means of self-expression, a key tool in her rebellion against the male-dominated language and literature that have excluded many women. One such critic, Hélène Cixous, suggests that to symbolize her search for a language expressive of her own female body and essence, the woman writer should use an indelible and invisible white ink, thereby creating a hermetic inscription out of mother's milk. This new "script" would symbolize her alienation from the patriarchy and her community with other female forgers of new truths.[49] Although Bogan would have scoffed at the idea of white ink symbolizing female creativity, she uses a similar image in the "Meadow Milk" of "The Crossed Apple"; furthermore, in three poems that focus on mythological women as sources of power, she employs silence as a tool similar to Cixous' "white ink," though without the consciousness of a feminist vision. The absence of a speech that is present, like the invisibility of an ink that flows, represents women's paradoxical "repressed expression"—her gift of silent speech, her passive resistance to patriarchal dictates. Alongside silence as a dominant image is solitude, which Bogan depicts as a companion-source of creative nourishment, a way by which the female quester can attain the freedom of one whose "body [may] hear no echo save its own."[50] Silence and solitude, then, are the central images of her most revealing poems about the muse.

A solitude not chosen is implicit in the fate and voice of Cassandra, the female prophet of Greek mythology punished by Apollo for insubordination by being awarded a gift of prophecy to which no one would listen. In "Cassandra" Bogan treats this mythic figure's plight as a metaphor for that of a woman poet:

> To me, one silly task is like another.
> I bare the shambling tricks of lust and pride.
> This flesh will never give a child its mother,—
> Song, like a wing, tears through my breast, my side,
> And madness chooses out my voice again,
> Again. I am the chosen no hand saves:
> The shrieking heaven lifted over men,
> Not the dumb earth, wherein they set their graves.[51]

Cassandra's stance as a female prophet dissociated from other women and from other prophets parallels Bogan's view of herself as a woman poet, alienated from other women and their "silly tasks" as well as from male poets. Like Cassandra, doomed by her own plaintive cry, the poet is isolated by her poetic gift, at once a debilitating and an empowering force. Neither the poet nor Cassandra chooses her gift of isolation, and both are ambivalent toward this power imposed by forces beyond their control. Cassandra's song literally attacks her, tearing through her breast and side; its source, madness, overwhelms its unwilling victim again and again. Ironically, then, both strength and weakness lie at the root of Cassandra's gift of prophecy. She is chosen for divinity yet not saved from suffering, empowered with song but ignored by all. Yet from this same song she derives her power.

Cassandra's mad, screaming voice provides a significant contrast to the deliberate predictions of other prophets from mythology—the blind Tiresias, for example, or Isaiah. Instead, her warnings might be likened to those of the oracle of Delphi, whose prophecies often went unheeded because their complexity defied mortal interpretation. Cassandra's plight and its attendant powers recall the conflict that Bogan describes in "The Daemon," as the poet is forced to recount repeatedly "the words . . . the flesh, the blow" to "the lot / Who little bore." Clearly Bogan perceives herself as a modern version of Cassandra, plagued and yet empowered by an insistent muse to speak not in a bardic voice, but in an oracular one.[52] In "Cassandra," Bogan finds her own seer's truths through the potent voice of a woman twice disenfranchised: by the madness that "chooses out my voice again, / Again," and by the alienating yet restorative silence that receives her unheeded cries, turning them back upon themselves.

Silence forms the core of "Medusa," a poem in which Bogan directly confronts her own demonic aspect in the guise of the terrifying Gorgon, who according to classical myth turns onlookers into stone. Rather than being a totally debilitating encounter, however, this confrontation helps the poet to assume some of Medusa's frozen, silent power. The poem begins with a description of the awesome meeting:

I had come to the house, in a cave of trees,
Facing a sheer sky.
Everything moved,—a bell hung ready to strike,
Sun and reflection wheeled by.

When the bare eyes were before me
And the hissing hair,
Held up at a window, seen through a door.
The stiff bald eyes, the serpents on the forehead
Formed in the air.[53]

As the poet encounters Medusa, a whirlwind carries the reflection of house, trees, and sky into the poet's range of vision. This image of reflection is especially crucial, since according to legend, the Gorgon's hideous face must be viewed only indirectly, lest the observer be petrified with fright and cast into stone. Significantly, however, the poet confronts the "bare eyes" and "hissing hair" directly. This act of boldness recalls the male quester of another Bogan poem, "A Tale," who finds endurance only "where something dreadful and another / Look quietly upon each other." It also anticipates later poems, such as "March Twilight," where a watcher gazes into "another face," only to see "Time's eye"; or "Little Lobelia's Song," where the childlike speaker sees reflected in her own face the image of a potent Other.[54] As these later poems suggest, this notion of an eye-to-eye encounter between speaker and shadow, that other self both frightening and recognizable, is crucial to Bogan's poetic imagery and to her perception of the poet-muse relationship. Only by looking squarely at the "beast within," Bogan believes, can the poet come to terms with her own hidden powers.

The last three stanzas of "Medusa" describe a scene transformed, as both time and motion are suspended in the wake of the Gorgon's power:

This is a dead scene forever now.
Nothing will ever stir.
The end will never brighten more than this,
Nor the rain blur.

The water will always fall, and will not fall,
And the tipped bell make no sound.
The grass will always be growing for hay
Deep on the ground.

And I shall stand here like a shadow
Under the great balanced day,
My eyes on the yellow dust, that was lifting in the wind,
And does not drift away.

Medusa exercises her powers of transformation by recasting her surroundings into silence and stasis, a state that parallels the perpetual suspension of the scene on Keats' Grecian urn. Ironically, however, the poet's insistent voice emerges from this silence. Although Bogan calls this a "dead scene," life flourishes amid the stasis ("the grass will always be growing for hay / Deep on the ground"), and her description conveys a tentative resolution. As the poet stands "like a shadow / Under the great balanced day," she becomes a new Medusa, a passive-aggressive goddess capable of controlling herself and her craft, of "killing" life into art. Medusa's silence provides Bogan a powerful, if static, stance from which to speak. The poet's usurpation of the goddess's strength recalls Yeats' enigmatic question at the end of "Leda and the Swan": "Did she put on his knowledge with her power / Before the indifferent beak could let her drop?"[55] Unlike Leda, who was forced by Zeus into female subservience, the poet confronts her goddess as a same-sex equal, and that makes all the difference. Bogan does assume both the knowledge and the power of Medusa, her demonic muse, and through this power she redefines stony silence as creative energy.

The transference of power from goddess to poet is a central theme also of "The Sleeping Fury," another poem of homage to a female muse. Medusa, Cassandra, the Amazon of "The Dream," the temptress of "The Crossed Apple"—virtually all of Bogan's strong, demonic women fuse here into the single evocative image of the fury, "my scourge, my sister," once violent and vengeful but now at rest. This demonic alternate self alludes, of course, to the maenads of Greek mythology, those orgiastic "madwomen" who avenged Clytaemnestra and dismembered Orpheus, and who are generally associated with matriarchal rule. For Bogan, the fury represents an awesome and frightening aspect of her self, one that she has difficulty accepting but that she must confront and control if her art is to flourish. An imagery of transformation dominates the poem, as the fury's destructive vengeance is rejected in favor of a hard-won harmony, a reconciliation of opposing forces: noise and silence, fear and calm, rage and release, demonism and beneficence, war and peace. Ultimately at one with her fury, the poet affirms her own vital powers born of silence, solitude, and strength gleaned from the goddess-muse.

The poem's first two stanzas describe the "raging beast" now sleeping peacefully:

> You are here now,
> Who were so loud and feared, in a symbol before me,
> Alone and asleep, and I at last look long upon you.
>
> Your hair fallen on your cheek, no longer in the semblance of serpents,
> Lifted in the gale; your mouth, that shrieked so, silent.
> You, my scourge, my sister, lie asleep, like a child,
> Who, after rage, for an hour quiet, sleeps out its tears.

Confrontation and transformation are key motifs here, as the poet assesses this symbol that has become a reality—a force to be gazed at, reflected upon, and reckoned with. The fury once was overpowering: a Medusa whose hair writhed with deadly serpents, a Cassandra whose shrieking voice would not be silenced. Aware at last, however, of her close link to this female force, still awesome yet paradoxically childlike, Bogan accepts the fury as both scourge and sister. As she reflects in tranquility, she derives new meaning from what was once a symbol of horror; her fury becomes a tool for transforming chaos into creative energy. Bogan goes on to describe the furies' fierce nocturnal pursuits, as they travel *en masse* on a reign of terror, avenging themselves through sacramental offerings and clamoring for sacrificial blood. "Hands full of scourges, wreathed with . . . flames and adders," Bogan's fury, the "you" of the poem, is particularly vindictive: "You alone turn away, not appeased; unaltered, avenger." Significantly, this shouting, insatiable fury is both separate from and part of the poet, bound to the speaker's side like a shadow: "You alone turned away, but did not move from my side."

Although revenge is the furies' chief occupation, Bogan suggests, these goddesses also manifest powers of revelation. Stanzas six and seven recount the confrontations insisted upon by the furies, as they expose at dawn "the ignoble dream and the mask, sly, with slits at the eyes, / Pretence and half-sorrow, beneath which a coward's hope trembled." Unmasking the coward, the false lover, the liar is a process crucial to both fury and poet, Bogan implies, and one that must begin with inward exploration. The autonomous self can emerge, however, only after meeting the awesome fury:

> You who know what we love, but drive us to know it;
> You with your whips and shrieks, bearer of truth and of solitude;
> You who give, unlike men, to expiation your mercy.
>
> Dropping the scourge when at last the scourged advances to meet it,
> You, when the hunted turns, no longer remain the hunter
> But stand silent and wait, at last returning his gaze.

As in "Medusa" and a host of other poems, Bogan employs here the image of face-to-face confrontation to symbolize the transference of power from goddess to mortal woman, muse to poet. As the eyes of the scourged meet those of the scourge, as the hunted advances to face the hunter, the fury's whip and knives are laid to rest, her shouts silenced.

At last the poet's affirmative voice assumes control, a voice emerging from the quiet aftermath in a manner reminiscent of the last line of "Poem in Prose": "it is silence which comes from us." Having exorcised the demon with the power of the "daemon," Bogan confronts a solitary and powerful female self:

> Beautiful now as a child whose hair, wet with rage and tears
> Clings to its face. And now I may look upon you,
> Having once met your eyes. You lie in sleep and forget me.
> Alone and strong in my peace, I look upon you in yours.[56]

This chapter began with questions essential to an understanding of Louise Bogan's poetry and poetics: who or what does Bogan perceive as her muse, and what images does she use to mythologize her relationship to this inspirational source? And to what extent is Robert Graves correct in asserting that the woman poet must "be her own muse"? As indicated in poems about creative inspiration, the muse for Bogan is an aspect of the self, a shadow figure at once demonic and sustaining, silent and vocal, solitary and strong. The balance achieved when scourge and sister attain a reconciled peace provides the poet with a primary source of artistic nourishment. In turn, her art, specifically her "aesthetic of silence," is a crucial tool by which she learns to control her furies, in order to keep them from controlling her. In Bogan's case, therefore, Graves' assertion is accurate. By invoking strong female figures who serve as both sources and manifestations of her creativity, the woman poet becomes her own muse.

This is not to say that Bogan completely overcomes her creative ambivalence; her reconciled peace is tentative at best, her hold on it tenuous. Her conflicts over the woman poet's "singular role and precious destiny" continue throughout her life, permeating both her poetry and her prose.[57] "It is a dangerous lot, that of the charming, romantic public poet, especially if it falls to a woman," Bogan claims in an essay on Edna St. Vincent Millay, and she goes on to reveal her own conflicted vision of the aging female creator:

> It is difficult to say what a woman poet should concern herself with as she grows older, because women poets who have produced an impressively bulky body of work are few. But is there any reason to believe that a woman's spiritual fiber is less sturdy than a man's? Is it not possible for a woman to come to terms with herself, if not with the world; to withdraw more and more, as time goes on, her own personality from her productions; to stop childish fears of death and eschew charming rebellions against facts?[58]

Clearly Bogan is not certain what is possible for the woman poet, or even what is desirable. Aware of the need to "come to terms with herself," insistent that her own "spiritual fiber" equals a man's, she still is entrapped by the notion that art requires an extinction of self—that, in the words of T. S. Eliot, the "man who suffers" must be separate from "the mind which creates."[59] For Bogan as for many other women poets of her time, especially heterosexual poets, male-defined and devoid of female community, the public and private selves must remain distinct. Yet her poems and essays reveal the painful psychic fragmentation that a lifetime of personal and artistic struggle may bring.

Despite Eliot's admonition and her own insecurities, however, Bogan refuses to extinguish the creative self; indeed, she often revels in its powers and perversities. "Like scales, cleanly, lightly played," she admits, "myself rises up from myself."[60] By confronting the shadow-self, Bogan moves closer to an affirmation of self and art. In the words of Adrienne Rich, Bogan's work represents "a graph of the struggle to commit a female sensibility, in all its aspects, to language. We who inherit that struggle have much to learn from her."[61]

"Write, Write or Die": The Goddess Muse of H.D.

This must be my stance,
my station: though you brushed aside

my verse,
I can't get away from it,
I've tried to;

true, it was "fascinating . . .
if you can stand its preciousness,"
you wrote of what I wrote;

why must I write?
you would not care for this,
but She draws the veil aside,

unbinds my eyes,
commands,
write, write or die.[1]

This passage from H.D.'s last volume of poetry, *Hermetic Definition*, reveals the frustration, ambivalence, and power at the root of her attempt to forge a strong creative identity. "This *must be* my stance, my station," the poet insists, distressed at the devaluation of her work by the patronizing "you" of the poem. H.D.'s pain and anger surface as she quotes the critic's condescending words: "fascinating . . . if you can stand its preciousness."[2] Also apparent here is her own ambivalence toward an art that produces the indictment of faint praise. "True," she admits of the critic's assessment, implicitly affirming his judgment. She has "tried to . . . get away from" her poetry, she continues, but its powers are greater than her own. Despite a negative critical reception and her private reservations, H.D.'s voice will not be silenced.

"Why must I write?" the poet wonders rhetorically; who or what inspires this persistent and controversial poetry? H.D. identifies her inspirational source as a potent female muse, a goddess who unveils, unbinds, and subsequently commands the poet to "write, write or die." The relentless "She" of this poem is

Isis, most protean of Egyptian deities, who, according to Erich Neumann, "corresponds to the archetype of the Great Mother and also discloses suggestions of the primordial archetype of the Feminine"; but Isis is one of many names for H.D.'s muse.[3] In her Imagist poems the inspiring forces appear as women from Greek mythology, transformed by the poet from secondary figures in a patriarchal drama to powerful wellsprings of female creative identity. Often H.D. invokes Artemis, the Greek goddess of chastity, the moon, the hunt, with whom the poet feels a special affinity.[4] In "Amaranth," a fragment from the *Collected Poems*, the goddess is an unnamed "lady of all beauty," an Aphrodite figure who claims the poet as priestess and daughter: "she too is of my host/ . . . she is my poet."[5] In *Trilogy*, H.D.'s tripartite epic of World War II, the muse is "Our Lady," who appears not with the traditional holy child, the Savior of Christian legend ("the Lamb was not with her, / either as Bridegroom or Child"), but with a blank book, "the unwritten volume of the new."[6] In *Helen in Egypt*, H.D.'s major epic poem, the questing Helen seeks affirmation from Thetis, the maternal sea goddess, a fertile source of the woman poet's creative rememberings: "O Thetis, O Sea-mother, . . . let me remember, let me remember. . . ."[7] In "Sagesse," from *Hermetic Definition*, the poet pays homage to the "Grande Mer," patron saint of female life and art, who instructs her as a daughter: "listen, my child, fear not the ancient lore."[8] And in "Winter Love," the last section of *Hermetic Definition*, the muse represents an alternate female self, as the persona, Helen, invokes the crippled "Grande Dame," a thinly veiled version of the elderly H.D., to serve as a midwife at the birth of her *Espérance*.[9] Throughout her poetic career H.D. was fascinated with the goddess as a metaphor for female creativity.

What characteristics does H.D. attribute to her muse, and what role does the muse play in her mythology of the poet-goddess-self? The muse for H.D. may be an erotic force, a spiritual love object, or a verse inspirer. As part of the "ancient wisdom" that informs the woman poet's movement toward personal identity and spiritual insight, the muse allows her to confront, explore, and come to terms with herself as a latter-day female version of the "sacred scribe." The goddess is not the only figure upon whom H.D. relies; she also calls upon male deities and paternal figures for poetic inspiration. But she often demythologizes traditional gods in order to assert a balanced spiritual vision that regenerates and revenerates their female counterparts. Most poems have female personae, and the source to whom these speakers most consistently turn for assistance is not a male mentor but a female muse. As the H.D. scholar Susan Stanford Friedman explains, the poet's efforts to name and claim a female source of inspiration are central to her "revisionist mythmaking":

> H.D.'s work began immersed in patriarchal imagery: Freud's psychoanalysis and esoteric mysticism. She used these images to restore the bond with her mother, to resurrect the Goddess, to revise woman as a cultural symbol, and thus establish a valid dimension of women's quest.

> In this process of cultural transformation, the role of the artist is crucial. The Goddess is a Muse, "mother" to art as well as vision. The artist's re-visionist myth-making is "revolutionary" . . . for her art is a creative act that helps establish a new cultural tradition.[10]

The goddess, then, is a personification of the poet's own creative genius, through which she unravels, interprets, and re-visions the ancient mysteries and the sacred logos.

In much of H.D.'s later work the muse emerges as a maternal figure; indeed, the poet's quest for a strong creative identity parallels the daughter's search for reunion with the mother, the primal source of nourishment, inspiration, and love. "The mother is the Muse, the Creator, and in my case especially, as my mother's name was Helen," H.D. claims.[11] In *Tribute to Freud*, the poet acknowledges her artistic mother, Helen Wolle Doolittle, as a key source of her creative ability: "Obviously, this is my inheritance. I derive my imaginative faculties through my musician-artist mother."[12] H.D.'s identification of female creativity with her mother and with the maternal principle was influenced by her forays into psychoanalysis. During the 1930s she spent several years as Sigmund Freud's analysand, in the hope that he would help her interpret a series of occult experiences. The most striking of these, which H.D. calls the "writing-on-the-wall" episode, occurred at Corfu in 1920 and projected, among others, three major figures: the silhouette of an airman's head in visored cap; a Delphic tripod, the sacred symbol of oracular prophecy; and a goblet or cup, a "mysterious chalice." As H.D. watched, she imagined herself as Perseus confronting the Gorgon head, that demon she also must confront as a woman poet. Other figures appeared on the wall, the most interesting a wingless Nike, the symbol of victory, on whose interpretation H.D. and Freud disagreed. For H.D., who viewed Nike as "my own special sign or part of my hieroglyph," Nike was wingless because "Victory could never, would never fly away from Athens."[13] To Freud, however, Nike's winglessness represented woman's incompleteness, a sense of loss manifested as penis envy. Nevertheless, as H.D. explains, she and Freud did agree that these images were part of her quest for the lost mother: "the professor translated the pictures on the wall, or the picture-writing on the wall of a hotel bedroom in Corfu, the Greek Ionian island, that I saw projected there in the spring of 1920, as a desire for union with my mother. I was physically in Greece, in Hellas (Helen). I had come home to the glory that was Greece."[14]

That H.D.'s imagination was fired by Freud's interpretation of her "mother fix," as she called it, can be seen in a letter to her lifelong companion, Bryher (Winifred Ellerman), written shortly after the psychoanalytic sessions had begun:

> Freud says mine is absolutely FIRST layer. I got stuck at the earliest pre-OE stage, and "back to the womb" seems to be my only solution. Hence islands, sea, Greek primitives, and so on. It's all too, too wonder-making.[15]

H.D. realizes that the primitive imagery of her early verse—the sea, the islands, her cold, remote goddesses—was linked to her desire to go "back to the womb." And in later poems she claims the magical name of Helen as a persona, assuming the mother's identity and seeking her inspirational powers.

H.D.'s epic quest is not rooted merely in her wish for union with her biological mother, however; she also invokes the "Grande Mer," the mother-goddess at the root of female creative inspiration and the matriarchal principle at the core of "ancient wisdom," "spiritual realism." In *Bid Me to Live*, a *roman à clef*, H.D. asserts the woman poet's need to claim a maternal muse and thereby affirm herself as autonomous creator. "I can see it through your eyes, through Van Gogh's," the poet-protagonist Julia Ashton tells Rico, a character modeled after D. H. Lawrence. "You are driven by your genius. You will express love. Why does it drive you mad, that desire to create your mother? . . . I could not be your mother. Anyhow, I need a great-mother as much as you do."[16] Not content to be a muse to the male poet, eager to assert her needs before this rival talent, the woman poet seeks a maternal source of inspiration not because she is "driven mad" but because she values the mother's love and sustenance.

This quest for the "great-mother" at the core of female life and art is for H.D. a restorative search, an affirmation of the devalued female principle that she considers paramount. In *The Gift*, an autobiographical account of her Moravian heritage, she asserts the preeminence of the mother as a symbol of divine inspiration:

> Mary, Maia, Miriam, Mut, Madre, Mère, Mother, pray for us. . . . This is Gaia, this is the beginning. This is the end. Under every shrine to Zeus, to Jupiter, to Zeus-pater or Theus-pater or God-the-father . . . there is an earlier altar. There is, beneath the carved superstructure of every temple to God-the-father, the dark cave or grotto or inner hall or cellar to Mary, Mère, mut, mutter, pray for us.[17]

The maternal force crucial to human creation and sustenance has long been suppressed, H.D. suggests; the woman poet's task is to revalue the mother-goddess, to restore her to her rightful place of veneration and centrality.

This effort to re-vision the maternal muse may be illustrated by a passage from *Tribute to the Angels*. Having rejected the "death cult" of patriarchal culture—specifically, the "seventy-time-seven / bitter, unending wars" prophesied by John of the biblical Book of Revelation—H.D. sets out to "collect the fragments of the splintered glass / . . . now shattered in the shards men tread upon." In so doing, she begins to re-invoke and re-create the healing female principle. For H.D., such re-creation can occur only through linguistic alchemy, with the potent logos, the poet's revisionary tool, as an elixir:

> Now polish the crucible
> and in the bowl distill
>
> a word most bitter, *marah*,
> a word bitterer still, *mar*,

sea, brine, breaker, seducer,
giver of life, giver of tears;

Now polish the crucible
and set the jet of flame

under, till *marah-mar*
are melted, fuse and join

and change and alter,
mer, mere, mère, mater, Maia, Mary,

Star of the Sea,
Mother.[18]

Through poetic language, with its transformative force, *marah*, "most bitter," gives way to "Star of the Sea, / Mother," and H.D. names a potent muse.

As these passages suggest, H.D.'s transformation of the mother to the goddess-muse is grounded in a complex theory of language. "*In the beginning / was the Word*," the poet asserts in *The Walls Do Not Fall*, and she goes on to describe poets as maternal vessels who nourish the cryptic yet fertile word; "spinners" of the binding thread of language; linguistic voyagers, "*discoverers / of the not known*."[19] H.D.'s perceptions of the sacrosanct quality of language and of her own role as linguistic alchemist can be seen in three key images: the palimpsest, the hieroglyph, and the hermetic definition. Each image reflects her view of language as a veil that both conceals and reveals ultimate reality. The palimpsest, a parchment whose writings have been erased to accommodate new sacred texts, is an appropriate symbol of H.D.'s richly textured, multilayered verse. Perceived through a glass darkly, such poetry must be unearthed layer by fragile layer in a process transcendent of time and place. Complex and enigmatic like the palimpsest, the hieroglyph adds a horizontal perspective to H.D.'s work, a surface structure to complement the deep structure of her poems. Picture-writing must be read from side to side as well as up and down: likewise, the would-be decoder of H.D.'s hieroglyphics must employ an aesthetic strategy of moving two ways at once—a technique of seeing, in the fullest visual and prophetic sense of the word, the horizontal as well as the vertical "writing-on-the-wall."[20] Finally, hermetic definition connotes a poetic language and vision both airtight, secure within itself, yet protean in its flexibility and multiplicity. A definition that is hermetic must be eloquent yet cunning like the trickster god Hermes, vital and transformative like the legendary patron of alchemy, Hermes Trismegistus, whom H.D. invokes in *Tribute to the Angels*. As a skilled weaver of intricate words and ideas, H.D. places herself at the foreground of that company of "nameless initiates" who serve as "keepers of the secret."[21]

Taken together, these three metaphors—the palimpsest, the hieroglyph, and the hermetic definition—provide a paradigm for H.D.'s view of the dialectic between poet and poem. Or, more appropriately, they suggest the trihedron in which poet, poem, and the muse, or "ancient wisdom," are bound. Each image alludes to the poet's dual role as initiator and decipherer, decoder of ancient truths as well as creator of the art that reveals them; and each is connected to the mysteries of Greek and Egyptian antiquity by etymology as well as definition. Most important, all three images have strong female associations. The folds and layers of the palimpsest recall the female genitalia, and the term's Greek etymon, *palimpsestos*, means literally "scraped again," a phrase that connotes the pains and pleasures of the womb and offers a metaphor for the social and political plight of women throughout history, as "texts" that have been undervalued and denied, written upon only to be erased. H.D.'s palimpsest anticipates the French theorist Jacques Derrida's term "invagination," which describes the "inward refolding" of a text, its outer edges overlapping in an endless series of pockets, an internal labyrinth.[22]

Although less overtly a feminine image than the palimpsest, the hieroglyph recalls the sacred writings of ancient priests and scribes, whom H.D. frequently describes in female imagery. Furthermore, there is an etymological and mythological link between hieroglyphic writing and the hierophant, a female initiate in the Eleusinian mysteries. Finally, the hieroglyph serves as a metaphor for the poet herself, who must be deciphered, translated, re-visioned. This metaphoric use can be seen in *Helen in Egypt*, as the questing Helen analyzes her prophetic powers:

> I was not interested,
> I was not instructed,
> nor guessed the inner sense of the hieratic,
>
> But when the bird swooped past,
> that first evening,
> I seemed to know the writing,
>
> as if God made the picture
> and matched it
> with a living hieroglyph.[23]

The third symbol, the hermetic definition, also occurs in H.D.'s work as an elaborately coded pseudonym: H.D., Hilda Doolittle, the poet herself as the most complex hieroglyph to be deciphered. "She herself is the writing," H.D. says of Helen, whom Achilles curses as "witch," "hieroglyph." So is Hilda Doolittle herself the writing, the chief hieroglyph of her canon, and a private exploration of her female self complements her poetic quest for "ancient wisdom" through the aid of a female muse.

"LADY OF ALL BEAUTY": THE IMAGIST MUSE

H.D.'s earliest efforts to invoke a female muse occur in her Imagist poems, characterized by linguistic compression, dramatic juxtaposition of images, and frequent mythological allusions. *Collected Poems* and *Red Roses for Bronze* are filled with goddesses and mythological women whom H.D. treats as muses: figures who guide the poet-speaker on her quest for creative identity, women who themselves speak and with whose struggle for voice the female poet identifies. As a young expatriate poet in England during the years of World War I, H.D. was surrounded by such dominant—and often domineering—literary figures and personal mentors as Ezra Pound, D.H. Lawrence, and Richard Aldington.[24] Her interactions with these men often led to internal conflict: was she to be muse to these male writers, or was she to be poet? Because of this insecurity, perhaps, as well as for aesthetic purposes, she frequently writes from within the protective armor of what Jeanne Kammer has labeled the "diaphoric" mode, a highly compressed, elliptical verse "better understood as configuration rather than statement." Speaking of the "linguistic parsimony" that characterizes the poetry of Emily Dickinson, Marianne Moore, and the early H.D., Kammer suggests that "this shared impulse to compressed speech may arise in part from habits of privacy, camouflage, and indirection encouraged in the manner of the gently-bred female. Moreover, for the reclusive, emotionally vulnerable personality . . . the ambiguity of saying and not saying may be the only acceptable axis for communication."[25] While Imagism for her male counterparts might best be envisioned as an offensive strategy, a means of asserting a new modernist aesthetic, for H.D. it seems to have been a way of saying and not saying, an ambiguous, defensive stance from which to venture into the male world of poetry. It is from this silent aesthetic, therefore, that H.D.'s female muse first emerges.

To understand the muse's role in H.D.'s Imagist poetry, we must first examine the young poet's ambivalence toward her own creativity. Several early works reveal her struggle to overcome what one critic has called the "anxiety of her own imminent nothingness."[26] Uncertain how much creative power she can justly claim, unsure whether her inspirational fire is kindled from without or within, she often creates personae who allow her to confront this uncertainty via the "safe" realm of poetic detachment. In several early works, H.D. joins women poets from Dickinson to Rich in envisioning these alternate selves as male—a predictable impulse, given traditional prejudices against the creative woman. As Rich notes regarding Dickinson, "a woman's poetry about her relationship to her daemon—her own active, creative power—has in patriarchal culture used the language of heterosexual love or patriarchal theology"—or, in H.D.'s case, patriarchal mythology.[27] Thus in the "Murex" section of her novel *Palimpsest*, H.D. describes her own conflict as well as that of the protagonist, Raymonde Ransome, when she refers to woman's creative power as a force outside of and beyond herself, male in its potency and thrust. As Hilda Doolittle assumes the sex-neutral *nom de plume* H.D., so Raymonde identifies her creative impulse as other than female by writing under the pseudonym Ray Bart: "From far and far and far, Ray Bart would always sleuth and trail and track her. . . . It was Ray Bart who always checkmated her. It was Ray Bart who caught her open-handed. . . . It was the poet, the young spearman who was Raymonde's genius."[28]

This portrayal of the creative self as masculine is also seen in "Pygmalion," an early poem in which H.D.'s male persona, the mythological Greek sculptor enthralled with his own creation, assesses the dangers inherent in not distinguishing subject from object, creator from creation. Early in the poem Pygmalion establishes what is perhaps the central conflict experienced by any budding artist but one intensified in the woman, whose powers have so long been denied. How powerful *is* my art, the sculptor asks, and to what extent must the creative act be a narcissistic enterprise, a means of envisioning and hence creating the self?

> Shall I let myself be caught
> in my own light?
> . . . .
> does this fire thwart me
> and my craft,
> or does my work cloud this light?
> which is the god,
> which is the stone
> the god takes for his use?

This effort toward defining and limiting the artistic self continues in stanza two, as the poet employs elemental imagery to depict the highly charged tension among art, artist, and artifact:

> Which am I,
> the stone or the power
> that lifts the rock from the earth?
> am I master of this fire,
> is this fire my own strength?

The rest of the poem suggests the young H.D.'s answers to her own questions, her attempt to walk the tightrope between a justifiable pride in one's artistry and an arrogant usurpation of divine creation. Although Pygmalion pays lip service to Pallas and Hephaestus as sources of inspiration, he is heady with his own power; in his hubris he oversteps human bounds, claiming the gods as his own invention: "I made the gods less than men, / For I was a man and they my work." But neither art nor artist is omnipotent, the poet quickly concludes, as the gods reiterate their own power and perfection. "*You are useless*," their spokesman hurls at the human interloper. "*No marble can bind me, / no stone suggest*."

For the poet-persona, however, the narcissistic conflict is not resolved easily. Pygmalion continues to reject his own Otherness, to rebel against his inferior status: jolted into an awareness that he cannot re-create divinity in his art, he refuses to be stifled by the angry gods, to be rendered useless. After an agonizing period of self-doubt—"my work is for naught"—Pygmalion reasserts his artistic self, with an urgency and force tempered only slightly by his perplexed questioning:

> Now am I the power
> that has made the fire
> as of old I made the gods
> start from the rocks?
> am I the god?
> or does this fire carve me
> for its own use?[29]

Although others of the *Collected Poems* employ male personae, most of H.D.'s Imagist poems feature female speakers who pay homage to the goddesses who sustain them. "Triplex," for instance, invokes multiple goddesses—Athene, Aphrodite, and Artemis:

> Maid
> of the luminous grey-eyes,
> Mistress
> of honey and marble implacable white thighs
> and Goddess,
> chaste daughter of Zeus,
> most beautiful in the skies.

"Let them grow side by side in me, / these three," the quester continues, as she identifies each deity by appropriate flower imagery—the royal violet for Athene, the passionate rose for Aphrodite, and the wild hill-crocus for her favorite of the three, Artemis, set apart by the appellation "Goddess."[30] Throughout the *Collected Poems* H.D. is ambivalent toward Aphrodite, whom she sees as awe-inspiring but also frightening, and mistrustful of Athene, who in "Pallas" is praised as "most kind" but is also criticized as "high and far and blind."[31] It is Artemis with whom the poet most closely identifies, perhaps because of her asexual nature. Like great goddesses of old, Artemis is virginal, isolated, wild—a protector of women, a communer with nature.

Three of Artemis' features particularly attract H.D.: her rejection of Apollonian rationality and order; her self-imposed alienation and its attendant autonomy; and her role as moon goddess and huntress, comrade of women. The first two characteristics can be seen in the Artemis of "All Mountains," an untamed natural force again identified with the "wild / exquisite hill-crocus / from Arcadian snows." Eschewing ordinary human interaction ("let Phoebus keep the fervid marketplace"), Artemis claims as her territory higher realms, "the islands of the upper air, / all mountains / and the towering mountain trees." Her milieu is also broader in scope than Apollo's, protean and imaginatively charged:

my islands
shift and change,
now here, now there,
dazzling,
white,
granite,
silver
in blue aether.[32]

The Artemis of *Hippolytus Temporizes* also refuses human intercourse; literally the virgin of old, she who is unto herself, she opts for isolation and concealment. "I must be hidden / where no mortals are," she insists, and she ensures that efforts to contain her are to no avail:

Someone will come
after I shun each place
and set a circle,
blunt end up,
of stones,
and pile an altar,
but I shall have gone
further,
toward loftier barrier,
mightier trees.[33]

Artemis' power would seem to lie in her elusiveness; she prefers to keep her devotees at a distance. As one of these devotees, the poet identifies with the goddess's wildness and alienation: she too "must be hidden" if her art is to go further, be "loftier . . . mightier."

It is in her roles as goddess of the moon and the hunt, however, that Artemis functions most directly as a muse-figure for H.D. In "Huntress," the speakers are Amazons in hot pursuit of their elusive goddess, eager to cajole new members into their ranks:

Come, blunt your spear with us,
our pace is hot
and our bare heels
in the heel-prints—
we stand tense—do you see—
are you already beaten
by the chase?

In her early poems H.D. often uses the image of the spear carrier as a symbol for the questing poet; Raymonde Ransome's "genius," Ray Bart, for example, is a "young spearman." The Freudian implications of such a title are obvious, yet this designation suggests not H.D.'s longing for the missing phallus so much as her wish for powers perceived as male: the force of genius, the "weapon" of the word, the ecstasy of the heroic quest. As the title "Huntress" indicates, the heroic warriors here are spear*women*, their leader the elusive Artemis; and neither the goddess nor her spokespersons have patience with those too weak to undertake or persevere at the hunt:

> Spring up—sway forward—
> follow the quickest one,
> aye, though you leave the trail
> and drop exhausted at our feet.[34]

In "Moonrise," too, the female questers invoke the moon goddess to "fling your spearhead on the shore" so that their subsequent music might lure wayward members back into the fold:

> O flight,
> bring her swiftly to our song.
> She is great,
> we measure her by the pine trees.[35]

H.D. is especially attracted to Artemis' physical prowess. In the novel *Hermione*, for instance, the protagonist wishes to be "straight and strong like some girl athlete from Laconian hill slopes, straight and brave like the maiden Artemis."[36] Only by emulating the goddess's powers, H.D. suggests, can the female initiate find strength; the female poet, voice.

H.D.'s long-term interest in Artemis can be seen in *The Hedgehog* (1936), a story written for her daughter, Perdita. As Susan Gubar has pointed out, the story's young protagonist, Madge, sets out in search of "secret symbols" embodied in the hedgehog of the title. She is guided in her quest not only by a Doctor Blum, a figure modeled after Freud, but also by the moon goddess Artemis. In *The Hedgehog* H.D. describes Artemis as one who "loved little girls and big girls who ran races just like boys along the seashore." Gubar explains Artemis' centrality in Madge's search for linguistical power and hence for selfhood:

> This vision of Artemis . . . embodies Madge's distinctive female joy and her sense that, existing as she does in both the mythic past and the secular present, she contains multitudes. Far from seeking male forms of power, then, Madge manages to see and make of the enigmatic signs of her culture a new and sustaining story of female freedom.[37]

Although Artemis is a favorite goddess-muse of H.D.'s early poetry (especially in her first volumes, *Sea Garden* and *The God*), the poet also pays homage to Aphrodite, the Greek goddess of sexuality and love. Many of the poems in *Heliodora* are explicitly to or about Aphrodite, and often she is invoked as muse. In "Amaranth," for example, a female speaker defers willingly to the greater powers of an Aphrodite figure, "she the shameless and radiant." Like Pygmalion, this speaker has moments of self-doubt: "Am I blind? / am I the less ready for her sacrifice?" But the speaker perseveres in her pilgrimage toward the goddess-muse, to whom she will offer her love, her art, her self: "Nay I give back to my goddess the gift / she tendered me in a moment / of great bounty." She refuses to founder beneath the weight of the gift:

Ah no—though I stumble toward
her alter-step,
though my flesh is scorched and rent,
shattered, cut apart,
and slashed open.

In stanza three the petitioner eschews identification with the cold calm of Apollo and, by extension, with the rational "masculine" principle. Instead, she embraces female eroticism and creativity:

Lady of all beauty,
I give you this:
say I have offered but small sacrifice,
say I am unworthy your touch,
but say not, I turned to some cold, calm god,
silent, pitiful, in preference.

At last, in a passage that anticipates the interdependence of Helen and Thetis in *Helen in Egypt*, the goddess speaks to and for the persona, as the roles reverse and muse extols poet:

She too is of the deathless,
she too will wander in my palaces
where all beauty is peace.

She too is of my host
that gather in groups or singly wait
by some altar apart;
she too is my poet.

. . . .

Turn if you will from her path
for one moment seek
a lesser beauty
and a lesser grace,
but you will find
no peace in the end
save in her presence.[38]

H.D. also invokes mythological women who model the art of self-inspiration. Eurydice has traditionally been portrayed as passive, a tragic heroine rescued from Hades by her husband, the poet-singer Orpheus, only to be cast back into darkness by his untimely glance. H.D.'s Eurydice is at times both passive and despairing: nothing can change the fact that she must live forever in Hades. But if Eurydice is physically "trapped," the poet suggests, she can be imaginatively free, re-creating and redefining her own "prison." Thus H.D. reconstructs this classical myth of passion, abandonment, and despair from the woman's perspective. Eurydice's initial attitude is one of anguish and hopelessness, as she blames Orpheus for her plight: "so for your arrogance / I am broken at last." But Eurydice does not remain "broken" or "lost" for long. Like women writers from Anne Finch, who scorned her status as "cipher," to Germaine Greer, who politicized the term "female eunuch," H.D. rebels at woman's status as Other, as "nothing." With passion and fury, this Eurydice challenges Orpheus' superiority, his "light":

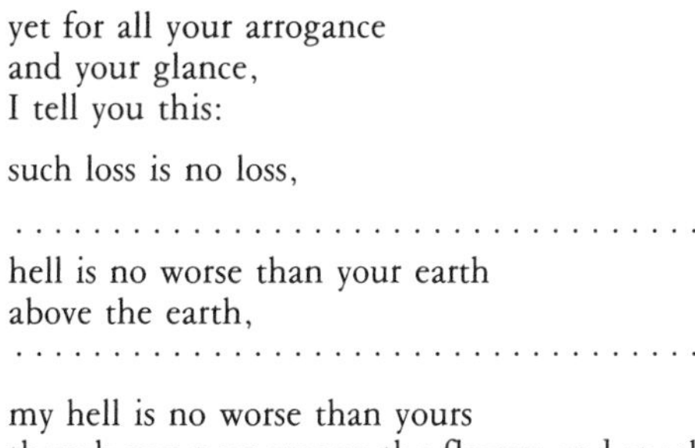

yet for all your arrogance
and your glance,
I tell you this:

such loss is no loss,

. . . .

hell is no worse than your earth
above the earth,

. . . .

my hell is no worse than yours
though you pass among the flowers and speak
with the spirits above earth.

Heady in her newly found power as subject, as presence, Eurydice goes on to chart Hades as female territory and to claim herself as inspiration:

At least I have the flowers of myself,
and my thoughts, no god
can take that;
I have the fervour of myself for a presence
and my own spirit for light;

and my spirit with its loss
knows this;
though small against the black,
small against the formless rocks,
hell must break before I am lost,

before I am lost,
hell must open like a red rose
for the dead to pass.[39]

This poem is especially interesting in light of an exchange between D. H. Lawrence and H.D. recounted fictionally in *Bid Me to Live*. Criticizing a draft of a poem about Eurydice written by Julia Ashton, fellow artist Rico (Lawrence) insists that Julia write only of her own sex and hence forego any attempt at "universality." "I don't like the second half of the Orpheus sequence as well as the first," Rico writes. "Stick to the woman speaking. How can you know what Orpheus feels? It's your part to be woman, the woman vibration, Eurydice should be enough. You can't deal with both."[40] The poem referred to here was perhaps a version of the "Eurydice" later published in *The God*, and it is conceivable, as Rachel Blau DuPlessis suggests, that H.D. did indeed revise the poem in accordance with Lawrence's wishes.[41] But one can also read "Eurydice" as H.D.'s disavowal of Lawrence as mentor and muse, by drawing parallels between Eurydice's rejection of all that Orpheus stands for, her virtual invocation of *herself* as muse, and H.D.'s own rebellion against Lawrence's dicta. In a later letter (which, significantly, is never mailed) Julia argues that both male and female perspectives are essential to any writer in search of "the *gloire*," a rarefied state of heightened perception:

> Perhaps you would say I was trespassing, couldn't see both sides, as you said of my Orpheus. I could be Eurydice in character, you said, but woman-is-woman and I couldn't be both. The *gloire* is both.

In the next few paragraphs, however, Julia associates the *gloire* not with "both sides" but with female circularity, maternity, and creativity:

> The child is the *gloire* before it is born. The circle of the candle on my notebook is the *gloire*, the story isn't yet born. While I live in the unborn story, I am the *gloire*. I must keep it alive, myself living within it.[42]

H.D. recognizes that the woman poet must find the *gloire* within herself, that she must nourish the light of inspiration as a child in her womb. Like Eurydice, H.D. must "live in the unborn story" of herself and her art.

As these poems indicate, H.D. sees herself as a poet-priestess paying homage to the goddess-muse-self, a source of inspiration through which she begins to construct a complex mythology—spiritual and erotic and creative. Like H.D., these goddesses rebel against patriarchal forces; they attain power by replacing unyielding, restrictive "male" values with more fluid "female" ones. Significantly, it was during this Imagist period that H.D. strove to free herself from her role as muse for Aldington, Pound, and Lawrence and that she began what was to be a lifelong relationship with Bryher. In 1919, when H.D. was pregnant, gravely ill, and alone, Bryher nursed her back to health. And on at least one occasion during the "writing-on-the-wall" episode at Corfu in 1920, Bryher served quite literally as H.D.'s muse. As the poet watched the hieroglyph form on the wall before her, she sought her friend's advice as to whether she should "allow" her vision to continue:

> I say to Bryher, "There have been pictures here—I thought they were shadows at first, but they are light, not shadow. They are quite simple objects—but of course it's very strange. I can break away from them now, if I want—it's just a matter of concentrating—what do you think? Shall I stop? Shall I go on?" Bryher says without hesitation, "Go on."[43]

That H.D. recognized the importance of this shared artistic and mystical experience is evident from her retrospective evaluation:

> . . . I knew that this experience, this writing-on-the-wall before me, could not be shared . . . with anyone except the girl who stood so bravely there beside me. This girl had said without hesitation, "Go on." It was she really who had the detachment and the integrity of the Pythoness of Delphi. But it was I, battered and dissociated from my American family and my English friends, who was seeing the pictures, who was reading the writing or who was granted the inner vision. Or perhaps in some sense, we were "seeing" it together, for without her, admittedly, I could not have gone on.[44]

Although H.D.'s and Bryher's relationship was complex and volatile, they lived together for much of the poet's life. Given this primary relationship and Bryher's role as a source of inspiration for H.D., it seems little wonder that she invokes female muses as representatives of a healing matriarchal vision. Although her Imagist poems represent no *sustained* effort toward such a vision, the goddesses H.D. depicts foreshadow the mythology of female inspiration she creates in later works. They constitute the bottom layer (or perhaps the top) of a richly evocative female palimpsest.

"THE SECRET OF ISIS": TRILOGY AS FEMALE PALIMPSEST

In a poem from *Red Roses for Bronze* entitled "Chance Meeting," H.D. contrasts her own aesthetic with that of another poet, presumably male and possibly modeled after Aldington. Glib like the male protagonist in the poem "Heliodora," to whom the female poet loses in a battle of images designed to determine poetic superiority,[45] the "you" of this poem is nonetheless "left comfortless" by his easy art:

You thought as poets think,
suavely it's true,
and you could turn
intricate river-runnels into words,
tell
wave-lengths in brave metres;
all the same,
the spell
had passed you,
left you comfortless.

Although her own art lacks such facility, the poet suggests, it casts a different "spell":

the things I have
are nameless,
old and true;
they may not be named;
few may live and know.[46]

Having encountered "ancient wisdom," H.D. chastises this other poet for letting the "true-rune" pass by. In a sense, however, her rebuke may also be self-directed. As an Imagist poet, H.D. was often "left comfortless" by her efforts to give form to the formless, to name the unnameable. This poem may explain her gradual shift from the "diaphoric" compression of her early poems to the long, sequential poems written after 1940, in which she creates a female mythos through a radical transformation of the poetic logos.

During the 1930s, H.D. found many "not knowns" to explore: spiritualism, Moravian mysticism, Kabbalism, gnosticism, cinema art, astrology, the tarot, and most significantly, psychoanalysis.[47] As *Tribute to Freud* indicates, her experience as Freud's analysand had a profound influence on her perceptions of herself and her art. On the one hand, it alerted her to the complexities and significance of her own psychic visions, the most intense of which was the "writing-on-the-wall" episode. Freud viewed this occult experience as her most "dangerous symptom," not because of her "neurotic" attachment to her mother but because of a "perverse" wish for female divinity and power.[48] That H.D. associated this vision with both ambition and creativity is evident:

> We can read my writing, the fact that there was writing, in two ways or in more than two ways. We can read or translate it as a suppressed desire for forbidden "signs and wonders," breaking bounds, a suppressed desire to be a Prophetess, to be important anyway, megalomania they call it—a hidden desire to "found a new religion" which the professor ferreted out in the later Moses picture. Or this writing-on-the-wall is merely an extension of the artist's mind, a *picture* or an illustrated poem, taken out of the actual dream or daydream content and projected from within (though apparently from outside).[49]

The poet recognizes what the psychoanalyst does not: that her visions may be not an unnatural megalomania but a natural extension of the artist's mind—pictorial representations of the poet's art.

H.D.'s study with Freud (for she viewed herself as pupil as well as analysand) caused her to push beyond her own self-imposed barriers regarding myth and thought and art. Yet despite her great admiration and respect for "the Professor," she sometimes challenged him: "I do not yet quite see why he picked the writing-on-the-wall as the danger-signal, or omitted what to my mind were tendencies or events that were equally important or equally 'dangerous.'"[50] Although she goes on to assess this event from a typically Freudian perspective, doubts as to the accuracy of Freud's interpretations appear often. In a poem entitled "The Master," for example, based on her experience with Freud, H.D. admits anger toward his unwillingness to give credence to her belief in immortality, her "mysteries":

> I was angry with the old man
> with his talk of the man-strength,
> I was angry with his mystery, his mysteries
> I argued till day-break.[51]

In her journal entry for March 10, 1933, H.D. again records her disagreement with Freud, this time because of his misogyny:

> I was rather annoyed with the Professor in one of his volumes. He said (as I remember) that women did not creatively amount to anything or amount to much, unless they had a male counterpart or a male companion from whom they drew their inspiration. Perhaps he is right and my dream of "salting" my typewriter with the tell-tale transference symbol is further proof of his infallibility.[52]

How much of this latter statement is ironic, how much indicative of intimidation, and how much genuinely hypothetical is hard to say. At any rate, from H.D.'s perspective, "the Professor was not always right."[53]

However much Freud and H.D. disagreed on such issues as eternal life and female creativity, it is clear that H.D.'s view of herself as woman and as poet changed radically as a result of her analysis. In fact, her exchange with Freud may well have freed her from the writer's block she experienced through most of the 1930s. Her first major work subsequent to her psychoanalysis, *Trilogy*, is a poetic triptych written during World War II. As a poet intrigued by words as "secret symbols," H.D. turns to the poetic logos as a means of restoring order to a society in chaos. In its power to transform reality, to reshape and hence redefine human experience, language is a means of "reconstituting the world," as Adrienne Rich puts it; and H.D. is aware that her world—London during the blitz of the early 1940s—desperately needs reconstitution. For H.D., this reconstruction entails a rejection of the "masculine" principle responsible for the current destructive tide, in favor of an ancient "feminine" principle symbolized by the charred mayapple tree that miraculously blossoms anew.

The Walls Do Not Fall opens with a stark description of London during the bombings of World War II, ironically juxtaposed against the "Spirit" and "Presence" of poetic inspiration, which asserts itself amid the chaos. Although H.D. and her fellow poets "know not nor are known" within such environs, they are nonetheless privy to "Pythian pronouncements"; they continue to "pass the flame," even as they wonder "what saved us? what for?"[54] The answer comes quickly. Like the priestess of Delphi, whose pronouncements could be read two ways, so the key to understanding the horror of the present lies in the secrets of the past:

> gods always face two-ways,
> so let us search the old highways
>
> for the true rune, the right-spell,
> recover old values.[55]

To "recover old values," then, is H.D.'s chief goal, specifically those old values that attempt to restore primacy to the mother-goddess of antiquity, "Isis, Aset or Astarte." Angry that patriarchal mythologists have labeled this goddess "harlot," that they view anyone who "hankers after old fleshpots" as "retrogressive," H.D. challenges both the rhetoric and the misogyny of this stance.[56] In decrying those who would devalue the goddess, H.D. revels in her own implicit demonism, accepting with a conspiratorial zest accusations that "your rhythm is the devil's hymn / your stylus is dipped in corrosive sublimate." Yes, she shouts in reply, the woman poet *must* "scratch out / indelible ink of the palimpsest / of past misadventure" to replace it with a palimpsestic revision of her own making.[57] The "past adventure" of patriarchal fragmentation and alienation, after all, has led to the havoc of world war, H.D. alleges. Necessity calls the re-visionist poet to her task: the recovery of a female mythos and "protection for the scribe" who undertakes such a quest.

The language H.D. employs in her search for the "true-rune" is couched in female imagery: the tightly enclosed mollusk shell, which, "firm in its own limited orbit," begets "self-out-of-self, / selfless, / that pearl-of-great-price"; the "industrious worm," which "spins its own shroud," emerging from its chrysalis as Psyche, the female emanation of creativity and rejuvenation.[58] But the female quester must begin at the top layer of the palimpsest, and so H.D. looks first for "ancient wisdom" through the "fathers":

> Ra, Osiris, *Amen* appeared
> in a spacious, bare meeting-house;
>
> he is the world-father,
> father of past aeons,
>
> present and future equally;
> beardless, not at all like Jehovah.[59]

Despite the power of Eastern gods, the poet fears that they may be bound to Jehovah as part of the "beautiful yet static, empty / old thought, old convention."[60] She has rejected the "Christos-image," "most difficult to disentangle," for its association with "pain worship" and "death symbol" indicts this myth as destructive. Now the poet must turn away from the Egyptian god Amen, "our Christos," through whom she had hoped to go "home" to Egypt, to be reborn like the phoenix, that "bennu bird," which symbolizes nourishment and reawakening.[61] Because male deities no longer suffice, H.D. finally dispenses with "illusion of lost gods," which can lead only to "*reversion of old values, / oneness lost, madness*.[62] Despairing of this leg of her journey, the poet rejects her own

> imagery
>
> done to death; perilous ascent,
> ridiculous descent; rhyme, jingle,
>
> overworked assonance, nonsense,
> juxtaposition of words for words' sake,
>
> without meaning, undefined.[63]

As a final remonstrance, she implores,

> let us not teach
> what we have learned badly
>
> and not profited by.[64]

What must be taught instead, the poet suggests in a new burst of creative inspiration, is "love, the Creator" in her quintessential maternal form. We must entreat Hest,

Aset, Isis, the great enchantress,
in her attribute of Serqet

the original great-mother,
who drove

harnessed scorpions
before her.[65]

Joseph N. Riddel suggests that H.D.'s invocation of Isis as "great enchantress" indicates her own "modest affirmations," her implicit realization that woman's role is not as autonomous creator but instead as muse, weaver of spells for some great (and presumably male) god. But H.D.'s assessment of the powers of Isis' "enchantment" belies Riddel's view that the poet is "embracing her own limitations."[66] In an unpublished work entitled *Pilate's Wife*, H.D.'s protagonist speaks of Isis' "enchantment" as a source of divine female wisdom and love, a healing power unparalleled in Greek mythology:

> Isis was a magician and a goddess of wisdom. The Greeks, for all their immense pragmatism and logical philosophy, had had to split the perfect image of the perfect Woman, say here is Love, faithless [Aphrodite] and here is Wisdom, loveless [Athene]. Yet even Aphrodite and Athene, remodelled, flung into some blasting furnace, to return, one perfectly welded figure, would yet lack something—something of the magic that Isis held in Egypt.[67]

The "magic that Isis held in Egypt"—her "enchantment"—is a complex combination of love and wisdom, a potent antidote to what H.D. later calls the "masculine iron-ring" of the patriarchy. Thus when the poet cries, "let us substitute / enchantment for sentiment, / re-dedicate our gifts / to spiritual realism," she is not "embracing her own limitations," as Riddel would have it. Rather, she is substituting her female creative power, drawn from Isis, for the "old values" that the "Christos-image" represents.[68] As "great enchantress," the "original great-mother," Isis is a formidable female muse: a witch, a sorceress, a potent purveyor of the magic of the word.

In the final stanzas of *The Walls Do Not Fall*, the "one-truth" emerges from H.D. through the metaphysical medium of language. According to H.D.'s theory, words can transform reality, naming and thus effecting spiritual truths. Words are "anagrams, cryptograms, / little boxes, conditioned / to hatch butterflies."[69] Therefore, linguistic anagrams must be used to "recover the secret of Isis."[70] For H.D., hope for a return to a "spiritual realism" unscathed by war and hatred lies in the reveneration of the Great Goddess and the reconstruction of the female principle she represents. But how to effect such a reconstitution? As *Walls* ends, H.D. is uncertain, although she seems hopeful that her goal can be attained:

we know no rule
of procedure,

we are voyagers, discoverers
of the not-known,

the unrecorded;
we have no map;

possibly we will reach haven,
heaven.[71]

Tribute to the Angels begins with the invocation of Hermes Trismegistus, patron of alchemy, as H.D. conjures up an image of the poet as criminal trickster, gleeful panderer of language. This initial invocation also signals H.D.'s shift from "Amen-worship" to "Isis-worship," from masculine to feminine mythos through the alchemical poetic word. The centrality of language to H.D.'s revisionist mythmaking can be seen in a passage from *Bid Me to Live* in which H.D. views herself as a "trader in words":

> She was self-effacing in her attack on those Greek words, she was flamboyantly ambitious. The words themselves held inner words, she thought. If you look at a word long enough, this peculiar twist, its magic angle, would lead somewhere, like that Phoenician track, trod by the old traders. She was a trader in gold, the old gold, the myrrh of the dead spirit. She was bargaining with each word.[72]

As a merchant of linguistic myrrh, the poet must "collect the fragments of the splintered glass" that are patriarchal culture,

melt down and integrate,

re-invoke, re-create
opal, onyx, obsidian,

now shattered in the shards
men tread upon.[73]

Thus she turns to a female image, the alchemical bowl, where "*marah*," "most bitter," is combined with "*mar*," "giver of life, giver of tears." To reimagine the world, "*marah-mar*" must be "melted, fuse and join / and change and alter." The result of this alchemy, the poet suggests, is a re-vision of the matriarchal muse as "Star of the Sea, / Mother."[74]

The poet goes on to invoke "Venus, Aphrodite, Astarte," goddesses devalued by patriarchal religion and society:

. . . knaves and fools

have done you impious wrong,
Venus, for venery stands for impurity

and Venus, as desire
is venerous, lascivious,

while the very root of the word shrieks
like a mandrake when foul witches pull

its stem at midnight . . .[75]

Female sexuality, H.D. asserts, must be reestablished as a powerful aspect of female divinity; Venus must be re-visioned as "O holiest one," "venerator."[76] Female strength has long been maligned as female demonism, the poet recognizes; language has been manipulated to obscure the true etymology of Venus. Neither misrepresentation must continue.

This rejuvenation sets the stage for the appearance of the major muse figure in *Tribute to the Angels*, the mysterious "Our Lady," who "knocks" casually, catching the poet unawares. Although she does not at first recognize the lady, H.D. links her to the crescent moon and hence to both Artemis and Thetis.[77] Clearly this lady has many manifestations in Judeo-Christian traditions as well, H.D. notes, as "Our Lady of the Goldfinch, / Our Lady of the Candelabra, / Our Lady of the Pomegranate, / Our Lady of the Chair." "The painters did very well by her . . . / they never missed a line," the poet states wryly. Yet such artistic depictions are inadequate, for "none of these, none of these/ suggest her as I saw her."[78]

The difference between H.D.'s version of the Lady and other versions is that in *Tribute to the Angels* she appears with "none of her usual attributes; / the Child was not with her."[79] Although H.D. drops this piece of information casually, it represents a crucial aspect of this goddess, sufficient unto herself. The child traditionally depicted with Isis, Mary, and other variations of the Great Goddess is male, an infant-consort who, with the advent of patriarchy, gradually attained greater prominence, eventually surpassing that of the mother.[80] To cast off such associations, H.D. implies, this goddess must come alone. Furthermore, instead of the child, she carries a book; hence H.D. establishes Our Lady as a poetic muse:

So she must have been pleased with us,
who did not forego our heritage

at the grave-edge;
she must have been pleased

with the straggling company of the brush and quill
who did not deny their birthright;

She must have been pleased with us,
for she looked so kindly at us

under her drift of veils,
and she carried a book.[81]

This description recalls H.D.'s muse in "Amaranth," the "lady of all beauty" pleased with the poet-daughter ("she is my poet"). Moreover, it suggests an association with other mythological and religious figures: Santa Sophia, the Holy

Ghost, the new Eve—"she brings the Book of Life, obviously."[82] But such efforts to identify the Lady are too pat, H.D. insists. After all, "she wasn't hieratic; she wasn't frozen, / she wasn't tall." She *is* the "Bona Dea" with a new cult, true, but she is "all that and much more." Her book is not "the tome of ancient wisdom" but "the blank pages / of the unwritten volume of the new"—or, to return to H.D.'s image in *Bid Me to Live*, the "*gloire*," the "unborn story."[83] The goddess herself is "unwritten," as yet unformed:

> she is not shut up in a cave
> like a Sibyl; she is not
>
> imprisoned in leaden bars
> in a coloured window;
>
> she is Psyche, the butterfly,
> out of the cocoon.[84]

Furthermore, the goddess has come to assert her affinity with H.D. and other re-visionist poets:

> her attention is undivided,
> we are her bridegroom and lamb;
>
> her book is our book; written
> or unwritten, its pages will reveal
>
> a tale of a Fisherman,
> a tale of a jar or jars,
>
> the same—different—the same attributes
> different yet the same as before.

As the poem ends, poet and muse merge, are mutually affirming.

> She carried a book, either to imply
> she was one of us, with us,
>
> or to suggest she was satisfied
> with our purpose, a tribute to the Angels.[85]

In part three of *Trilogy, The Flowering of the Rod*, H.D. again rejects destructive male values in favor of a nurturing female consciousness. The blank slate of the goddess's book assumes the properties of a snowy landscape, as the poet gives birth to her story:

> I go where I love and where I am loved,
> into the snow;
>
> . . . let us leave
> The place-of-a-skull
> to those who have fashioned it.[86]

In lieu of Golgotha, the poet seeks Bethlehem, her own birthplace in Pennsylvania and the Christian setting of birth and beginnings. If she reaches her destination, the poem's female quester will be offered an "alabaster jar" of healing and rejuvenating myrrh, a gift attainable from Kaspar the Mage, a central figure in *Flowering*. To coax this myrrh from Kaspar, the poet invokes "this other Mary," Mary Magdala, transformed by patriarchal theology into a whore and an outcast but reclaimed by H.D. as a key spiritual force. Only through Mary can the poet reach her destination and assume her symbolic place among the divine triad of mother-goddess, poet-daughter, and lover-son:

> I am Mary, she said, of Magdala,
> I am Mary, a great tower;
>
> through my will and my power,
> Mary shall be myrrh.[87]

In subsequent sections of *Flowering*, H.D. describes the singular nature of the encounter between Mary and Kaspar, which "some say . . . never happened, / some say . . . happens over and over."[88] Mesmerized by the mysterious presence of the enigmatic Mary, Kaspar experiences a psychic vision that convinces him to relinquish the alabaster jar. During his dream Kaspar undergoes a transformative moment of what Virginia Woolf calls "thinking back through our mothers."[89] Led by Mary, he confronts the reality of an older matriarchal truth:

> he might whisper tenderly, those names
> without fear of eternal damnation,
>
> Isis, Astarte, Cyprus
> and the other four;
>
> he might re-name them,
> Ge-meter, De-meter, earth-mother
>
> or Venus
> in a star.[90]

In a transcendent vision, Kaspar realizes that the "star of David" is indeed the "star of Venus," that these "daemons" are "not inalterably part of the picture." Freed from his former state, he now can hear "an echo of an echo is a shell," the shell of matriarchal consciousness.[91] Hence he receives "the title Magian . . . *Wise Man*" and comprehends "Paradise / before Eve."[92]

Having subverted the traditional Christian myth, H.D. returns to the seven female "daemons" at the root of Mary Magdala's powers and to their transmitted message. For H.D., both the message and the prehistory it reveals have distinctively female origins.

Lilith born before Eve
and one born before Lilith,
and Eve; we three are forgiven,
we are three of the seven
daemons cast out of her.[93]

As Susan Gubar has suggested, this passage implies "that a matriarchal genealogy has been erased from recorded history when this ancient female trinity was exorcised as evil, cast out of human consciousness by those who would begin with a second Eve who brings death into the garden."[94] Like Lilith and Eve after her, H.D. as woman poet has attempted the forbidden: she not only identifies with these seven female "daemons," muses all, but she insists that they be restored to their original positions of veneration.

At the end of *Trilogy*, H.D. pays homage to a new version of the "sufficient family" with which each of her epic works concludes.[95] As Mary reaches Bethlehem and receives the myrrh from Kaspar, he realizes that the fragrant attar emanates not from his gift but from the child, that "bundle of myrrh / she held in her arms."[96] Mother-muse and child-creation together effect the "flowering of the rod," a restoration of the ancient female principle to its original position of power and influence. Similar matriarchal constructs are imaged in both ancient and modern art: consider, for example, the numerous reliefs of Demeter and Kore with Demeter's messenger, Triptolemus; or the various renderings, foremost of which is Leonardo da Vinci's, of the Virgin, St. Anne, and the boy-child. In offering a woman-centered paradigm, H.D. peels back the layers of the modern patriarchal family to rediscover an older nurturing unit: two women with a less powerful male figure. From matriarchal consciousness, the poet implies, stems the hope for survival of the "childhood of the race," which is also the "childhood of the individual."[97]

"SHE HERSELF IS THE WRITING": HELEN AS HIEROGLYPH

All Greece hates
the still eyes in the white face,
the lustre as of olives
where she stands,
and the white hands.

All Greece reviles
the wan face when she smiles,
hating it deeper still
when it grows wan and white,
remembering past enchantments
and past ills.

Greece sits unmoved,
God's daughter, born of love,
the beauty of cool feet
and slenderest knees,
could love indeed the maid,
only if she were laid,
white ash amid funereal cypresses.[98]

In this "crystalline" rendering of the mythological woman who perhaps most thoroughly captures H.D.'s imagination, the poet portrays Helen sympathetically as a passive and vulnerable victim of circumstance, "God's daughter, born of love." How can Greece *not* be moved, the poet implies, by this tragic figure who shares the very name of her country, Hellas? Like Mary Magdala, whom H.D. re-visions from whore to goddess in *Trilogy*, Helen of Troy has been maligned by patriarchal myth. Nearly forty years after writing her first "Helen," therefore, H.D. sets out to re-member and re-mythologize "Helena, Helen hated of all Greece."[99]

For H.D., the name Helen represents not wantonness and evil but classical beauty, female creativity, and maternal love. "The mother is the Muse, the Creator," H.D. declares, and she goes on to quote from Poe's "Helen," whose portrait she associates with her own mother:

On desperate seas long wont to roam,
  Thy hyacinth hair, thy classic face,
Thy naiad airs, have brought me home
  To the glory that was Greece
  And the grandeur that was Rome.[100]

H.D. is intrigued by the notion of being "brought . . . home" to the mother by way of "the glory that was Greece." Indeed, she experiences most of her psychic visions there: her "writing-on-the-wall" dream and her "Princess" dream, which caused Freud to complain that H.D. wished to be a "goddess," "founder of a new religion."[101] The validity of Freud's analysis of H.D.'s unconscious motives is, of course, debatable; but certainly a fascination with the mother as a symbol of divine wholeness informs her epic works. *Helen in Egypt* in particular illustrates the questing Helen's efforts to attain psychic unity and personal identity through Thetis, the divine mother-goddess. But before Helen can hope to merge with the "Grande Mer," H.D. recognizes that she must first attempt to *know* the mother, a feat possible only if she can begin to know herself as daughter, woman, and, by extension, creator. In search of "herself / her selves," then, H.D. gives her character her mother's name, as both poet and persona set out to "make real to myself what is most real."[102]

The structure of *Helen in Egypt* indicates both a personal and a universal quest. Through the transformative power of language, the poet deciphers the hieroglyphs of herself and explores her relationship to a female divinity. Like

Palimpsest and *Trilogy*, this work is a triptych, comprising three closely woven volumes. However, in *Helen in Egypt* H.D. has placed between the dense, oracular poems equally complex prose passages—authorial interpretations or, if you will, intrusions into her own text. In this work, then, the poet assumes a dual persona: the "real" H.D. looms as the central observer-speaker in the italicized prose passages, while the "other" voice, that of Helen, participates directly in this quest for spiritual insight and personal definition. Thus both poet and persona invoke as muse the goddess Thetis, participating jointly in an elaborate mythmaking ritual. As H.D. defines the myth, one might say, her "shadow," Helen, experiences it.

Part one of *Helen in Egypt*, "Pallinode," begins with H.D.'s alternate version of the traditional legend, which places Helen not in Troy but in Egypt. Like Stesichorus of Sicily, the author of the original *Pallinode*, and Euripides, who repeats Stesichorus' story, H.D. offers "a defence, explanation or apology" for Helen. Unlike her fellow apologists, however, the woman poet wishes to re-vision Helen as an active rather than a passive force. As Friedman suggests,

> H.D.'s pallinode is a far more complicated critique of tradition than Euripides' and Stesichorus' revisions of the Helen myth. They both established Helen's innocence by seeing her as a modest and chaste Penelope figure who waits patiently in Egypt for her husband to reclaim her. H.D., on the other hand, bases her defense of Helen on a redefinition of innocence that calls into question the male-dominated system of values victimizing Helen in the first place.[103]

To assert Helen's multiple facets, H.D. portrays her as a complex and contradictory figure, "both phantom and reality."[104] The essential paradoxes of *Helen in Egypt* are hence established, as the elusive Helen moves backward and forward in time and space, in and out of reality, in search of one self and many selves.

Despite the stigma under which she lives, Helen claims at first to have found peace in her Egyptian environs:

> fear nothing of the future or the past,
> He, God, will guide you,
> bring you to this place,
>
> as he brought me, his daughter,
> twin-sister of twin-brothers
> and Clytaemnestra, shadow of us all;
>
> the old enchantment holds,
> here there is peace
> for Helena, Helen hated of all Greece.[105]

This opening poem identifies Helen with Clytaemnestra, her twin sister and "shadow-self." Refusing to denounce her sister, Helen not only acknowledges Clytaemnestra as a twin but insists upon her universality, her connection to all women as "shadows of us all." By introducing Clytaemnestra early and prominently into her pallinode, H.D. implies a perverse pleasure in the demonic aspects of both Helen's and her sister's reputations. To be the object of such hatred, after all, is to wield power, albeit negative; like Eve and Lilith before her, Helen and Clytaemnestra as rebels take on a force otherwise unavailable to them. Through a rejection of acceptable feminine roles, Helen acquires an unnatural potency as "Helen, Daemon that thou art," "this evil philtre," "this curse of Aphrodite."[106]

Despite her paradoxical power, however, Helen will not accept her male-defined status as phantom and anathema, for it requires that she be object rather than subject. As the "Pallinode" progresses, Helen seeks to name herself according to her own definitions, definitions distinct from those of patriarchal mythology. To this end, she invokes the sea goddess Thetis, patron of women and mother of Achilles, Helen's lover and fellow quester. Significantly, Helen's first response to Achilles is not to the "god" himself but to his mother:

> How did we know each other?
> was it the sea-enchantment in his eyes
> of Thetis, his sea-mother?[107]

Although Achilles is described as "the New Mortal, / shedding his glory, / limping slowly across the sand," he has not yet been transformed from inviolate warlord to vulnerable lover-child. To come to terms with his Oedipal attachment to his mother, he must first turn to Helen, enacting the voice of traditional misogynistic myth.[108]

While Achilles speaks in accusing tones, however, Helen seeks to translate "*a symbol in time, into timeless-time or hieroglyph or ancient Egyptian time*."[109] To effect such a translation, Helen must employ what H.D. calls "*intuitive . . . rather than intellectual*" knowledge. Helen's art, the poet tells us, is a complex aesthetic born of female instruction, enchantment, and inspiration:

> *From the depth of her racial inheritance, she invokes . . . the symbol or the "letter" that represents or recalls the protective mother-goddess. This is no death-symbol but a life-symbol, it is Isis or her Greek counterpart, Thetis, the mother of Achilles.*[110]

Through the goddess, Helen will attempt to decipher herself and to replace the death-force of the warlord Achilles with the life-force of the divine mother, Thetis.

When Helen first confronts Achilles, he reacts against her, exploding with invectives that have long been leveled against woman:

> "what sort of enchantment is this?
> what art will you wield with a fagot?
> are you Hecate? are you a witch?
>
> a vulture, a hieroglyph,
> the sign or the name of a goddess?
> what sort of goddess is this?"[111]

Achilles includes among his scathing epithets "hieroglyph," a term seemingly free of derogatory connotations yet here equated with "vulture" and "witch." This denunciation occurs again a few stanzas later: "O cursèd, O envious Isis, / you—you—a vulture, a hieroglyph."[112] In her accompanying prose passage H.D. explains Achilles' ire with casual aplomb—"*we must blame someone*"—and describes this final invective of "hieroglyph" as "*almost funny*." If this is humor, however, it is of the darkest sort, since Achilles attempts to strangle Helen. "*Can you throttle a phantom*?" H.D. wonders wryly. But Achilles' efforts are to no avail, since the powers Helen has begun to acquire through Thetis are greater than his own; hence his hatred turns to love. As Helen and Achilles embrace at the end of book one of "Pallinode," Helen is overwhelmed with contradictory emotions. "*Let me go out, let me forget, / let me be lost*," she prays as she lies with Achilles. But escape through love is not the answer, and again Helen turns from the son to the mother: "*O Thetis, O sea-mother / let me remember, let me remember, / forever, this Star in the night*."[113]

Throughout the "Pallinode" Helen wrestles with her ambiguous relationship with Achilles and her ambivalence toward herself as a mysteriously potent woman. "Perhaps he was right / to call me Hecate and a witch," she muses, guiltily accepting for the moment her role as monster. Further, as "living hieroglyph," Helen recognizes in herself and fears those powers beyond rational explanation:

> how did I know the vulture?
> why did I invoke the mother?
> why was he seized with terror?
>
> in the dark, I must have looked
> an inked-in shadow; but with his anger,
> that ember, I became
>
> what his accusation made me,
> Isis, forever with that Child,
> the Hawk Horus.[114]

Here H.D. links Helen specifically to the muse in her maternal guise, Isis "forever with that Child . . . / Horus." Since H.D. has already identified Isis and Thetis as one, she is reaffirming Helen's role as creator, mother to the hieroglyph of herself as Thetis is mother to Achilles and, symbolically, to the questing Helen as well. As Isis sought to reconstruct her lost brother-lover Osiris, H.D. suggests, so Helen must use her powers and those of the mother-goddess to wrest Achilles, and by extension all of humanity, from "Typhon, the Destroyer."[115] "Must death rule life?" Helen asks poignantly. "Must the lily fade in the dark?"[116]

Thus the poet returns to the central theme of *Trilogy*: how to replace the destructive patriarchal ethos with the healing female principle. In books three and four of the "Pallinode," Helen confronts this issue through Achilles, who as both lover and enemy threatens her female identity:

I must fight for Helena
lest the lure of his sea-eyes
endanger my memory
of the thousand-and-one-darts.[117]

Yet Achilles—and this is the "Pallinode's" central paradox—also pushes Helen relentlessly *toward* a confrontation with herself. Steeped in the passivity that a misogynistic mythology has forced upon her, Helen fears a direct encounter with her past, preferring instead to take refuge in her guise as phantom, illusion. But Achilles insists that Helen face her own legacy, that she answer his persistent question: "Helena, which was the dream, / which was the veil of Cytheraea?"[118] Besides its references to the veil of Aphrodite, which according to legend guided Helen's sailboat to Troy, this enigmatic query also alludes to a number of dualities with which Helen in her dream-trance must wrestle: time and timelessness, illusion and reality, Greek and Trojan, love and death. "*Is the 'veil of Cytheraea' or of Love, Death? Is the disguise of Death or the 'veil' of Death, Love? This is too difficult a question to answer*," H.D. explains in her prose commentary.[119] But comprehending the incomprehensible is Helen's assigned task, and to that end, therefore, she sets out to confront "Helen upon the Walls," the "traitor" whose powers of enchantment sent Troy to its fall and Achilles to his death. If Helen is ever to reconstruct her fragmented psyche, H.D. implies, she must solve the riddle of her own seemingly disparate identities: "how are Helen in Egypt / and Helen upon the ramparts, / together yet separate?"[120]

The first aspect of herself with which Helen must come to terms, then, is this demonic impulse so crucial to self-understanding—for H.D., an aspect of the self not innate but patriarchally imposed. Unlike such poets as Louise Bogan and May Sarton, H.D. generally does not view her muse-self as demonic. Yet she recognizes that women from Lilith to Eve to Venus have been *misread* as demonic; hence she explores this facet of female identification. For Helen, the naming of woman as evil, monstrous, is epitomized by her twin sister, Clytaemnestra, "doomed" according to legend as a vengeful murderess yet validated and universalized by Helen as "shadow of us all." In book five of "Pallinode," Helen is inextricably linked to her sister:

I am not happy without her,
Clytaemnestra, my sister;
. . . .

why should Helen be given
peace throughout eternity,
and Clytaemnestra doomed,

and slain by her son, Orestes?[121]

As the protean goddess Isis combines features of both the Terrible and the Good Mother, so Helen and Clytaemnestra represent multiple facets of a single female identity, mutually inclusive parts of a single whole. Only by affirming "my scourge, my sister," as Louise Bogan calls her demonic Other, can Helen solve the riddle of her identity.[122]

Helen's pallinode for Clytaemnestra centers upon the two women's crucial roles as mothers, creators and nurturers of life. As the twin sisters represent kindred psyches, Helen asserts, so, too, do their daughters: "Hermione, my child, / and Iphigenia, her child, are one."[123] In the poems that follow, Helen recounts the story of Iphigenia at Aulis, the near-sacrifice of Clytaemnestra's daughter as "a pledge to Death, / to War and the armies of Greece."[124] As two generations of "brides before the altar," mother and daughter fuse in Helen's mind into a single female entity, a sacrificial virgin with whom Helen, too, identifies, since all have been victims of the "iron-ring" of the warlords. It is against the entrapment and betrayal that this "iron-ring" symbolizes, H.D. suggests, that both Helen and Clytaemnestra have struggled.

Like Demeter wresting her beloved Kore from Hades, so Clytaemnestra challenges those warlords who would sacrifice her daughter. In a powerful passage near the end of the "Pallinode," H.D. images Clytaemnestra and Iphigenia as a swan and a cygnet invincible in an "iron-ring" of their own: that most passionate human bond, that of mother and daughter.

> Have you ever seen a swan,
> when you threaten its nest—
> two swans, but she was alone,
>
> who was never alone;
> the wings of an angry swan
> can compass the earth,
>
> can drive the demons
> back to Tartarus,
> can measure heaven in their span;
>
> one swan and one cygnet
> were stronger than all the host,
> assembled upon the slopes
>
> and the hills of Aulis.[125]

As a mother swan will do anything to protect her nest, H.D.'s analogy implies, so Clytaemnestra is moved to murderous wrath as her daughter's life is threatened by her husband and his cronies. Perhaps H.D. is suggesting that any crime that Clytaemnestra later commits is justifiable. "It is true that she lay with her lover," Helen explains in defense of her sister, "but she could never forget / the glint of steel at the throat / of her child on the altar."[126]

Yet Helen does not seem completely convinced by her own apologia; she is ambivalent toward her sister's plight and toward her own female identity. One of Helen's responses to Clytaemnestra is conspiratorial guilt; they are Eve and Lilith caught in one inextricable web. "*Does she possibly feel that her deser-*

tion of Menelaus is comparable to her sister's murder of Agamemnon?" H.D. wonders of Helen. "*Do they share Nemesis together?*"[127] As twins,

> Clytaemnestra gathered the red rose,
> Helen, the white,
> but they grew on one stem,
>
> one branch, one root in the dark.[128]

Despite the common darkness of their origins and their destinies, however, Helen's life has differed from her sister's. For Helen, the maternal bond once proved secondary to the sexual, for in going with Paris she also abandoned her daughter, Hermione. At this point in her quest, however, Helen is not able to confront the issue of her own maternal desertion. Instead, she must examine first her relationship to Clytaemnestra. "Hermione and Iphigenia / are protected," Helen therefore rationalizes, "they need no help."[129] Rather, it is Helen who needs help, she who must "*re-create the whole of the tragic scene. Helen is the Greek drama. Again*, she herself is the writing."[130]

As the author of her own text and the central character therein, Helen must both accept Clytaemnestra as a shadow-self and eschew the violent "Will to Power" that her sister has chosen. "Does it even the Balance / if a wife repeats a husband's folly?" H.D. wonders, as she recounts Agamemnon's return from Troy with Cassandra and his subsequent death at the hands of Clytaemnestra and Aegisthus.

> Never; the law is different;
> if a woman fights
> she must fight by stealth,
>
> with invisible gear;
> no sword, no dagger, no spear
> in a woman's hands
>
> can make wrong, right.[131]

This passage has aroused controversy among critics of *Helen in Egypt*, several of whom interpret it as H.D.'s acquiescence to the "truism" of female passivity and subservience.[132] But given H.D.'s war phobia, revealed poignantly in *Trilogy* and discussed at length in *Tribute to Freud*, this passage more likely reflects H.D.'s strong pacifistic sentiments, her wish to substitute a life-affirming female principle for the destructive "iron-ring" of patriarchy.[133] Certainly this poem, along with Thetis' earlier monologue ("a woman's wiles are a net"), asserts the power of female "craft"—a term that suggests not only woman's cunning and subtlety but also her subversive art, the "net" by which she "captures" language and attains poetic subjectivity.[134] Woman's weapons may be less overt than those traditionally wielded by the warlords, H.D. implies, but they are not necessarily less apocalyptic; they, too, are empowered to destroy and create anew.

As the giver and nurturer of life, woman must be dedicated to its preservation, H.D.'s argument asserts; she must redefine herself in terms of her life-giving, life-sustaining capacities, eschewing all links to male violence and bloodshed.

For Helen, therefore, to redefine herself is to re-vision her alternate self, Clytaemnestra. Although she does not condone her sister's murder of Agamemnon, Helen nonetheless wishes to name her sister anew, to purge her of prior identities. As part of this reinterpretation, Helen associates her sister with Astarte, a primitive goddess who both destroys and creates. In Helen's mind, Clytaemnestra

> is not Nemesis, as you named her,
> nor Nephythys, but perhaps Astarte
>
> will re-call her ultimately.[135]

As so Astarte does. Re-visioned and revalidated by her sister, Clytaemnestra is "called to another Star, / Ashtoreth, Ishtar, / Astarte"—to the protean goddess in her multiplicity. Having laid her sister's ghost to rest at last ("be still, O sister, O shadow"), Helen resumes her own journey toward self-definition.[136]

In part two, "Leuké," Helen is transported in time and space to "l'isle blanche," where she attempts further to remember her past and re-member herself by casting off old stereotypes:

> I am not nor mean to be
> the Daemon they made of me;
> . . . .
>
> I remember a dream that was real;
> let them sing Helena for a thousand years,
> let them name and re-name Helen,
>
> I can not endure the weight of eternity,
> they will never understand
> how, a second time, I am free.[137]

Eschewing the names given her by others, Helen attempts to come to terms with self-chosen roles. To this end, she turns from Egypt and Achilles and Thetis to journey both backward and inward. On Leuké, male figures replace Thetis as Helen's guide into her past: Paris, the former lover through whom Helen must recall the rebellious Helen of Troy and the sensual Helen Dendritis; and Theseus, the king who long ago stole her from Sparta to be his child bride. As Helen soon realizes, however, there is a problem in choosing either Paris or Theseus as "psychopomp." Despite their supposed objectivity, both would rewrite Helen's story, each according to his own design. Thus Helen must detach herself from any masculine vision of reality and turn instead to her own voice: "do you hear me? do I whisper? / there is a voice within me, / listen—let it speak for me."[138]

This movement toward an independent language and vision at first intimidates Helen, since she must confront frightening manifestations of herself. The first of these is "*an heroic voice, the voice of Helen of Sparta.*"[139] "Do I love War?" Helen asks herself in terror/ "Is this Helena?"[140] Remembering Theseus' advice, she fights off her fears and allows another voice, her lyric side, to take over. This other voice reminds her that Helen of Sparta is merely one facet of her identity, that as "Persephone's sister" and thus Demeter's daughter, she is also linked to "Cypris, Cypria, Amor, / . . . Thetis / . . . Clytaemnestra . . . Astarte / or Nephthys, twin-sister of Isis, / and Isis is Cypris, Cypria."[141] This circular catalog of goddesses reveals to Helen her own protean nature, her many selves:

> Helen—Helen—Helen—
> there was always another and another and another;
> the rose has many petals,
>
> or if you will, the nenuphar,
> father, brother, son, lover,
> sister, husband and child;
>
> beyond all other, the Child,
> the child in the father,
> the child in the mother,
>
> the child-mother, yourself.[142]

From the mother that is herself, the infant Helen must be born, fully aware of her multiple identities and voices.

Thus Helen at last confronts those dualities that have plagued her throughout her quest, and in so doing asserts herself as "Helen in Egypt, / Helen at home, / Helen in Hellas forever."[143] As part of a larger world order, H.D. suggests, Helen must recognize the paradox at the center of herself; she is both Helen in Egypt and Helen in Hellas, two irreconcilable halves at once a perpetual whole—not an androgynous male-female combination but an autonomous female-female self, virgin and matron, fused and complete. With this understanding, the poet explains, "*Helen is at peace, she has found the answer, she will rest.*"[144] For nourishment and sustenance, Helen must return to the womb of the eternal mother, the source of all beginnings:

> I am only a daughter,
> no, I am not Demeter,
> seated before an altar,
>
> your brazier, there,
> I am Koré, Persephone; . . .
> . . . .
>
> . . . only let Thetis,
> the goddess hold me for a while
> in this her island, her egg-shell.[145]

Reemerging from the "egg-shell" of Leuké, Helen needs to "renew the Quest," to "read here/ in my crystal, the Writing."[146] Thus in part three, "Eidolon," she returns to Egypt for a reunion with Achilles and a final reconstruction of herself. No longer "King of the Myrmidons," Achilles like Helen must come to terms with a new identity, or a new series of identities. First, he must recognize himself as "the royal Sacred High Priest of love-rites"—not the rapacious "love-rites" of the Greek warlords, but the essential rituals of love and death, as in the Eleusinian rites. "We are in Eleusis," H.D. explains as Helen and Achilles are reunited. "Helen is Persephone, / Achilles is Dis, / (the Greek Isis-Osiris)."[147] For the first time, Helen and Achilles meet as fellow questers, equals, brother and sister as well as lovers.

The pivotal figure around whom both Helen's and Achilles' struggles center is the mother-goddess Thetis. The title "Eidolon" refers to a bronze figurine of the sea goddess that Achilles has cherished as a child and that later rests at the head of his ship, "a mermaid, Thetis upon the prow."[148] As Achilles engages in a classic Oedipal struggle for both separation from and identification with the mother, he recognizes that his earlier violent reaction toward Helen was the pent-up hostility of the son for his mother, that powerful force that he would both claim and deny.[149] As Helen has separated momentarily from Thetis in order to "name" herself independently, so Achilles must experience a release from the "ecstasy of desolation, / a desire to return to the old / thunder and roar of the sea."[150] He must also admit his fury toward the mother responsible for her son's vulnerability, having forgotten to dip his heel in the river Styx. In other words, he must recognize the mother as both creator and destroyer, as the dual-faceted matriarchal goddess of old.

As Achilles wrestles with his Oedipal conflicts, Helen must confront an area of her past with which she has not come to terms on Leuké: her abandonment of her daughter, Hermione. Recalling Theseus' advice that she should acknowledge her disparate facets, Helen sets out to remember that which she has long sought to repress:

> now I remember, I remember
> Paris before Egypt, Paris after;
> . . . .
>
> my Lord's devotion, my child
> prattling of a bird's nest,
>
> playing with my work-basket;
> the reels rolled to the floor
> and she did not stoop to pick up
>
> the scattered spools but stared
> with wide eyes in a white face,
> at a stranger—and stared at her mother,

a stranger—that was all;
I placed my foot on the last step
of the marble water-stair

and never looked back;
how could I remember all that?[151]

As Helen's old grief resurfaces, she realizes that she and her daughter are destined to be "strangers," communicating only through vague stares that belie any true recognition. As Friedman has noted, this passage represents H.D.'s strongest attack on the expectations of female passivity and conformity that patriarchal marriage and motherhood impose upon a woman.[152] At the same time, however, Helen does not free herself from blame for leaving her child behind. In admitting responsibility for her own choice, she must feel again the pain of this excruciating loss.

If Helen has lost her daughter through her rebellion, however, she has gained self-knowledge. Aware of this "rhythm as yet unheard," she reimagines her experiences at Troy, this time through her own eyes. Re-visioning such complex dualities as Apollo and Aphrodite, Greece and Troy, the dream and the veil, Paris and Achilles, Helen attains a more realistic perspective on her Trojan experience:

So it was nothing, nothing at all,
the loss, the gain; it was nothing,
the victory, the shouting

and Hector slain; it was nothing,
the days of waiting were over.[153]

Relieved of this final obstacle to self-understanding, Helen is able finally to declare, "I think I see clearly at last."[154] By reconciling herself to her losses, that is, Helen may gain the elusive self.

What Helen "sees clearly" in the last two books of *Helen in Egypt* is the crucial role of the maternal muse, Thetis, in the formation or re-formation of her own and Achilles' identities. "*The enchantment, the magic . . . is overpowering*," the poet insists; "*it could not have been endured but 'for her'* ":

For her, it is clear,
(are you near, are you far),
for her, we are One,

not for each other . . . [155]

Through Thetis, Helen realizes, both she and Achilles have come to know themselves in all their protean complexity, as they shift through time and space, "*centralized by a moment, 'undecided yet.'* "[156] Like the frozen figures on Keats' Grecian urn, Helen and Achilles simultaneously live in the past, the present, and the future. Through a cyclical process, sexual and creative, Helen gives "miraculous birth" to a son, Euphorion, at once "the child in Chiron's cave," the young Achilles, and the "frail maiden" abducted by Theseus, Helen herself. The divine triad of Thetis-Helen-Achilles, mother-daughter-son, is thus complemented by "the child in the father, / the child in the mother, / the child-mother, yourself."[157]

In *Tribute to Freud* H.D. discusses her view of "the hieroglyph of the dream" through which "man" can interpret and comprehend human experience:

> The picture-writing, the hieroglyph of the dream, was the common property of the whole race; in the dream, man, as at the beginning of time, spoke a universal language, and man, meeting in the universal understanding of the unconscious or the subconscious, would forego barriers of time and space, and man, understanding man, would save mankind.[158]

In depicting Helen as a hieroglyph ("she herself is the writing"), the poet offers a female paradigm of salvation: woman saving all humanity. In so doing, she also affirms her own personal and poetic identities. Through Helen as a shadow-self and Thetis as a mother-muse, H.D. in *Helen in Egypt* claims herself through her art and validates her art through herself.

"WHY MUST I WRITE?": H.D. AS HERMETIC DEFINITION

> I wanted to free myself of repetitive thoughts and experiences—my own and those of many of my contemporaries. I did not specifically realize just what it was I wanted, but . . . at least, I knew this—I would . . . stand aside, if I could (if it were not already too late), and take stock of my possessions. You might say that I had—yes, I had something that I specifically owned. I *owned* myself.[159]

What does it mean for a woman poet to "own" herself, and how do the "*hachish supérieur*" of visionary dreams and the writing that it inspires enable H.D. to achieve autonomy, especially in her old age? These questions suggest the primary themes of her last volume of poetry, *Hermetic Definition*. Like its major predecessors, this work is composed of three parts: "Hermetic Definition," "Sagesse," and "Winter Love." Although less closely linked in theme and tone than the triptychs of H.D.'s two earlier epics, these three poems elaborate the elderly poet's perceptions of the creative process and her lifelong battle for poetic subjectivity.

"Hermetic Definition" comprises three sections: "Red Rose and a Beggar," "The Grove of Academe," and "Star of Day." In the first section the poet depicts herself alternately as a "red rose," the flower of youthful passion, and a "beggar," an impoverished seeker who envisions passion as a means of creative inspiration. "Red Rose and a Beggar" begins with a halting tribute to Lionel Durand, a young *Newsweek* editor whom H.D. had met in Paris, and a querulous assessment of her sexual and creative reawakening:

Why did you come
to trouble my decline?
I am old (I was old till you came);

the reddest rose unfolds,
(which is ridiculous
in this time, this place,

unseemly, impossible,
even slightly scandalous),
the reddest rose unfolds.[160]

H.D. pays homage to the "you" of the poem as her *raison d'être*: "you are my whole estate; / I would hide in your mind / as a child hides in an attic."[161] This image of the poet as child and the lover as protective inner space is expanded by a similar association in the next poem, where Durand is portrayed as the child in need of nurture. As the man from Paris, "Par-Isis," he is identified as the son of Isis, Horus, and thus connected to the maternal muse, whom H.D. calls forth once more in this work.

If the "you" of the poem, presumably Durand, elicits such devotion and engenders such a creative outpouring, why then does he not function as the poet's muse? According to traditional definitions, Durand would seem to qualify as a male version of Graves' "sister of the mirage and echo," an "inspiring animus" to the female poet. But H.D. attributes her newly awakened powers not to Durand himself but the unfolding of the "reddest rose," the rejuvenation of the female self. Durand is not the inspiration for H.D.'s poetry but an eidolon of poetry itself. That a force greater than Durand is responsible for the poet's creative renewal is made clear in the fifth poem of "Red Rose and a Beggar," the poem with which this chapter began:

why must I write?
you would not care for this,
but She draws the veil aside,

unbinds my eyes,
commands,
write, write or die.[162]

Since "She" is subsequently identified as Isis, the protean ancient goddess who appears also in *Trilogy* and *Helen in Egypt*, this passage asserts the crucial bond between female poet and female muse.

As "Red Rose and a Beggar" continues, H.D. further develops the identities of Isis as Muse-self and Durand as Horus, the child-creation. In the sixth poem she "prays to" Paris, "Par-Isis," and to his mother, "Isis-self, Egyptian flower, / *Notre-Dame*."[163] References to Notre Dame occur partly because of its location in Paris and hence its association with Durand; however, the poet also alludes to Robert Ambelain's theory in *Dans l'Ombre des Cathedrales* (1939), a hermetic work by which she was greatly influenced. This study links "Christian symbolism as evidenced in the portals of Notre Dame and traditional hermetic schemes like those lingering from Isis and Par-Isis, her son."[164] If Ambelain is correct, H.D. suggests, there continues to operate an ancient matriarchal hierarchy, of which Isis is an early manifestation and the Virgin Mary merely one modern emanation. According to the poet's spiritual hermetics, she and Durand as Isis and Par-Isis are part of this "ancient wisdom."

The second section of "Hermetic Definition," "The Grove of Academe," describes H.D.'s encounter with the French poet St. John Perse, here called "Seigneur," whose poetry she greatly admires. As the poem explains, his assistance saved her once from falling during an awards ceremony in New York:

> you are my own age,
> my own stars;
> I accepted acclaim
>
> from the others,
> for the honour,
> unexpectedly thrust upon me,
>
> . . . .
>
> and I might have fallen
> but your hand reached out to me.[165]

Associated with the mythological Perseus, slayer of the Gorgon Medusa, Perse for H.D. represents supernatural powers and poetic rejuvenation; his touch validates both personal and creative selves. Furthermore, the brief encounter between H.D. and Perse reveals the disparity between male and female aesthetics:

> I cherish my personal treasures,
> now that I discover
>
> how different yours are;
> we meet in antitheses;
> no need to speak, to heed one another.[166]

As the male slayer of the female monster, however, Perseus also threatens the woman poet. Admitting her ambivalence about her art ("if I had hidden as I wanted to, / fearing acclaim, / I would not have met you"), H.D. is overwhelmed by Perse's poetry. But she is not rendered silent by it; paradoxically, she is freed to acknowledge her own power once she has paid tribute to his. "I am swept away / in the orgy of your poetry," she declares to Perse; "you draw me out / to compete with your frenzy; / . . . your words free me."[167] Despite this affirmation, however, the poet continues at times to be self-deprecatory: "by antitheses, I become ant or eel, / nothingness slides off this rock."[168] Ultimately, the "antithetical centre" that Perse represents becomes too imposing a force. Eschewing Perse as mentor, she would return instead to her own "creation," the "child" Durand, who continues to haunt her imagination.

> I want my old habit,
> I want to light candles;
> *Seigneur*, you must forgive my deflection,
>
> I can not step over the horizon;
> I must wait to-day, to-morrow or the day after
> for the answer.[169]

"Star of Day," the third section of "Hermetic Definition," is dominated by metaphors of pregnancy and rebirth, as the poet conceives and gives birth to her new creation. Ironically, the occasion for this celebration of new life is death: H.D. had learned in January 1961 of Durand's death a few days before Christmas.[170] The poet's grief gives way to fecundity, as she mythologizes herself as the ancient Saïs and Durand as the conception, the "Star of Day":

> they say Saïs brought forth the Star of Day,
> at midnight when the shadows are most dense,
> the nights longest and most desperate,
>
> it was Plutarch spoke of Saïs . . .
> we know the rest,
> Isis, Cybele (Atys), *Notre Dame*.[171]

For a mind as complexly associative as H.D.'s, the "coincidence" of having met Durand nine months prior to his death, along with his death at Christmastime, weaves a rich web of archetypal connotations. Confronted with the irony of his dying "just as my Christmas candles had burnt out," the poet re-visions him in a "new circle, / one of the zodiac angels" whom Ambelain mentions. She also images herself as the maternal force responsible for generating this new cycle, by linking her "Star of Day" to Isis' instructions to "write, write or die":

> It was April that we met,
> and once in May;
> I did not realize my state of mind,
>
> my "condition" you might say,
> until August when I wrote,
> *the reddest rose unfolds*,
>
> I did not realize that separation
> was the only solution,
> if I were to resolve this curious "condition,"
>
> you were five months "on the way,"
> I did not realize how intimate
> the relation, nor what lay ahead;
>
> I did not know that I must keep faith
> with something, I called it writing,
> *write, write or die*.[172]

H.D. now realizes that her creative rejuvenation came not from Durand himself but from the muse, Isis, who "ordained or controlled this." No longer inclined to "walk into" her lover, the poet acknowledges her own control over her art: "I did not think of it the other way, / that it was you who walked into me."[173]

The final poems of "Hermetic Definition" are filled with further allusions to pregnancy and childbearing, as the poet speaks again of her "condition," of the "cut cord," of her "nine months to remember." When Durand failed to write after their second meeting, the poet recalls,

> I felt cast out, I was thrown away,
> and to recover identity,
>
> I wrote furiously,
> I was in a fever, you were lost,
> just as I had found you,
>
> but I went on, I had to go on,
> the writing was the un-born,
> the conception.[174]

Having affirmed her art as a source of sustenance, the poet moves toward autonomy. No longer governed by sexual passion ("now I draw my nun-grey about me"), she is sustained by greater force, her creativity. She is complete within herself:

> I only know,
> this room contains me,
> it is enough for me,
>
> there is always an end;
> . . . .
> Night brings the Day.[175]

The initial impulse behind "Sagesse" is the poet's identification with a white scops owl held captive in a London zoo, which reminds the ailing poet of her own "captivity" in a Swiss hospital. "May those who file before you feel / something of what you are—that God is kept within / the narrow confines of a cage, a pen."[176] So the poet addresses the owl, her comrade, punning on the word *pen*, the source of her entrapment and yet her means of attaining freedom. In fact, her *pen* causes the poet difficulty in dealing with her "wardens," since the hospital staff and particularly her own doctor, here called Germain, would tear her from her work, "fearing my abstraction":

> "why are you trembling?
>
> what are you thinking?
> I don't know where you are;
>
> you must come out, the car will come to-morrow,
> you haven't been out for a week."[177]

The poet has not "been out" because her journeys have been inward ones. As she falls in and out of consciousness, she flows between past and present as part of an effort to re-member, to render whole the vulnerable self. From the "pen," the hospital room in which she is confined, the poet reinterprets her past with that other pen, the instrument of her creativity.

Early in the poem H.D. associates the owl with Athene, whose feminine strength and clarity of vision the poet seeks. In the face of physical weakness, however, strength is difficult to maintain. Thus H.D. turns for support to two crucial forces: her art and her muse. Advised by Germain that " 'your weakness and your nerves / are due to apprehension; if you write like this, create, / you must expect reaction,' " the poet rebels: " 'nothing like this happened when I wrote before.' " Refusing to stop writing, she invokes " 'Marah,' the *Grande Mer*, patron and protectress, / sword-lilies on their stalks, / *Créatrice de la Foi*."[178] As "*Sombre Mère Sterile*" and "*Brilliante Mère Féconde*," this female protector draws upon the power of the word, the poetic logos, through the imagery of the whispering shell:

> you hold it to my ear,
> " 'listen, my child, fear not the ancient lore,
>
> (*Gymnosophes, Philosophes*), this echo is for you,
> listen, my child, it is enough,
>
> the echo of the sea, our secret
> and our simple mystery, *Grande Mer* . . . ' "[179]

Rejuvenated by this powerful voice, the poet continues to call upon the "Grande Mer" for validation. Near the end of "Sagesse" she invokes the goddess as "Our Lady":

> O most fair; unworthy, we would pray
> your intercession for us; grant us strength,
>
> a little strength to serve your Power.[180]

In "Winter Love," H.D. brings her work full circle, again imaging herself as Helen. Although Helen of "Winter Love" at times recalls her counterpart in *Helen in Egypt*, this new persona has little to do with Paris or Achilles or, for that matter, even Thetis. Instead, she takes as a "winter lover" Odysseus, prototypical Greek hero and male quester, a figure who may well represent her youthful lover Ezra Pound. But H.D. imbues Helen with the potency generally attributed to the mythical Odysseus as slayer of the Cyclops, outwitter of Circe, most cunning and creative of men. Through her female *bildungsroman*, a retrospective validation of herself as woman hero, the poet attempts to "come home" to her self. "There was a Helen before there was a War," H.D. insists, echoing the earlier Helen, "but who remembers her?"[181] This plaintive query begins H.D.'s final search for affirmation and validation.

Since no one else remembers Helen, the poet must re-member her once more, through the magic of the poetic word:

The-tis, Sea-'tis, I played games like this;
I had long reveries, invoked the future,
re-invoked the past, syllables, mysteries, numbers;

I must have turned a secret key, unwittingly,
when I said Odysseus—when did I say Odysseus?
how did I call you back, or how did I come back?[182]

Even as she denies her linguistic alchemy H.D. employs it, creating a new Helen born of the old. Once more the poet insists on the power of language to re-create, to raise from the dead. Helen has "come back," the poet reveals, having narrowly escaped the watchful eye of her "grandam," a grim elderly matron who serves as "warden" of the young, vital Helen. In a series of exquisite strophes and antistrophes, the poet celebrates Helen's escape and affirms the female sexuality and power that "Helios-Helen-Eros" represents.[183]

Such freedom must be temporary, however, as Helen realizes when she peers into the mirror of herself:

There was a Helen before there was a war,
but who remembers her? O grandam, you, you, you,
with faded hair—you answer, you descend,

ascend, from where? it was all over,
I was wrapped in a tight shroud,
but you appear; the death-bands fall away;

you have come, grandam, no toothless grin,
no *corbeau sur une crâne*:
"remember," you say, "Helen, remember?"[184]

Perhaps past and present *can* be reconciled, H.D. suggests; wholeness can be attained. After all, the youthful poet and her elderly counterpart must coexist in harmony. According to this appealing vision, Helen and the "grandam" can merge as mother and daughter, protected in their solitary cocoon:

Grande Dame, I will carry your crutch for you,
you needn't hobble, hobble any more,
you will tell me what was true,

what wasn't true,
we will walk miles over the sand.[185]

In the last five books of "Winter Love," however, the elderly poet turns on her youthful self, rejecting this idyllic future in favor of her only real choice, the hope of living on through her art. Thus the grandam becomes a *Grande Dame*, a midwife to the fecund Helen. Despite Helen's pleas ("grandam, mid-wife, *Sage-Femme*, / let me rest, let me rest, / I can't struggle any more"), she must sacrifice her old self to give birth to a new:

grandam, midwife, *Sage-Femme*,
I pray you, as with his last breath,
a man might pray, keep *Espérance*,

our darling from my sight,
for bliss so great,
the thought of that soft touch,

would drag me back to life
and I would rest;
grandam, great *Grande Dame*,

midwife and *Sage-Femme*,
you brought Him forth in darkness,
while I slept.[186]

As further punishment-reward, Helen must suckle her creation, even though it stays her breath. "Cruel, cruel midwife, / so secretly to steal my phantom self," Helen cries, as the "*Sage-Femme*" holds the child to its mother's breast, forcing her to bear the "terrible . . . weight of honey and of milk,"—of life itself.[187] As "Winter Love" ends, the poet-midwife administers the last rites to Helen, who dies giving nourishment to her own creation:

I die in agony whether I give or do not give;
cruel, cruel *Sage-Femme*,

wiser than all the regents of God's throne,
why do you torture me?
come, come, O *Espérance*,

Espérance, O golden bee,
take life afresh and if you must,
so slay me.[188]

Hermetic Definition represents H.D.'s most comprehensive mythologizing of herself as woman artist, inextricably linked to birth, death, and regeneration. However, the poet explores this same theme in a work roughly contemporaneous with *Hermetic Definition*: *Vale Ave*, a long poem written during the summer of 1959. The central figure of *Vale Ave* is Lilith—like Helen, a woman hero reviled in patriarchal lore. But H.D.'s Lilith is a powerful female creator, and through her the poet again celebrates the muse as female,

An invisible Circe or disguised Lilith,
or Helen, Guinevere, Semiramis,

that we invoke as graces, even Virtues,
not for their beauty only, but for their implacable search

for the *semblable*, the haunting first cause,
the *primum mobile* that gave both Hell and Paradise to Dante.

"Perhaps I boast," the elderly poet goes on to speculate,

> perhaps I should be cowed and disciplined,
> a woman of seventy, lying—no—not helpless,
>
> for I called for light,
> and *Dieu qui inspire*, Light came.[189]

This poignant passage about creative inspiration and rejuvenation captures the essence of H.D.'s mythology of the woman-goddess-self. Throughout her canon this poet gives credence to the claim of many contemporary women writers: women are becoming midwives at their own births, exploring new ways of regenerating and revenerating their female creativity and the muse within themselves.

4

"Toward Durable Fire": The Solitary Muse of May Sarton

"We have to make myths of our lives," May Sarton says in *Plant Dreaming Deep*. "It is the only way to live them without despair."[1] Of the many twentieth-century American women poets who are mythmakers, Sarton speaks most urgently and often about what it means to be a woman and a writer and about the female muse as a primary source of poetic inspiration. In the fourth "Autumn Sonnet" from *A Durable Fire*, she describes the crucial relationship between the woman poet and her muse:

> I never thought that it could be, not once,
> The Muse appearing in warm human guise,
> She the mad creature of unhappy chance
> Who looked at me with cold Medusa eyes,
> Giver of anguish and so little good.
> For how could I have dreamed that you would come
> To help me tame the wildness in my blood,
> To bring the struggling poet safely home?[2]

As "sister of the mirage and echo," Sarton's muse parallels in some respects the quasi-erotic, mystical inspirer invoked by Robert Graves, her "whom I desired above all things to know."[3] Furthermore, in her "warm human guise," Sarton's source of inspiration represents a female variation on the contemporary poet Gary Snyder's theme of the muse as the "clearest mirror," the "human lover."[4] But for Sarton the muse is also a demonic shadow, a crucial Medusa-self against whom the poet struggles and yet through whom she ultimately transforms the "wildness in my blood" into vital creative energy. In the words of Hilary Stevens, Sarton's poet-protagonist and alter-ego in *Mrs. Stevens Hears the Mermaids Singing*, "the muse destroys as well as gives life, does not nourish, pierces, forces one to discard, renew, be born again. Joy and agony are pivoted in her presence."[5]

To understand Sarton's theory of the muse, we must examine her view of female creativity, which centers on the antithesis between artist and woman. "I was broken in two / By sheer definition," she exclaims in "Birthday on the Acropolis," and though she is reacting here to the "pitiless clarity" of the stark Greek light and landscape, the statement describes as well her conflict in attempting to reconcile her femininity with her art.[6] Like writers from Emily Dickinson to Virginia Woolf to Adrienne Rich, Sarton struggles to overcome psychic fragmentation, a feeling of self versus self. For Sarton, this quest to name and claim her female creative identity is complicated by an acceptance of the patriarchal definition of woman as Other—as beloved rather than lover, object rather than subject; in short, as inherently "other than" active creator. She aligns herself with a perspective both Jungian and ahistorical in assuming an archetypal feminine principle innately separate from an active masculine principle. This assumption has enormous implications for her poetics, which posits an inevitable dichotomy between the feminine and the artistic sensibilities. "The woman who needs to create works of art," Hilary Stevens asserts, "is born with a kind of psychic tension in her which drives her unmercifully to find a way to balance, to make herself whole. Every human being has this need: in the artist it is mandatory. Unable to fulfill it, he goes mad. But when the artist is a woman, she fulfills it at the *expense* of herself as a woman."[7]

"At the *expense* of herself as a woman"—this statement recalls Robert Southey's famous pronouncement to Charlotte Brontë in 1837: "literature is not the business of a woman's life, and it cannot be."[8] For May Sarton, Southey's assertion contains a modicum of truth. "After all, admit it," Mrs. Stevens says to Jenny Hare, her youthful interviewer and a budding writer, "a woman is meant to create children, not works of art. . . . It's the natural order of things that [a man] constructs objects outside himself and his family. The woman who does so is aberrant."[9] Sarton's argument hinges on an acceptance of traditional definitions of *masculine* as active, objective, dynamic, and of *feminine* as passive, subjective, static. Any woman who writes seriously, according to this paradigm, assumes a masculine role. "I settled for being a woman," Hilary's mother-in-law tells her. "I wonder whether you can."[10] Like Aphra Behn, who spoke of "my masculine part, the poet in me," Sarton suggests that the aggressive, male side of the female self, the Jungian animus, creates literary works.[11] Yet Sarton neither claims nor desires to "write like a man"; as Peter Selversen, Hilary's other interviewer, says of her work, "the style is masculine; the content is feminine."[12] Sarton is aware of the difficulties the woman writer confronts in attempting to reconcile her gender and her creativity. How, then, does she incorporate her view of the creative enterprise as a masculine phenomenon into her definition and perception of herself as a woman writer?

For one thing, she views the woman writer's aberrance not as a liability but as an asset, a source of unique creative power. In this respect she takes issue with Sandra M. Gilbert and Susan Gubar, who suggest that in the nineteenth century, at least, the woman who writes typically "experiences her gender as a painful obstacle or even a debilitating inadequacy."[13] According to Sarton's schema, in contrast, the woman writer's aberrance serves as a constructive rather than a destructive force, for it catapults her not toward neurosis but toward health. Anxiety is especially acute in the creative woman, Sarton acknowledges, as are frustration, fragmentation, rage; but these feelings of being "rent in two . . . most of the time," as Jenny describes herself in *Mrs. Stevens*, are precisely the raw material from which female art is sculpted, the female self validated.[14] In a sense, therefore, Sarton agrees with Southey: literature is *not* a woman's business if the woman in question expects or wishes to assume traditional female roles as well as the nontraditional guise of artist. If the woman writer accepts and indeed relishes her incongruity, however, if she celebrates her aberrance as a source of artistic nourishment, literature becomes life's *only* business. "For the aberrant woman," Mrs. Stevens explains, "art is health, the only health! It is . . . the constant attempt to rejoin something broken off or lost, to make whole again. It is always integrating."[15]

Once her aberrance is acknowledged as a given, the woman writer can set about the process of self-discovery, which Sarton believes lies at the root of meaningful art, especially of poetry. Although she has worked for fifty years in three genres—in addition to fourteen volumes of poetry, she has published eighteen novels and six nonfictional works—Sarton focuses her theory of female creativity on poetry and the process of attaining poetic autonomy. "Poetry and novels are absolutely different," she asserts in *World of Light*, a film about her life and work. Whereas a novel represents a dialogue with others, poetry focuses on the inner world: "you write poetry for yourself and God."[16] In *Journal of a Solitude* she muses further on this subject: "Why is it that poetry always seems to me so much more of a true work of the soul than prose? I never feel elated after writing a piece of prose, though I have written good things on concentrated will. . . . Perhaps it is that prose is earned and poetry given."[17] Poetry, then, is a gift; the poet an instrument. One elects to be a novelist but is "chosen" to be a poet: "you have to be willing . . . to give something terribly intimate and secret of yourself to the world—and not care."[18]

As the crucial source that inspires the poet, Sarton's muse "throws the artist back upon herself," thereby facilitating this essential psychic exchange. "When the Muse comes," Hilary explains, "the dialogue begins. . . . The Muse opens up the dialogue with oneself and goes her way."[19] "The Muse is always a question," she continues. "That's what sets up the dialogue . . . not with the Muse, but with oneself."[20] In some respects, Sarton's muse resembles the classic, passive inspirational source of the male poet, the traditional female lover: she is mysterious, she cannot be pinned down, she "goes her way." But as a shadow to the woman poet, she also represents a vital, active aspect of the poetic process, a potent and demonic force against whom the poet is constantly pitted. "Think of a mixture of properties in a chemical test tube," Hilary says to Jenny and Peter; "sometimes when two elements are mixed, they boil; there is tumult; heat is disengaged. So in the presence of the Muse, the sources of poetry boil;

the faculty of language itself ferments."[21] Like Plato, Sarton believes that creative energy is often a product of irrationality, "frenzy," and that the primary source of this tumult is the "honeyed muse."

Whether she manifests herself as a serene visitant or a tempestuous "precipitating presence," the muse for Sarton is irrevocably and quintessentially female; there neither is nor can be, she asserts, a male muse. "What seems to me valid and interesting," Peter tells Jenny before they meet Hilary Stevens,

> "is the question posited at such huge length by Robert Graves in *The White Goddess*—who and what is the Muse? Here we have a poet who has gone on writing poems long after the Muse, at least in a personal incarnation, has become irrelevant. What sustains the intensity? Is there a White God?" he asked, and immediately felt how funny it sounded. They both laughed.
>
> "Of course not!"[22]

Later, when Peter toasts the muse, "whoever she or he may be," Hilary Stevens protests. " 'Whom I desired above all things to know. Sister of the mirage and echo!' . . . the Muse, young man, is *she*!"[23] For Sarton, this female muse is erotic, demonic, and maternal. In her guise as human lover, feminine inspiration incarnate, Sarton's muse resembles alternately Plato's Diotima, Petrarch's Laura, and Dante's Beatrice; she evokes either passionate love—Plato's "frenzy"—or a strong sense of spiritual connectedness, or both. Yet the extreme tension that Sarton considers essential to the exchange between poet and muse often suggests not a meeting of lovers but a collision of wild, animal-like forces: "I am the cage where poetry / Paces and roars."[24] These two extremes—the muse as lover and the muse as demon—merge finally in the image of the mother, Sarton's ultimate metaphor for poetic inspiration. "My mother still remains the great devouring enigma," Hilary Stevens admits, "the Muse, you see . . ."[25]

This concept of the muse as mother suggests the complex struggle for female identity that the woman writer experiences: how to bring into her scope the Other, whether lover or demonic shadow or mother, without destroying the self. As psychologists and anthropologists from Sigmund Freud to Dorothy Dinnerstein have pointed out, human awe of and ambivalence toward the mother spring from her dual nature: as nurturer of life, she also holds the power of negation, destruction, and death. In the woman this ambivalence may be especially acute, since the biological mother is a powerful same-sex role model whom the daughter must simultaneously reject and emulate.[26] If the muse is ultimately the mother, as Sarton claims, she represents for the woman poet a source not only of love and nurture but also of anger and ambivalence. From the tension engendered by these conflicting emotions, Sarton concludes, springs impassioned poetry.

Although the female muse is the most crucial ingredient in the "witch's brew" that Sarton as a poet boils, a second element is also very important: solitude.

"I have become enamored of solitude . . . my last great love," she admits in the film *World of Light*, and indeed silence and isolation provide her with a major source of artistic nourishment. As the condition that breeds art, solitude is especially important to the woman poet, who frequently has had little access to a "room of her own." "Solitude itself is a way of waiting for the inaudible and the invisible to make itself felt," Sarton explains. "And that is why solitude is never static and never hopeless."[27] Neither is it always easy, however. "The value of solitude—one of its values—is, of course, that there is . . . nothing to help balance at times of particular stress or depression."[28] Such attacks from within, she insists, force the woman artist to struggle with her art. For Sarton, then, female creativity is fertilized through a solitude shattered by visitations from the muse, who both intrudes upon and enhances this delicate but crucial way of living. The ideal result of such exchanges is a sense of balance, a reconciliation of selves.

Sarton's aesthetic views will be clarified and elaborated if we examine her depictions of the muse in *Mrs. Stevens Hears the Mermaids Singing*, a novel that might be considered poetic theory in the guise of fiction. The novel's protagonist, Hilary Stevens, serves as Sarton's double, mirror and mouthpiece for her creator. Like Sarton, she objects to her lack of serious critical attention, and she wishes to be considered foremost as a poet rather than a novelist. Hilary Stevens and May Sarton each lives alone in a remote New England house to which each is strongly attached. Finally, both women discuss frankly their lesbianism, particularly as it affects their art.[29] As the poet's double, Hilary reveals Sarton's poetic theory, elaborates her perception of the female muse, and paints a lyrical portrait of several female incarnations of this muse.

Three distinct inspirational sources, or three aspects of a single muse, emerge in *Mrs. Stevens*: the detached lover, the demonic Other, and the all-pervading mother. Hilary Stevens must come to terms with all three forces during her interview with Peter and Jenny. The first incarnation of the muse that she recalls is the lover, distant and remote. Surfacing initially in Hilary's re-memberings is her former governess Phillippa Munn, the impetus behind the young poet's sexual and artistic awakening, her initial "instrument of revelation." Spurned by Phillippa, who views her as child and student, the youthful Hilary turns to poetry to express her "multiplicity of sensation":

> Everything could now be *said*—this was the intoxicating discovery Hilary made. She could go the limit with her feeling; she could come to terms with it by analyzing it through the written word.[30]

From this response to Phillippa, Hilary produces her first poetry, "a series of crude, passionate love poems" whose intensity shocks the governess and frightens their creator. Recalling Phillippa, the adult Hilary recognizes the value of this adolescent epiphany:

> The sign of the Muse, she thought: impossible, haunting, she who makes the whole world reverberate. Odd that I recognized her at fifteen! And she felt some remote tenderness for that quaking, passionate being whose only outlet had been poetry—, bad poetry, at that!—But who had learned then to poise the tensions, to solve the equation through art.[31]

A much later manifestation of the lover-muse, Willa MacPherson, is another force behind Hilary's ongoing efforts to "poise the tensions, to solve the equation through art." After years of intellectual exchange, Hilary becomes emotionally involved with Willa almost by accident: she brings her a recording of the Brandenburg Concerti and learns from Willa's violent response of her former liaison with a well-known musician. Hilary's awareness of Willa's unrequited passion arouses her own, and she unleashes a torrent of new poems that she presents to Willa, who accepts them with a detachment reminiscent of the attitude that medieval troubadours and Renaissance sonneteers attributed to their ladies:

> Willa listened. She accepted the poems as the true Muse does with detached, imaginative grace; she brought to bear her critical intelligence, illuminated by something like love, the inwardness, the transparency which had been opened in spite of herself. . . . Above all, she succeeded in making Hilary accept that the poem itself was the reality, accept, at least at first, that together, for some mysterious reason, they made possible the act of creation. It was intimacy of a strange kind.[32]

Despite her detachment, Willa differs from the male poet's courtly muse in her willingness to take Hilary's art seriously, to help the poet define and refine the power of the poetic word. She is distant, that is, but not disdainful. This relationship ends painfully, yet the elderly poet acknowledges Willa as a key inspirational force. "After all, the poems existed. That strange marriage of two minds, from which they had flowed, still lived there on the page."[33]

The passion that Hilary Stevens unleashes at times toward both Phillippa and Willa suggests a second manifestation of the muse as a demonic Medusa-self, violent yet essential to the tension that produces poetry at "white heat." "Women are afraid of their demon, want to control it, make it sensible like themselves," Hilary asserts; indeed, much of her artistic struggle hinges upon the recognition that one's demons must be confronted instead of denied.[34] Hilary's most incorrigible demons are "they," those "enemy" voices that accompany old age with its attendant forgetfulness, its doubts as to one's creative capacities. "Who were *they* exactly?" Mrs. Stevens asks herself. "Old fool, *they* are your own demons, . . . the never-conquered demons with whom you carry on the struggle for survival against laziness, depression, guilt, and fatigue."[35] This effort is at times exhausting, the poet admits, but it can also be energizing, particularly when "they" become "she," a demonic lover-muse against whom the poet is pitted and through whom she is mirrored and defined.

For Hilary, this muse appears forcefully in Dorothea, a sociologist with whom she lived during middle age. Unlike Willa, who accepted poems as a goddess might receive supplicants, Dorothea and Hilary interact as equal forces; hence their exchanges are charged with a "concentrated violence." Through Dorothea, Hilary is "once more in the presence of the Muse, the crucial one, the Medusa who had made her understand that if you turn Medusa's face around, it is your own face. It is yourself who must be conquered."[36] As a source of renewed vitality, Dorothea forces Hilary to confront "the enemy," herself, with a vengeance at once "a strange sort of love."

> But whatever it was, the poems began to pour out. Hilary walking down Fifth Avenue on the way to her job, would be pursued by poems, lines running through her head, lines of dialogue. Day and night, it seemed, she was struggling like a little bull against the wall, and the wall was Dorothea. Well, she thought, I have met my match.[37]

As Hilary's "match," a powerful Other who is also a part of the self, Dorothea evokes an ambivalence that emerges finally as a "devastating, destructive rage." This hostility kills any hope of dialogue between poet and muse, as the two engage in a furious battle of wills. At last Hilary realizes that "the creative person, the person who moves from an irrational source of power, has to face the fact that this power antagonizes. Under all the superficial praise of the 'creative' is the desire to kill. It is the old war between the mystic and the nonmystic, a war to the death."[38] Mystic versus nonmystic, artist versus social scientist, Other versus self—despite their apparent differences, Hilary and Dorothea mirror each other; each sees in the other a self whom she feels driven to destroy. "I was the enemy, the anarchic, earth-shaking power," Hilary can admit years later. Broken into irrevocable halves, Hilary and Dorothea separate so that each may reconstruct herself. But Hilary learns a valuable lesson through her shadow: "It would have been better . . . to let the furies out instead of trying to contain them. I got split up, and those poems were the means of trying to knit myself together again."[40] With poets such as Louise Bogan and Muriel Rukeyser, Sarton acknowledges the importance of controlling her furies in order to keep them from controlling her. "She of the disciplined mind had had to come to terms with the anarchic Aphrodite buried so deep in herself," Hilary Stevens declares. Yet both she and Dorothea gain much from their mutual agony. "We had turned the Medusa face around and seen our *selves*. The long solitude ahead would be the richer for it."[41]

As a final act of self-discovery, Hilary Stevens confronts the muse as mother—not only the literal, biological mother but also the Great Goddess in her fierce duality: angry as well as loving, life-denying and life-affirming. The interaction of maternal muse and female poet, Mrs. Stevens claims, "is what is meant by fertilization."[42] Early in the novel Hilary acknowledges both awe and ambivalence toward her mother, whom she remembers in two ways: as a tired woman sitting at a desk, "overwhelmed by what she had failed to accomplish," and as a rare intelligence who "flourished in social situations, loved good conversation with a passion, enjoyed pitting her mind and her personality against those of her peers."[43] Yet like many children sent away to boarding school or summer camp, the young Hilary feels painfully rejected by her mother, to whom she is never totally reconciled.

Despite this resentment, it is her mother with whom Hilary holds her most crucial dialogue. In recalling her mother's death, the poet recognizes in her a compelling force that the daughter seeking artistic and personal validation must confront. "Yes, let us end this dialogue with the beginning," she says to Peter and Jenny. "I have sometimes imagined that my last book might be about my mother; it is time to die when one has come to terms with everything. My mother still remains the great devouring enigma . . . the Muse, you see."[44] If reconciliation between mother and daughter is impossible, Sarton suggests, the poet must come to terms with the maternal principle in and through her art. In this sense, therefore, the mother functions as a muse to the poet-daughter, as "she whom I desired above all things to know."

Paralleling and complementing Sarton's theory of female creativity in *Mrs. Stevens* is her poetry itself—half a century's worth, written from 1930 to the present. "We are whole or have intimations of what it means to be whole when the entire being—spirit, mind, nerves, flesh, the body itself—are concentrated toward a single end. I feel it when I am writing a poem," she claims in *Journal of a Solitude*. "Art is always integrating. . . . I have written every poem . . . to find out what I think, to know where I stand."[45] The scope and nature of the poetic process, particularly that of the woman writer, provide the theme of "My Sisters, O My Sisters," an early poem in which Sarton explores the link between female writing and female power. In the first section, the poet looks back through her literary foremothers and affirms the difficulties the woman artist faces in her movement from silence to speech:

> Dorothy Wordsworth, dying, did not want to read,
> "I am too busy with my own feelings," she said.
>
> And all women who have wanted to break out
> Of the prison of consciousness to sing or shout
>
> Are strange monsters who renounce the treasure
> Of their silence for a curious devouring pleasure.
>
> Dickinson, Rossetti, Sappho—they all know it,
> Something is lost, strained, unforgiven in the poet.

Sarton argues that women writers are a breed apart, "strange monsters" who must set aside traditional female passivity to uncover the "curious devouring pleasure" of creativity. Such "sacrifices" are often problematical, the poet admits, and she offers a catalog of "aberrant" women writers to support her argument: George Sand, who "loved too much"; Madame de Stael, "too powerful for men"; Madame de Sévigné, "too sensitive." Yet only through the self-imposed renunciation of traditional roles, she suggests, have authentic female voices emerged.

The contemporary woman writer, Sarton continues, has much to learn from her forebears' attempts to break out of the prison of silence. In order to become "more simply human," she must come

> . . . to the deep place where poet becomes woman,
>
> Where nothing has to be renounced or given over
> In the pure light that shines out from the lover,
>
> In the pure light that brings forth fruit and flower
> And that great sanity, that sun, the feminine power.

Sarton links herself to women poets from Emily Dickinson to H.D. in appropriating as a metaphor for "feminine power" the traditional symbol of masculine energy and potency, the sun. As writing women, the poet suggests, she and her peers must find that "deep place" from which to celebrate the "pure light" of creativity.

Sarton defines "that great sanity . . . the feminine power" as a revaluation of those qualities typically associated with woman: fecundity, nurture, and love. These "riches," which have heretofore sustained men and children, "these great powers / Which are ours alone," must now be used by women to fertilize one another, to stimulate their own creativity. As models of the precarious balance for which women must now strive, she offers two biblical foremothers with equally valuable but very different heritages: Eve and Mary. The reconciliation of passion and wisdom that these two women represent is important to Sarton's paradigm, since she believes that women, especially artists, must be governed by both attributes. Like H.D. in *Trilogy*, Sarton rejects misogynistic notions denouncing Eve as evil incarnate and offering as the sole model Mary, a symbol of feminine wisdom yet also of feminine purity and passivity. Instead, she re-visions and celebrates both women as active female forces:

> To be Eve, the giver of knowledge, the lover;
> To be Mary, the shield, the healer and the mother.
> The balance is eternal whatever we may wish.

The women poet's complex task, the poet concludes, is to affirm both branches of this full-bodied tree.

Yet Sarton acknowledges the difficulties inherent in such a quest. "Where re-join the source / The fertile feminine goddess, double river?" In the final section she offers female creativity, woman's solitary art, as a means to "re-join the source" and thus attain balance and clarity of vision. Taking to task herself and other women who have "asked so little of ourselves and men / And let the Furies have their way," the poet calls upon women to claim the "holy fountain" of creative imagination, transforming it into a wellspring of feminine song. Only by appropriating the "masculine and violent joy of pure creation," the poet suggests, can women "come home to the earth," giving birth to themselves as artists. "That great sanity, that sun, the feminine power" will become a reality, Sarton concludes, when women "match mens' [sic] greatness" with their own art.[46]

Other Sarton poems also describe the woman poet's efforts to "re-join the source," to assert a vital female voice. This struggle provides the underlying dialectic of "Poets and the Rain," which addresses the problem of poetic stasis and subsequent rejuvenation. In the first stanza the poet-persona is debilitated by the rain, which reflects her own inertia and despair; she speaks not as an active creator but as a passive receptacle for the words of others. "I will lie here alone and live your griefs," she declares. "I will receive you, passive and devout." Yet as she offers such disclaimers, the poet's creativity stirs, faint but intelligible. Plagued by "strange tides" in her head, she distinguishes three voices, each of which offers a different vision of life and art.

The first singer, an old man, "looks out and taunts the world, sick of mankind," his voice "shriller than all the rest." In an interesting reversal of a stereotype, Sarton associates shrillness not with a hysterical female voice but with a male cry of pessimism and derision. Although part of her sympathizes with this doomsday prophet, she ultimately rejects the model that he offers. She will "dream a hunting song to make the old hawk scream," but she will not adopt such a voice herself. Contrasted to this male voice are two female speakers whose visions, when combined, posit for the poet a more balanced and optimistic stance. The first woman represents the traditional female voice, that of nurturer, comforter, inspirer:

> Here is the woman, frustrate and most pure,
> Who builds a nest of blessings and there sits
> Singing the lighted tree and the dark stone
> (Many times to this woman I have come),
> Who bids us meditate and use our wits
> And we shall, with the help of love, endure—

Comforted by the love that this woman's song exudes, the poet herself is inspired to become a voice of feminine wisdom and maternal love. This choice, however, is not enough for the creative woman: the singer is "frustrate"; her purity and nest building are passive postures. Despite her connection to traditional female arts, or perhaps because of it, this woman's song is too simple and static a model for the poet.

The speaker is most moved by the "blurred" yet potent voice of a "great girl, the violent and strong,"

> Who walks accompanied by dreams and visions,
> Speaks with the blurred voice of a giant sleeping
> And wakes to hear the foreign children weeping
> And sees the crystal crack, the fierce divisions,
> Asking deep questions in her difficult song.[47]

This description recalls Denise Levertov's celebration in "In Mind" of a "turbulent moon-ridden girl . . . who knows strange songs," or Louise Bogan's "The

Dream," in which a "strong creature . . . another woman" leaps and shouts until her passive counterpart is prodded into life-saving speech and action.[48] In Sarton's poem, the great girl's "deep questions" and "difficult song," her fierce commitment to her art and her beliefs, offer the questing poet her most inspirational model. Although she realizes the difficulties of such a vision, the persona determines that her voice, like the girl's, must emerge from an emotional and intellectual complex, a "labyrinth of mind":

> A sudden sweep of raindrops from the cloud,
> I stand, rapt with delight, though deaf and blind,
>
> And speak my poem now, leaves of a tree
> Whose roots are hidden deep in mystery.[49]

In rejecting stasis for dynamic song, the poet celebrates the complexity of her own imagination, its ability both to merge with nature and to transform it. Significantly, however, the speaker's celebration is not without its price, nor is her choice without ambivalence, for she is rendered deaf and blind in the wake of her song. She is able to sing, but she must acknowledge her impediments even as she asserts her newly found voice.

The special danger inherent in the woman poet's effort to "speak aloud," to re-vision as her own the "masculine and violent joy of pure creation," is also the subject of "Journey toward Poetry." The poet's structuring of her imaginative experience, Sarton suggests, is analogous to a dangerous journey across foreign yet somehow familiar terrain, a haunting interior picaresque that produces ultimately for the chary traveler the ideal word or image or perspective. For Sarton, such a psychic voyage usually begins in chaos, concentrated violence:

> First that beautiful mad exploration
> Through a multiple legend of landscape
> When all roads open and then close again
> Behind a car that rushes toward escape,
> The mind shot out across foreign borders
> To visionary and abrupt disorders.

An array of intensely surrealistic images accompanies such "mad exploration": hills winding and unwinding on a spool; rivers running away from their beds; a geranium bursting open to reveal a "huge blood-red cathedral"; "marble graveyards" falling into the sea. One is reminded of Yeats' "blood-dimmed tide": "the center cannot hold," Sarton implies, when the imagination runs unchecked.

Yet the center does hold. Once the poet's errant imagination is stayed, her inner landscapes soften, become pastoral. From disorder, to paraphrase Wallace Stevens, emerges a violent order:

> After the mad beautiful racing is done,
> To be still, to be silent, to stand by a window
> Where time not motion changes light to shadow,
> Is to be present at the birth of creation.[50]

Reconstructing her universe from a position of silence and stasis, the poet transforms mundane objects—"the field of wheat, the telephone pole"—into something altogether new. In Hilary Stevens' words, "intensity commands form."[51] "Journey toward Poetry" serves as Sarton's metaphoric depiction of the poetic process, fraught with danger for any poet but intensely so for the woman. Beginning in rage or anxiety, at "white heat," the poet's "beautiful mad racing" ultimately gives way to that fruitful ripening of image and idea that informs "the birth of creation."

Central to the creative process for Sarton is the female muse, perceived by the poet as "always a question . . . what sets up the dialogue" with oneself.[52] As the pivotal force upon which poetry centers, the muse, like the protean poet, wears multiple masks. Sarton is especially vocal about the inspirational power of the muse as lover: "You learn a lot from the person you love. I'm talking about women mostly. That's the whole thing for me. Women have been the muse, and it's the more aggressive side of me which falls in love with women. I feel more able to write and more myself than I do at any other time." During relationships with men, Sarton continues, she felt drained of creative energy. "With a woman, on the contrary, I felt very excited, wrote poems, you see. And that is the only way I can judge."[53]

In her poetry this erotic manifestation of the muse appears sometimes as a human lover-visitant, sometimes as a goddess or mythological woman. One recurring figure is Aphrodite, the Greek goddess of love and sexuality, who also is linked to ancient Eastern mother-goddesses, such as Ishtar, Isis, and Astarte.[54] Because the goddess's powers are both matriarchal and sexual, Sarton often envisions Aphrodite as a primordial figure of fecundity. Such a goddess is found in "These Images Remain," an early sonnet sequence in which the poet confronts the sexual tension at the heart of the poet-muse relationship. As the epitome of female beauty and eroticism, Aphrodite inspires the poet to become free and fertile:

> And you are here at last, and you are free
> To stand like Aphrodite on her shell,
> Wrapped in the wind, the net of nerves undone,
> So piercingly alive and beautiful,
> Her breasts are eyes. She opens in the sun
> And sees herself reflected in the sand
> When the great wave has left her naked there,
> And looks at her own feet and her own hand
> As on strange flowers and on her golden hair
> As on some treasure given by the seas
> To one who holds the earth between her knees.

Yet this "silent consummation" between poet and muse is as precarious as quicksand, Sarton suggests in the fifth sonnet; any union with Aphrodite must be transitory, fleeting. She images herself as a male sculptor whose creation grows "out of deprivation . . . / out of a self-denying rage," inspired by intense longing and frustration. "He gladly yields for the sake of those lips," Sarton says of the sculptor-poet, "That savage throat that opens the whole chest, / Tension so great between him and the stone, / It seems he carries vengeance in his wrist." The poet can never possess the muse, Sarton realizes, but the effort to possess results in the sculptor's images, "great and severe." From the encounter between poet and muse, from "difficult love," comes a lasting art.[55]

Though the poet is periodically estranged from her muse, such separation is rarely long-lived. "The Muse is never wholly absent," Hilary Stevens explains to Peter and Jenny, discussing her own rejuvenation after writer's block. "One must at least glimpse the hem of her garment, as she vanishes into her radiant air."[56] In "The Return of Aphrodite," Sarton describes a reencounter with the muse:

> From deep she rises, poised upon her shell.
> Oh guiltless Aphrodite so long absent!
> The green waves part. There is no sound at all
> As she advances, tranquil and transparent,
> To lay on mortal flesh her sacred mantle.
>
> The wave recedes—she is drawn back again
> Into the ocean where light leaves a stain.[57]

Transparency is central to Sarton's muse as an extension of the self, the Medusa through whom one can gaze upon oneself. Unlike the poet's confrontation with Medusa, however, her exchange with Aphrodite is depicted in images of silence and tranquility, pure light rather than white heat. Sarton's imagery is also richly erotic: as the mortal poet receives the goddess's "sacred mantle," the "green waves part," receding at once after the sacred consummation and leaving in their wake a faint "stain" of light.

The erotic muse appears as devouring in "A Divorce of Lovers," a sonnet sequence on the poet's efforts to restore her lapsed poetic powers after a devastating love affair. In *World of Light* Sarton explains that these poems were written "in batches" during an extremely high fever; and her subsequent discussion of the muse as "a woman who focuses the world for me," whether in a pleasant or a painful way, suggests a connection between the lover in the poems and the muse. The lovers here are imaged as "two warring halves . . . cut in two," wounded perhaps beyond repair. In an effort to heal her wounds, the poet invokes the "surgeon," Reason, doubting all the while that this "doctor" has the power to rejuvenate her poetic energies: "We shall see / How Reason operates on Poetry." As the surgeon wields the scalpel, images of destruction dominate: "Old Fate" snapping the threads of life and love; a flower dying, cut at full bloom. As her wounds heal, however, the poet numbs to pain and feels instead the disorientation of a "blundering bird," a "baffled wanderer" on a "lost journey . . . out of this wilderness."

Eventually, the poet realizes that the loss of the lover can be endured; it is the loss of creativity that must be challenged. To "force Fate at a crucial pass," she invokes solitude as a healing balm: "Where these words end, let solitude begin."[58] Like Louise Bogan, Sarton recognizes that harsh words and cacophonous music must give way to an interim silence before the creative voice can be restored to its full resonance.[59] In Sonnet 17 she celebrates silence as a companion:

> As thoughts like clouds traverse my human eyes,
> Silence opens the world that I explore:
> Mozartian gaiety, the lightest presence,
> At last I welcome back my wandering soul
> Into these regions of strange transcendence,
> And find myself again, alive and whole.[60]

The reintegration of the self and the restoration of the poet's creative power are made possible, Sarton suggests, by a "turning back upon the self," which illuminates and indeed transforms both self and world.

Sarton's image of the muse as the beloved is especially prominent in the title sequence of *Letters from Maine*, a recent volume of poetry. The poet's "November Muse" is not the fierce, angry lover of her youth; rather, she gives "wisdom and laughter, also clarity." Even when the muse is absent, the speaker declares in the third poem, "I am floated on her presence, / Her strong reality, swung out above / Everything else that happens." But the erotic muse in these poems is also spiritual, an "Old Woman" who, according to a legend of the Nootka Indian tribe, is a "Primal Spirit, one with rock and wave":

> Old Woman I meet you deep inside myself.
> There in the rootbed of fertility,
> World without end, as the legend tells it,
> Under the words you are my silence.

The impact of this inspirational source becomes poignantly clear when the muse rejects the poet. Without inspiration, Sarton explains, "nothing can be said." Ultimately, however, the creative impulse perseveres, as the poet transforms painful experience into a lyrical and analytical assessment of the erotic muse's function:

> When the muse appears after long absence
> Everything stops except the poem. It rises
> In an unbroken wave and topples to silence.
> There is no way to make it happen by will.
> No muse appears when invoked, dire need
> Will not raise her pity.
>   She comes when she can,
> She too, no doubt, rising from the sea
> Like Aphrodite on her shell when it is time,
> When the impersonal tide bears her to the shore
> To play a difficult role she has not chosen,
> To free a prisoner she has no reason to love.
>
> What power is at work, then, what key
> Opens the door into these mysteries?[61]

The muse for Sarton also appears as a demonic force, a fury with whom the poet must come to terms in order to maintain creative energy. "Every visitation of the Muse is disturbing," Hilary Stevens declares, unsettling because it evokes such a conflicting array of responses: love and joy, guilt and rage. This ambivalence toward one's inspirational source is not new; women poets from Emily Dickinson to Emily Brontë to Louise Bogan have viewed their muse as a hostile force, sometimes male, sometimes female, frequently demonic. The poet, of course, is pitted against this muse in a fierce struggle for power. Sarton's demonic muse resembles Brontë's and Dickinson's in the tension it evokes, but like Bogan and other modern women poets, Sarton envisions her muse as a female shadow rather than a male Other. Rebellious but potent, this muse stimulates the poet's creative energy but also arouses feelings of anger, shame, and ambivalence. "The deep collision is and has been with my unregenerate, tormenting, and tormented self," Hilary Stevens admits. "Women are afraid of their daemon," she continues, "want to . . . make it sensible like themselves."[62] Sarton realizes, however, that one's demons cannot and should not be "made sensible." Instead, they should be acknowledged and re-visioned as a source of vital energy, creative rage.

The muse as a fury out for vengeance and retribution appears frequently in poems on the demise of a relationship and the subsequent loss of creative energy. In the fourth sonnet of "A Divorce of Lovers," for example, Sarton accuses her lover of "chasing out the furies and the plagues of passion" rather than attempting to come to terms with them:

> My guess is that the weapon's name was Pride.
> It is a word the Furies understand;
> Their ghosts are gathering on every side,
> And they will raise the hair upon your hand.[63]

In awe of the monsters who plague her, the poet nonetheless needs such "ghosts" if they can be re-visioned. When angels and furies "fly so near," she explains, "they come to force Fate at a crucial pass."[64] This forcing of Fate, in turn, opens up a crucial dialogue with the self, which ultimately transforms the poet's violence into creative energy. "Have done, poor beast," Sarton exhorts her fury. "I have come back into my world of no one . . . / And I am nourished here after the famine."[65]

In "The Furies" the poet explores the difficulties in reconciling herself to her demonic aspects. Here Sarton proffers a central psychological and aesthetic question: "How then to recognize / The hard unseeing eyes, / Or woman tell from ghost?" The woman poet's furies are "almost" human, Sarton explains—"almost, and yet not quite." The danger inherent in one's furies lies in their capacity to strip the poet of her energy and wits, to "wrap you in glamor cold, / Warm you with fairy gold, / Till you grow fond and lazy, / Witty, perverse, and crazy." Only after coming to terms with the risks one takes as a creator, Sarton concludes, "can one drink [the Furies'] health . . . / And call the Furies kind."[66]

In this poem Sarton looks ironically at the problems she faces in confronting her demons. Yet despite her effort to distance through irony, her fear of the Furies is great. "Never look straight at one," she warns the reader, "for then your self is gone." At other times, however, she asserts the creative woman's need to confront these furious forces, admitting their power and thus claiming it as her own. Such is the theme of "A Storm of Angels":

> Anarchic anger came to beat us down,
> Until from all that battering we went numb
> Like ravaged trees after a hurricane.
> But in its wake we saw fierce angels come—
> Not gentle and not kind—who threshed the grain
> With their harsh wings, winnowed from waste.

Despite their harshness, these angels are rejuvenating rather than debilitating, for they come "as messengers of a true power denied." The angels "beat down" the poet, strip her of her pride, bring her agony, yet this energizing agony sets the poet free. It is a gift from the furies to their selected instrument: "Theirs is an act of grace, and it is given / To those in Hell who can imagine Heaven."[67]

Often Sarton replaces angels and furies with animals, demonic forces that must be re-visioned. In "Control," for example, the poet argues against any attempt to deny the tiger within. In restraining such a beast, Sarton explains, one exercises a heady power at great expense, for destroying the tiger's vitality also negates an essential part of the self:

> You may have complete control.
> There will be no roar or growl.
> But can you look into those eyes
> Where the smothered fire lies?[68]

If the tiger's "fire" is "smothered," Sarton concludes, the poet risks cooling the white heat that generates good poetry.

Yet Sarton is not always comfortable with the demonic part of the self. In "After the Tiger," her ambivalence toward the monster within surfaces, as she alternately affirms and laments this psychic conflict. When "the tiger, violence, takes the human throat," the speaker first rejoices, "glad of the blood, glad of the lust," because "that tiger strength—oh it is beautiful!" Much of the tiger's demonic beauty lies in its purity of form, its awesome presence. "It is all success," she says of the tiger's strength. "It feels like a glorious creation." In subsequent stanzas, however, Sarton's ambivalence toward the tiger's brute strength surfaces, as she wonders what should be done with this passionate animal. After all, such wild release—however euphoric—is ultimately unsettling. "Who was a tiger once" becomes then "weak and small, / And terribly unfit for all he has to do." The poet wonders "who is a friend here, who an enemy," for the wounds which the "ghostly tiger" inflicts "sometimes do not heal for centuries." Peace after violence is possible, Sarton posits tentatively, but only if the "peace maker" has the patience and courage to reconstruct bit by bit what the raging tiger has torn down:

> After the tiger we become frail and human
> The dust of ruins acrid in the throat.
> Oh brothers, take it as an absolution
> That we must work so slowly toward hope![69]

This poem makes an interesting companion to Bogan's "The Sleeping Fury," in which the "tiger" is a shrieking maenad who wreaks terror through the night. In both poems this fury, an aspect of the self, must "sleep off madness" after unleashed violence. Both furies are perceived as benevolent-malevolent forces: Sarton's tiger is "enemy" and "friend"; Bogan's fury is "my scourge, my sister." But while Bogan finds strength and sustenance through her encounter with the fury, Sarton remains shaken: "After the violence peace does not rise / Like a forgiving sun to wash all clean." For Sarton, who claims to write from her aggressive, masculine side, the violent forces that clash in "After the Tiger" are depicted here as male: the tiger is a "god"; the poet in whom the tiger resides, "he"; the audience whom the poet addresses, "brothers." Bogan's "scourge," in contrast, is at once a "sister," a crucial same-sex figure more comprehensible to the woman poet. Sarton here is overwhelmed by the masculine fury. She is "frail and human," ambivalent toward the tiger's powers and unconvinced of her own. Bogan, on the other hand, concludes on a more confident note, having transformed her fury's destructive rage into creative energy: "Alone and strong in my peace, I look upon you in yours."[70]

When Sarton perceives her demonic counterpart as a female shadow rather than a male Other, however, she often experiences a creative impetus similar to that which Bogan wrests from her sleeping fury. In "The Godhead as Lynx," for instance, the poet gleans nourishment from the beautiful yet cold mother-lynx:

> Kyrie Eleison, O wild lynx!
> Mysterious sad eyes, and yet so bright,
> Wherein mind never grieves or thinks,
> But absolute attention is alight—
> Before that golden gaze, so deep and cold,
> My human rage dissolves, my pride is broken.

Sarton often uses face-to-face confrontation to dramatize the dialogue between poet and demonic muse; here the speaker, though but a "child," nonetheless challenges the lynx by meeting her "obsidian" eyes. Rather than fearing confrontation and dreading its aftermath, the speaker undertakes it on her own terms.

She goes on to envision the lynx as a "prehuman" maternal goddess into whose womb the poet-daughter is tempted to crawl:

> I feel a longing for the lynx's bed,
> To submerge self in that essential fur,
> And sleep close to this ancient world of grace,
> As if there could be healing next to her,
> The mother-lynx in her prehuman place.
> Yet that pure beauty does not know compassion—
> O cruel god, Kyrie Eleison!

Like ancient goddesses, the lynx is linked to both creation and destruction. Despite her "essential fur," her maternal comfort, she "does not know compassion"; and she is "cruel . . . / lightning to cut down the lamb, / A beauty that devours without qualm." Beneficent and demonic, therefore, the lynx offers the poet both a model and a means of self-possession and self-affirmation. As "a cruel god who only says 'I am,'" the lynx represents unharnessed male power in female flesh; thus her splendor and unusual force awaken the poet's own strength. Through her encounter with the godhead as lynx, the poet becomes a "laboring self who groans and thinks."[71]

The demonic muse whom Sarton most often invokes is Medusa, the mythological monster whose hair writhed with serpents, whose glance turned men to stone. Because she could be viewed only indirectly and because of the mystery and danger associated with her powers, she suggests the woman poet's struggle *with* herself *for* herself. In "The Muse as Medusa" Sarton describes an encounter with this "fury" and her effort to re-vision the potent and dynamic relationship between poet and muse. In contrast to the speaker's ironic advice in "The Furies"—"never look straight at one, / For then your self is gone"—Sarton here meets Medusa as she has met the lynx: one-on-one, "straight in the cold eye, cold." Despite her "nakedness" and vulnerability, the poet transforms the legendary monster from a debilitating force to a source of creative rejuvenation.

> I came as naked as any little fish,
> Prepared to be hooked, gutted, caught;
> But I saw you, Medusa, made my wish,
> And when I left you I was clothed in thought . . .

Medusa's stony gaze does not destroy; it transfigures, "clothing" the naked speaker in the warm protective garment of perception. "Forget the image," Sarton exults, for this Medusa renews through her silent but vital presence: "Your silence is my ocean, / And even now it teems with life."

Yet Medusa herself is not responsible for this teeming life; it continues in spite of rather than because of her presence. Medusa, after all, "chose / To abdicate by total lack of motion," and abdicating is something the speaker refuses to do. Instead, Sarton creates a dynamic, fluid seascape of which this fury can become a part, her destructive rage used rather than denied. In re-visioning Medusa "in her own image," the poet acknowledges a vital female creativity and affirms the demonic part of herself: "I turn your face around! It is my face."[72] This final statement echoes Hilary Stevens' response to Dorothea: "she was once more in the presence of the Muse, the crucial one, the Medusa who had made her understand that if you turn Medusa's face around, it is your own face."[73] Sarton is eager to examine the causes of her pain, to heal herself, to speak out. In revising Medusa as a source of creative energy, she paradoxically affirms and challenges another of Hilary Stevens' assertions: "we are all monsters, if it comes to that, we women who have chosen to be something more and something less than women."[74]

The third aspect of the muse that Sarton explores in both *Mrs. Stevens* and her poetry is the mother as inspirational source. At times the mother appears as a potent demonic figure, as in "The Godhead as Lynx." In several poems, however, Sarton celebrates female fecundity and maternity without demonic trappings, invoking as muse a beneficent mother figure who inspires the woman poet through her greater wisdom. In an early poem, "She Shall Be Called Woman," for example, the poet celebrates one of her most maligned yet potent foremothers, the biblical Eve, as a symbol of maternal fecundity and sexual and spiritual rejuvenation. Stripped of the demonic associations accorded her by patriarchal culture and religion, Sarton's Eve is re-visioned as an Ur-Mother, created initially by God but re-created by herself, out of her own energy and will. Sarton's chronicle omits the Genesis II creation scene and instead describes Eve's first faint murmurs of self-identity, ironically coincidental with her initial sexual encounter. Although "she did not cry out / nor move. / She lay quite still," Eve, like Lilith before her, is nonetheless frightened and angered:

> She could not yet endure
> this delicate savage
> to lie upon her.
> She could not yet endure
> the blood to beat so there.
> She could not cope
> with the first ache
> of fullness.

In a radical re-vision of the Genesis myth, Sarton has Eve, "disrupted at the center / and torn," leave Eden and seek refuge in the maternal womb of the sea: "And she went into the sea / because her core ached / and there was no healing."

As with the muse as Medusa, however, so with Eve: "not in denial, her peace." Through her solitary journey into feminine consciousness, Eve learns not to deny her sexuality and creativity but to claim them as sources of power. She begins to derive pleasure and confidence from her physical self:

She was aware
down to extremity
of how herself was charged,
fiber electric,
a hand under her breast
could hear the dynamo.
. . . .
Nothing ever was
as wonderful as this.

In exploring her own body, Eve "clothes herself" with a female garment of sexuality, fecundity, and power. "She would not ever be naked / again," the poet insists. As "the core of life," Eve casts off the vulnerability and powerlessness that Genesis II portrays as woman's lot. Instead, she gives birth "out of the infinite" to an autonomous entity: " 'I am the beginning, / the never-ending, / the perfect tree.' " To depict Eve's birthing of the female self Sarton uses menstruation as a metaphor:

There were seeds
within her
that burst at intervals
and for a little while
she would come back
to heaviness,
and then before a surging miracle
of blood,
relax,
and reidentify herself,
each time more closely
with the heart of life.[75]

As Eve the foremother reidentifies herself through her menstrual cycle, she connects "more closely / with the heart of life." So, Sarton implies, must Eve's daughter, the woman poet, rejuvenate herself through her resurgent creativity.

The woman poet's need to become a mother to herself and her art can be seen in a poem about Sarton's own mother, Mabel Elwes Sarton. "An Observation" was by the poet's own admission very difficult to write. But a persistent image of her mother, at work in her garden with "a rough sensitivity," finally metamorphosed into a poetic tribute:

True gardeners cannot bear a glove
Between the sure touch and the tender root,
Must let their hands grow knotted as they move
With a rough sensitivity about
Under the earth, between the rock and shoot,
Never to bruise or wound the hidden fruit.
And so I watched my mother's hands grow scarred,
She who could heal the wounded plant or friend
With the same vulnerable yet rigorous love;
I minded once to see her beauty gnarled,

But now her truth is given me to live,
As I learn for myself we must be hard
To move among the tender with an open hand,
And to stay sensitive up to the end
Pay with some toughness for a gentle world.[76]

As inheritor of her mother's healing powers, Sarton received a crucial "truth": vulnerability must be accompanied by rigor, tenderness by toughness, else the plant, the delicate and valuable creation, is unlikely to grow. "You must remain vulnerable and tough," Sarton explained during a reading of this poem, "or else you'll die of it."[77] Vulnerability, growth, balance—the heritage that the mother-muse bequeaths the daughter-poet.

In one of her most provocative poems about female inspiration, "The Invocation to Kali," Sarton depicts the muse as both demon and mother, confronting what Hilary Stevens calls "the full motherhood, the full monsterhood" of those who try to be "something more and something less than woman."[78] By celebrating Kali as muse, Sarton affirms the close link that she perceives among demonic rage, maternal love, and female creativity. The poem opens with an epigraph from Joseph Campbell's *The Masks of God*, a description of "*the Black Goddess Kali, the terrible one of many names, 'difficult of approach,' whose stomach is a void and so can never be filled, and whose womb is giving birth forever to all things*." As this passage suggests, many of Kali's traits parallel those that numerous cultures have assigned to "evil" goddesses. She is elusive, loath to be controlled by man; she is devouring and insatiable; and she is constantly and oppressively fertile, fecund despite man's efforts to contain her. Like many matriarchal goddesses, therefore, Kali stands for both creation and destruction, life and death, but is usually associated only with the negative pole of this duality. As an aspect of the woman's creative self, Kali is thus both inspiring and threatening. Her dual powers intrigue the poet, yet an identification with Kali evokes shame, anger, and fear—that peculiar blend of self-love and self-loathing of one both trapped and freed by her art.

In section one Sarton sets forth this poem's central issue—how best to cope with Kali's demands:

There are times when
I think only of killing
The voracious animal
Who is my perpetual shame,

The violent one
Whose raging demands
Break down peace and shelter
Like a peacock's scream.

There are times when
I think only of how to do away
With this brute power
That cannot be tamed.

I am the cage where poetry
Paces and roars. The beast
Is the god. How murder the god?
How live with the terrible god?

Aware of the capacity for creation that accompanies Kali's power, the poet is nonetheless ambivalent toward this demonic force, for she recognizes also its potential for debilitation and entrapment. What then to do with Kali? the poet wonders. Is she to be murdered or lived with?

Section two suggests the futility of any effort to murder the goddess:

The kingdom of Kali is within us deep.
The built-in destroyer, the savage goddess,
Wakes in the dark and takes away our sleep.
She moves through the blood to poison gentleness.

. . . .

How then to set her free or come to terms
With the volcano itself, the fierce power
Erupting injuries, shrieking alarms?
Kali among her skulls must have her hour.[79]

Sarton's imagery of volcanic eruption recalls a comment by H.D. about her art: "A sort of *rigor mortis* drove me onward. No, my poetry was not dead but it was built on or around the crater of an extinct volcano. Not *rigor mortis*. No, No! The vines grow more abundantly on those volcanic slopes."[80] Although Sarton's "volcanic slopes" are far from extinct, she shares H.D.'s certainty that the explosive potential of poetry gives it its vital, living force. If Kali is denied, Sarton suggests, she will continue her bloody reign, and the result will be what H.D. so passionately fears: "*rigor mortis*." But if Kali is faced "open-eyed," her explosive powers will be revealed for what they are: forces necessary if creativity is to flourish. For every act of creation, Sarton insists, is preceded by some kind of destruction,

Every creation is born out of the dark.
Every birth is bloody. Something gets torn.
Kali is there to do her sovereign work
Or else the living child will be stillborn.

In the next sections of "The Invocation to Kali" Sarton expands the image of Kali as a metaphor for the societal violence of the twentieth century. "The Concentration Camps" is packed with gruesome images depicting the horrifying results of humanity's efforts to deny its furies, to pretend that violence does not exist. "Have we managed to fade them out like God?" she asks of the most tragic of Hitler's victims, children. In "having turned away" from the "stench of bones," she continues, we have "tried to smother" fires that desperately need to burn, as vital reminders of what happens when violence is repressed and then unleashed. "What we have pushed aside and tried to bury, / Lives with a staggering thrust we cannot parry," the poet asserts. All of us are guilty, Sarton's indictment implies; refusing to meet our demons is both a cultural and an individual sickness.

In Sarton's view, the only solution to this widespread ailment is "to reckon with Kali for better or worse," to accept her violence as an essential purging force. Thus the poet turns finally to the goddess's sacred altar, offering an invocation to this "terrible one":

> Kali, be with us.
> Violence, destruction, receive our homage.
> Help us to bring darkness into the light,
> To lift out the pain, the anger,
> Where it can be seen for what it is—
> The balance-wheel for our vulnerable, aching love.
> Put the wild hunger where it belongs,
> Within the act of creation,
> Crude power that forges a balance
> Between hate and love.
>
> Help us to be the always hopeful
> Gardeners of the spirit
> Who know that without darkness
> Nothing comes to birth
> As without light
> Nothing flowers.
>
> Bear the roots in mind,
> You, the dark one, Kali,
> Awesome power.[81]

In "The Invocation to Kali," Sarton explores the power of the demonic maternal muse, the woman poet's "great devouring enigma" and the destructive/creative force through whom she must "forge a balance / Between hate and love." As Adrienne Rich has noted, motherhood is a highly charged metaphor for the woman writer, "the great mesh in which all human relations are entangled, in which lurk our most elemental assumptions about love and power."[82] The woman writer, both Sarton and Rich would argue, inevitably associates her poetic creativity with the female capacity for giving bloody birth. As we have seen, images of maternal power inform many of Sarton's tributes to the muse: the erotic Aphrodite "holds the earth between her knees," taking it in as her lover and bearing it as her child; the cold Medusa "clothes" her poet-daughter in the comforting wrap of thought; even the demonic Kali fosters creation, however violent, "out of the dark." For Sarton, the sexual, demonic, and maternal aspects of the muse are joint attributes of a single violent yet essential force.

The final poem of *Halfway to Silence*, "Of the Muse," offers a powerful and moving assessment of Sarton's creative philosophy as it has developed over fifty years.

There is no poetry in lies
But in crude honesty
There is hope for poetry.
For a long time now
I have been deprived of it
Because of pride,
Would not allow myself
The impossible.
Today I have learned
That to become
A great, cracked,
Wide-open door
Into nowhere
Is wisdom.

When I was young,
I misunderstood
The Muse.
Now I am older and wiser,
I can be glad of her
As one is glad of the light.
We do not thank the light,
But rejoice in what we see
Because of it.
What I see today
Is the snow falling:
All things are made new.[83]

The transformative power of poetry, Sarton continues to claim, emerges from an intense encounter between the woman poet and her female muse, the symbolic source of poetic inspiration and sustenance.

Furthermore, this poem reveals Sarton's emphasis on the link between poetry and honesty, a concern of many contemporary feminist theorists and women poets. "We have been rewarded for lying," Adrienne Rich declares, yet "the unconscious wants truth, as the body does. The complexity and fecundity of dreams come from the complexity and fecundity of the unconscious struggling to fulfill that desire. The complexity and fecundity of poetry comes from the same struggle."[84] Rich's statement might well be Sarton's, so accurately does it describe the theory implicit in "Of the Muse." Struggling to fulfill its desire for truth, the woman poet's "fecund and complex" unconscious, Sarton suggests along with Rich, is awakened to vital insights and potent speech through her dialogue with that muse who is at once the self. Once misunderstood, the muse is now recognized by the aging poet as a force analogous to light. "We do not thank the light," Sarton explains, "but rejoice in what we see / Because of it." What we see is the "crude" but honest power of poetry, its transformative potential. Through the female muse, "all things are made new."[85]

5

"Nothing but Myself? . . . My Selves": The Communal Muse of Adrienne Rich

"I have to ask myself whether it is because I am a woman that the idea of the Muse seems so uninteresting to me," Adrienne Rich asserts in "Poetry, Personality and Wholeness," a 1972 essay exploring the relationship between poet and poem. Quoting Gary Snyder's definition of the muse as "anything other that touches you and moves you. . . . Man in his sexual nature has found the clearest mirror to be his human lover," she discusses the problems the muse poses for the woman poet:

> For woman in her sexual nature the Muse cannot be the human lover (as man) because it is man and man's world which makes it especially difficult for her as artist. Man may at various times exist for her as teacher, idol, guru, master, all dominating roles; he may also exist as a friend with whom she struggles in all the warmth and friction of her affections; but he is definitely not the Muse (unless indeed, the anti-Muse, the demon lover, like Sylvia Plath's "Daddy"). . . . Possibly the idea of the Muse is man's way of projecting and objectifying his own feminine principle—along with his negative feelings about that principle.[1]

Rich deplores the age-old objectification of woman as muse to the male poet, and she resents the implication that the woman poet should seek creative power and sustenance from a "superior" male force. Yet she reflects at length on the various sources of creative energy that underlie the woman poet's struggle to name herself as poet rather than muse, as potent female creator—sources fundamentally female in their origins and nature. Emily Dickinson's muse is her own soul, Rich argues; Edna St. Vincent Millay's is her feminine consciousness brought to bear on an intense and profoundly female experience; Emily Brontë is inspired by nature—"*her* nature." In disavowing "the idea of the Muse," therefore, Rich rejects the word *muse* with all its patriarchal trappings and hierarchical implications, but she gives credence to the notion of poetic inspiration or inner vision. Indeed, she affirms the woman poet's reliance on a powerful female source of imaginative energy.

The importance that Rich attributes to women's "interior power" can be seen in her analysis of Emily Dickinson's relationship to her art. Citing "He fumbles at your Soul" and "He put the Belt around my life," Rich suggests that these and other poems "about possession" represent not Dickinson's search for a male muse but her effort to establish an autonomous female poetic identity:

> These two poems . . . seem to me a poet's poems—that is, they are about the poet's relationship to her own power, which is exteriorized in masculine form, much as masculine poets have invoked the female Muse. In writing at all—particularly an unorthodox and original poetry like Dickinson's—women have often felt in danger of losing their status as women. And this status has always been defined in terms of relationship to men—as daughter, sister, bride, wife, mother, mistress, Muse. Since the most powerful figures in patriarchal culture have been men, it seems natural that Dickinson would assign a masculine gender to that in herself which did not fit in with the conventional ideology of womanliness.[2]

Rich further suggests that to "recognize and acknowledge our own interior power," women poets typically have had to take enormous risks.[3] "The archetype of the daemon as masculine is beginning to change," Rich concludes, "but it has been real for women up until now."[4]

"To recognize and acknowledge our own interior power" has been a central tenet of Adrienne Rich's poetry and poetics during her thirty-five-year career, and she has thus been instrumental in challenging "the archetype of the daemon as masculine." Like Dickinson, Rich in her early work sometimes personifies the muse as a male force. Beginning with *Snapshots of a Daughter-in-Law* (1963), however, she consciously refuses to distance her female self from her art; and by *The Will to Change* (1971), Rich's poems reveal a woman writing by, for, and about women. Since the early 1970s, her lesbian-feminist consciousness has profoundly affected both her politics and her poetics. In *Diving into the Wreck* (1973), *The Dream of a Common Language* (1978), and *A Wild Patience Has Taken Me This Far* (1981), Rich's informing poetic principle has been that "*primary presence of women to ourselves and each other* . . . which is the crucible of a new language."[5]

The phrase "*primary presence of women to ourselves and each other*," which Rich attributes to the feminist theologian Mary Daly, sheds light on the woman poet's relationship to her imagination. Robert Graves has said that women "must be their own Muse"; and this in one way is what Rich asserts—of Dickinson, Brontë, Millay, and, ultimately, herself. "It is finally the woman's sense of *herself*—embattled, possessed—that gives the poetry its dynamic charge, its rhythms of struggle, need, will, and female energy."[6] Yet Rich realizes that a woman's relationship to her creativity demands more than simply turning within for inspiration and nourishment; however necessary such a path might be, it alone is not enough. In addition to drawing upon her own soul, *her* nature, Rich insists that the woman poet also invoke the "ordinary woman"—not as

Other, but as friend, lover, mother, daughter, nurturer, and inspirer. In her words, "we desire a poetry in which the 'I' has become all of us, not simply a specific suffering personality and not an abstraction which is also an evasion of the poet's own specificities."[7]

This invocation of a collective self is strikingly evident in a recent Rich poem, "Integrity." "A wild patience has taken me this far," the speaker declares as the poem opens, and she goes on to elaborate the nature and purpose of her poetic quest. The effort of her lifetime, the poet suggests, has been to guide to shore a timeworn boat "with a spasmodic outboard motor," constantly aware of an intense and dangerous sun, "blotted like unspoken anger / behind a casual mist." "The length of daylight / this far north . . . / is critical," the poet asserts; light is a guiding instrument, a vital aspect of her journey. Yet however "critical" the light might be, she continues, its transformative power is secondary to that of the helmswoman herself:

> But really I have nothing but myself
> to go by; nothing
> stands in the realm of pure necessity
> except what my hands can hold.
>
> *Nothing but myself? . . . My selves.*
> After so long, this answer.
> As if I had always known
> I steer the boat in, simply.
> The motor dying on the pebbles
> cicadas taking up the hum
> dropped in the silence.[8]

Rich defines "my selves" as "anger and tenderness: the spider's genius / to spin and weave in the same action / from her own body, anywhere— / even from a broken web."[9] But "my selves" refers also to other women: friends, lovers, muses. By spinning and weaving "in the same action / from her own body," Rich suggests, the creative woman first affirms her own power. Then, sufficient unto herself, she can draw upon the inspiration of other women and thereby create a vital, woman-centered art.

In mythologizing the female self and the "ordinary" woman, Adrienne Rich defines a new female muse, a radical re-vision of the traditional male-defined figure. "Re-vision," Rich declares, "—the act of looking back, of seeing with fresh eyes, of entering an old text from a new critical direction—is for women more than a chapter in cultural history: it is an act of survival."[10] One such act is the reimagining of the woman poet's inspirational power, a force inherently and essentially female. Through the alchemy of a common female language, the muse is re-created, given nontraditional linguistic/semantic/poetic contexts. "They are our birth-pains, and we are bearing ourselves," Rich proclaims, her statement applicable not only to women's poems of anger but also to their quests for creative identity.[11] Hence "my self," the poet singular, becomes "my selves," the collective female poet, persona, voice, power, inspiration, and—despite Rich's reluctance to use the term—muse.

To understand Rich's perception of her female creativity, we need to examine her view of the nature and function of poetry. As she explains in an essay on Judy Grahn,

> Poetry is above all a concentration of the *power* of language, which is the power of our ultimate relationship to everything in the universe. It is as if forces we can lay claim to in no other way, become present to us in sensuous form. The knowledge and use of this magic goes back very far: the rune, the chant; the incantation; the spell; the kenning; sacred words; forbidden words; the naming of the child, the plant, the insect, the ocean, the configuration of stars, the snow, the sensation in the body. The ritual telling of the dream. The physical reality of the human voice; of words gouged or incised in stone or wood, woven in silk or wool, painted on vellum, or traced in sand.[12]

Rich associates poetry with other arts of mystery and divination: magic, runes, chants, spells, sacred rituals. She also refuses to separate art from artist, for poetry's magic is couched firmly in "the physical reality of the human voice" and in the forceful motion of the human hand producing its artifact: gouging or incising words in acts of intensity or violence; weaving and painting in moments of healing peace; tracing in sand, a collaborative effort that assumes a tradition on which to build. As a force that "we can lay claim to in no other way" besides the magical, poetry for Rich offers a dual-faceted power: "the *power* of language" and "the power of our ultimate relationship to everything in the universe."

Language is transformative and rejuvenating, Rich further explains, for "writing is re-naming": "For a poem to coalesce, for a character or an action to take shape, there has to be an imaginative transformation of reality which is in no way passive."[13] For the woman poet this transformation is especially complex, since it is not only linguistic and aesthetic but also personal and political. It must begin, Rich believes, with the reclaiming of words otherwise obscured, limited, or abused within their patriarchal contexts. "For many women," she explains,

> the commonest words are having to be sifted through, rejected, laid aside for a long time, or turned to the light for new colors and flashes of meaning: *power, love, control, violence, political, personal, private, friendship, community, sexual, work, pain, pleasure, self, integrity* . . . When we become acutely, disturbingly aware of the language we are using and that is using us, we begin to grasp a material resource that women have never before collectively attempted to repossess (though we were its inventors, and though individual writers like Dickinson, Woolf, Stein, H. D., have approached language as transforming power).[14]

At the heart of any re-vision of language, Rich asserts, is poetry, for poetry is "among other things, a criticism of language. In setting words together in new configurations, in the mere, immense shift from male to female pronouns, in the relationships between words created through echo, repetition, rhythm, rhyme, it lets us hear and see our words in a new dimension."[15] Poetry, then, is a practical means of female linguistic repossession, of "reconstituting the world."[16]

Poetry is also a tool for redefining and revaluing relationship, Rich argues. As the feminist critic Marilyn R. Farwell has pointed out, Rich's ideal poet-poem relationship is based on a feminist ethics, an effort to rectify the "terrifying dissociation of sensibility" characteristic of a society that separates the masculine principle (defined by Rich as reason, objectivity, separation) from its female counterpart (intuition, subjectivity, relation). To dramatize the misuse of language and power by the patriarchy, Rich explores the metaphor of rape. In Farwell's words, "Rich believes that rape is the metaphor by which men, and at times women, keep themselves untouched by the female principle of subjectivity and relationship; and it is this separation of the two fundamental sides of human existence that is unethical. Without the reciprocal and communal relationship of the male and female principles, people, nature, and language are forced into a situation of manipulation and use."[17] As an alternative to this male metaphor Rich posits the image of motherhood, for the ideal poet-poem relationship resembles the ongoing and essential dialogue between mother and child. It is characterized by clear and loving communication, not by an assertion of the solipsistic poet's suffering ego. The mother-daughter relationship is "the great unwritten story," Rich asserts in *Of Woman Born*, a work about poetic creativity as well as motherhood.[18] Rich elsewhere has likened the poet to a parent: "if I have been a good parent to the poem, something will happen to you who read it."[19]

This focus on dialogue with "you who read it" is crucial to Rich's poetic theory. Envisioning her readership as primarily if not exclusively female, she seeks an active, ongoing exchange with women who are her selves: "I believe increasingly that only the willingness to share private and sometimes painful experience can enable women to create a collective description of the world which will be truly ours."[20] This task of "collective description" falls first to the woman poet:

> The poet's relationship to her poetry has, it seems to me . . . a twofold nature. Poetic language—the poem on paper—is a concretization of the poetry of the world at large, the self, and the forces within the self; and those forces are rescued from formlessness, lucidified, and integrated in the act of writing poems. But there is a more ancient concept of the poet, which is that she is endowed to speak for those who do not have the gift of language, or to see for those who—for whatever reasons—are less conscious of what they are living through. It is as though the risks of the poet's existence can be put to some use beyond her own survival.[21]

As a woman seer, a new-age prophet, Rich asserts at once a private and a public vision. If the poet's voice is heard, Rich implies, she will paradoxically both inspire and be inspired: by "the self, and the forces within the self"; and by the selves, "those who do not have the gift of language."

Rich's view of the woman poet as speaker, singer, and interpreter for other women leads her to emphasize honesty, the cornerstone of any relationship between poet and poem, or poet and audience. In "Women and Honor: Some Notes on Lying" she posits "truth" as a means of "liberating ourselves from our secrets," including "the terrible negative power of the lie in relationships between women."[22] By "truth," however, Rich does not simply mean what Margaret Homans has called "literalization," "the naive wish for a literal language and the belief in poetry's capacity for the duplication of experience."[23] Instead, Rich's concept of truth reflects the poet's vital connection to her self, other women, and her art:

> The unconscious wants truth, as the body does. The complexity and fecundity of dreams come from the complexity and fecundity of the unconscious struggling to fulfill that desire. The complexity and fecundity of poetry come from the same struggle.[24]

This quest for a new and complex truth, Rich further explains, forces the woman poet to confront "the void," the "dark core" that is an essential "part of every woman." By going down into this void, woman can "re-form the crystal" of female experience and female creativity:

> We begin out of the void, out of the darkness and emptiness. It is part of the cycle understood by the old pagan religions, that materialism denies. Out of the death, rebirth; out of nothing, something.
>
> The void is the creatrix, the matrix. It is not mere hollowness and anarchy. But in women it has been identified with lovelessness, barrenness, sterility. We have been urged to fill our "emptiness" with children. We are not supposed to go down into the darkness of the core.
>
> Yet, if we can risk it, the something born of that nothing is the beginning of our truth.[25]

Rich alludes here to the recovery of Kore by Demeter, who traveled to the "darkness of the core" of Hades to reclaim her daughter. This reclamation, the heart of the Eleusinian mysteries, is for Rich paradigmatic of the woman's acquisition of creative power. "Something born of that nothing," the "beginning of our truth," she suggests, is also the beginning of female art. In relating the unconscious self to larger mythic structures, Rich asserts the power of a vital "creatrix" or "matrix" in every woman.

How does Rich envision her own link to this "matrix"? What myths and metaphors does she employ to depict her relationship to her creativity? Her very early poems sometimes assert a "masculine" consciousness or invoke a male version of the traditional muse. In *Snapshots of a Daughter-in-Law*, however, she begins to envision the muse as a demonic female force, a figure akin to Louise Bogan's sleeping fury and May Sarton's goddess Kali. During the last fifteen years Rich has offered three metaphors for female creative identity: the androgyne, the mother, and the lesbian.[26] Implicit in Rich's use of androgyny is an emphasis on reintegrating the male and female principles in art and life. Such a reintegration, Rich argued in the mid-1970s, requires all poets, male and female, to get in touch with the devalued female principle, "the mother in all women and the woman in many men."[27] The second metaphor, motherhood, celebrates the creative woman's capacity for "thinking through the body," for "converting our physicality into both knowledge and power."[28] Rich's most recent metaphor for female creativity, lesbianism, incorporates many of the characteristics of motherhood and yet adds the more complex dimension of female sexual relationship and its analogue, relationship in creativity. "It is the lesbian in us," Rich asserts, "who drives us to feel imaginatively, . . . who is creative, for the dutiful daughter of the fathers in us is only a hack."[29]

For Rich in the 1980s, therefore, poetry represents "the musing of a mind / one with her body." The creative woman must be committed to an honest language, a feminist ethic, and a radically transformative art—"a whole new psychic geography."[30] Finally, she must be a source of inspiration and power for herself and for other women. Rich's communal muse may be defined as the lesbian-feminist self in honest and nonhierarchical communion with her sisters, an individual and a collective female consciousness. "*Nothing but myself? . . . My selves*" thus reveals Rich's most recent metaphor for a female creative principle, the "drive to connect," the inspirational force at the root of her "dream of a common language."

"RINGED WITH ORDEALS SHE WAS MASTERED BY": THE "MASCULINE" MUSE

> In a young poet, as T. S. Eliot has observed, the most promising sign is craftsmanship for it is evidence of a capacity for detachment from the self and its emotions without which no art is possible. Craftsmanship includes, of course, not only a talent for versification but also an ear and an intuitive grasp of much subtler and more difficult matters like proportion, consistency of diction and tone, and the matching of these with the subject at hand; Miss Rich's poems rarely fail on any of these counts. . . .
>
> I suggested . . . that poems are analogous to persons; the poems a reader will encounter in this book are neatly and modestly dressed, speak quietly but do not mumble, respect their elders but are not cowed by them, and do not tell fibs: that, for a first volume, is a good deal.[31]

W. H. Auden's introduction to Adrienne Rich's *A Change of World*, her first volume of poetry and the recipient of the Yale Younger Poets Award for 1951, reveals the underlying assumptions of the masculinist tradition into which Rich was catapulted at twenty-one. "The more perfect the artist, the more completely separate in him will be the man who suffers and the mind which creates," T. S. Eliot once asserted, his remark destined to become a modernist and a New Critical truism.[32] As Auden's comments suggest, Rich's early poems evidence this "detachment from the self and its emotions without which no art is possible"; furthermore, they do so in a manner appropriately feminine. In the literary critic Albert Gelpi's words, these poems as Auden perceives them perpetuate "the stereotype—prim, fussy, and schoolmarmish—that has corseted and strait-laced women-poets into 'poetesses' whom men could deprecate with admiration."[33]

Rich has commented on the problems she confronted in coming as an outsider to the masculine world of poetry. Because her models for "serious" poetry were mostly male and because, as Auden's words suggest, only rigorous objectivity was likely to command critical praise, she turned to formal craftsmanship in order to establish herself as an artist. In Rich's view, the incipient woman poet

> is peculiarly susceptible to language. She goes to poetry or fiction looking for *her* way of being in the world, since she too has been putting words and images together; she is looking eagerly for guides, maps, possibilities; and over and over in the "words' masculine persuasive force" of literature she comes up against something that negates everything she is about: she meets the image of Woman in books written by men.[34]

Because of her susceptibility to masculine language—detached, impersonal language—and to the intrusive male image of woman, Rich in many early poems conceals more than she reveals. As a result, such poems are often "enchanting . . . endearing and delightful . . . sweet," but rarely, to Rich's mind, either satisfactory or satisfying.[35]

A poem that illustrates what Rich calls her "asbestos gloves" strategy is "Aunt Jennifer's Tigers," written while she was still at Radcliffe:

> Aunt Jennifer's tigers prance across a screen,
> Bright topaz denizens of a world of green.
> They do not fear the men beneath the tree;
> They pace in sleek chivalric certainty.
>
> Aunt Jennifer's fingers fluttering through her wool
> Find even the ivory needle hard to pull.
> The massive weight of Uncle's wedding band
> Sits heavily upon Aunt Jennifer's hand.
>
> When Aunt is dead, her terrified hands will lie
> Still ringed with ordeals she was mastered by.
> The tigers in the panel that she made
> Will go on prancing, proud and unafraid.[36]

In the first stanza Rich describes a colorful tapestry of prancing tigers, potent and awesome in their "sleek chivalric certainty." The figure of Aunt Jennifer is starkly antithetical to the image of the proud, autonomous creatures she creates. Unlike the tigers, who prance about at will, Aunt Jennifer is held in check by the "massive weight of Uncle's wedding band," an obstruction to her livelihood and her art. "When Aunt is dead," the poet concludes, her "terrified hands" will lie in perpetual dis-ease, "still ringed with ordeals she was mastered by." The tigers, in contrast, "will go on prancing," oblivious to the suffering of which they were a part.

Certainly this poem meets the criterion of detachment that Eliot and Auden espouse. The persona reveals no emotion toward the landscape she has drawn; instead, she remains aloof at the edge of Aunt Jennifer's world, isolated from the older woman's pain by her guise as an objective linguist, a dispassionate weaver of words. The poem's careful structure—its regular rhyme and rhythm pattern—reveals the close attention to craft of one "peculiarly susceptible" to the "masculine persuasive force" of words. Viewing her early work from the privileged position of hindsight, Rich admits to being "startled" by the "split I even then experienced between the girl who wrote poems, who defined herself in writing poems, and the girl who was to define herself by her relationships with men":

> "Aunt Jennifer's Tigers" . . . looks with deliberate detachment at this split. . . . In writing this poem, composed and apparently cool as it is, I thought I was creating a portrait of an imaginary woman. But this woman suffers from the opposition of her imagination, worked out in tapestry, and her life-style. . . . It was important to me that Aunt Jennifer was a person as distinct from myself as possible—distanced by the formalism of the poem, by its objective, observant tone—even by putting the woman in a different generation.[37]

As Rich's comments imply, the opposition between her own imagination and the strictures placed upon it by the literary establishment led her next to rely on male personae and masculine muses. If putting Aunt Jennifer in an older generation was safer for the young poet, assuming a male mask might prove equally free from risk. The poem "The Loser," for example, features a man who "*thinks of the woman he once loved: first, after her wedding, and then nearly a decade later.*" From the wide-angle lens of the masculine observer-participant, Rich offers a critique of traditional marriage and the objectification of women. "Your wedding made my eyes ache," the speaker declares, angry at the "bourgeois sacrament" that wrested his lover away. "Beauty is always wasted . . . /A face like yours cannot be loved / long or seriously enough." Part two, ten years later, reveals a worn housewife stripped of both youth and beauty, gathering wash from a "squeaking line," her body "weighed against the load." Though the woman is "squared and stiffened by the pull / of what nine windy years have done," her former lover desires her still—no longer for her beauty, but for her powers of survival:

> I see all your intelligence
> flung into that unwearied stance.
>
> My envy is of no avail.
> I turn my head and wish him well
> who chafed your beauty into use
> and lives forever in a house
> lit by the friction of your mind.
> You stagger in against the wind.[38]

Rich employs the male persona here as a means of revealing and rejecting traditional male views of woman. On the one hand, the speaker seems enlightened in his valuing of the woman's intelligence, the "friction of [her] mind." However, this "detached and objective" masculine consciousness goes on to reveal its own biases, for as the husband abuses the wife by making her a household servant, so the persona deems her his muse—an intelligent muse, to be sure, but nonetheless an idealized rather than a real woman. The envious speaker, after all, initially loves the woman for her beautiful face, and at the end of the poem congratulates the husband as a victor: "I . . . wish him well / who chafed your beauty into use." He seems to find little wrong with the woman's mind being used to light the home fires; his only regret is that it is not *his* home, *his* fires. Rich's anger toward two types of injustice toward women—the servitude of traditional marriage and the insult of idealization—lies just beneath the surface of this taut poem. The strategy that keeps the anger "in its place" is the use of the male persona.

"The Roofwalker," a later poem from *Snapshots*, dramatizes the young poet's struggle against psychological and poetic strictures. Again, the male persona serves as a distancing device, a means of attributing Rich's vulnerability and dissatisfaction to an outside source. "I feel like them up there: / exposed, larger than life, / and due to break my neck," the speaker admits, noting from afar the surreal builders perched atop "half-finished houses." He goes on to reflect on his own imaginative constructs:

> Was it worth while to lay—
> with infinite exertion—
> a roof I can't live under?
> . . . .
> A life I didn't choose
> chose me: even
> my tools are the wrong ones
> for what I have to do.

This admission forces the persona to confront his errors of judgment and imagination. "Ignorant," he will seek a new identity as a covert but daring roofwalker,

> a naked man fleeing
> across the roofs
> who could with a shade of difference
> be sitting in the lamplight
> against the cream wallpaper
> reading—not with indifference—
> about a naked man
> fleeing across the roofs.[39]

The struggle to wrest power from a masculine visionary force, a male muse, informs a number of Rich's early poems. In discussing the poetry of Dorothy

Wordsworth and Emily Brontë, Margaret Homans has suggested that for both poets, "the sources of poetic power are not felt to be within the self." Troubled by "the apparent otherness of her mind's powers," each poet invokes a male muse, eager for his creative strength, yet wrestles against that same force, afraid of being swallowed up.[40] Rich displays a similar ambivalence in "Lucifer in the Train," as the traveling poet, isolated in a foreign country, beseeches the fallen Satan to share with her his restorative powers:

Lucifer, we are yours who stiff and mute
Ride out of worlds we shall not see again,
And watch from windows of a smoking train
The ashen prairies of the absolute.
. . . .
O foundered angel, first and loneliest
To turn this bitter sand beneath your hoe,
Teach us, the newly-landed, what you know;
After our weary transit, find us rest.[41]

On first reading, this Lucifer would appear a benign if remote force, a silent but wise teacher from whom the weary speaker hopes to learn. But the phrase "we are yours" implies a previous encounter with this grim Satan, and the "stiff muteness" of the "we" suggests the powerlessness of one possessed. Beneath the measured voice of supplication is a hint of desperation, for the speaker is hurled relentlessly toward "the ashen prairies of the absolute." As an alien traveler, the poet identifies with the fallen Satan, but as a mute and weary petitioner she feels constrained by her parasitic relationship to this potent and diabolical force, this malignant "bird" who "flies to its young with carrion in its claw."

In "The Insomniacs" Rich employs both a male persona and a masculine muse, thus dramatizing the problem of the fragmented self, the artist's need for wholeness. Likening himself to an actor and his Other to a mystic, each of whom "wherever he has been, / Must know his hand before his face," the speaker directs his wry words to a silent alternate self:

So: we are fairly met, grave friend—
The meeting of two wounds, in man.
I, gesturing with practiced hand,
I, my my great brocaded gown,
And you, the fixed and patient one,
Enduring all the world can do.
I, with my shifting masks, the gold
The awful scarlet, laughing blue,
Maker of many worlds; and you,
Worldless, the pure receptacle.

The actor and the mystic obviously are two aspects of a single psyche; neither can exist without the other, yet each is tortured by his solitary, surrealistic vision. The mystic's "floating eyes reveal / What saint or mummer groans to feel"; the actor's "voice commands the formal stage," yet a "jungle thrives beyond the wings— / All formless and benighted things / That rhetoric cannot assuage." Unable to reconcile their disparate yet paradoxically related anguish, both the speaker and his silent shadow are like Rich's Aunt Jennifer, "ringed with ordeals [they are] mastered by":

Not my words nor your visions mend
Such infamous knowledge. We are split,
Done into bits, undone, pale friend,
. . . .
The flaw is in us; we will break.

The sole hope of reconciliation, the "actor" asserts, lies in the capacity of each self to bring new vision and song to the other:

O dare you of this fracture make
Hosannas plain and tragical,

Or dare I let each cadence fall
Awkward as learning newly learned,
Simple as children's cradle songs,
As untranslatable and true,
We someday might conceive a way
To do the thing we long to do—
To live in time, to act in space
Yet find a ritual to embrace
Raw towns of man, the pockmarked sun.[42]

The poem ends on a tentatively affirmative note: harmony is conceivable only if both poet and muse acknowledge each other as equally powerful forces. Significantly, the source that facilitates this equilibrium is language, the hosannas and cadences that the speaker must learn anew.

Rich's struggle to come to terms with this projection of herself as masculine culminates with "Orion," a poem in which the young poet both seeks and resists the power of her "fierce half-brother." In stanza one, Rich explains that she had once romanticized her male muse as "my genius . . . / my cast-iron Viking, my helmed / lion-heart king in prison." Although she now is able to see Orion for what he is—"dragged down / by . . . / the last bravado you won't give over"—she nonetheless continues to be moved by his fiery power:

But you burn, and I know it;
as I throw back my head to take you in
an old transfusion happens again:
divine astronomy is nothing to it.

As the poet feeds on the energy of Orion, her ambivalence surfaces; she both resents and rejoices in the power she acquires. Her immediate recourse, to stare the demon down, proves ineffective:

. . . when I look you back

it's with a starlike eye
shooting its cold and egotistical spear
where it can do least damage.
Breathe deep! No hurt, no pardon
out here in the cold with you
you with your back to the wall.[43]

The poet's weapon, the phallic spear with its "cold and egotistical" eye, does not satisfy her, but it is the only weapon she is able to wield. As Rich later noted, "Orion" was

> a poem of reconnection with a part of myself I had felt I was losing—the active principle, the energetic imagination, the "half-brother" whom I projected, as I had for many years, into the constellation Orion. It's no accident that the words "cold and egotistical" appear in the poem, and are applied to myself. . . . The choice still seemed to be between "love"—womanly, maternal love, altruistic love . . . ; and egotism—a force directed by men into creation, achievement, ambition, often at the expense of others but justifiably so. For weren't they men, and wasn't that their destiny as womanly, selfless love was ours? We know now that the alternatives are false ones.[44]

Although she later realizes the limitations of this masculine creative identification, Rich's early poems are filled with male personae and muses. These poems depict the developing poet's ambivalence toward her art and her female self. Seeking a strong female poetic identity, however, she turns next to a demonic female force, a shadow-self free of the patriarchal shackles that the masculine muse inevitably imposes.

"A THINKING WOMAN SLEEPS WITH MONSTERS": THE DEMONIC MUSE

A woman in the shape of a monster
a monster in the shape of a woman
the skies are full of them[45]

So Rich begins "Planetarium," a "companion poem to 'Orion' " and a tribute to the astronomer Caroline Herschel (1750–1848), who discovered eight comets but failed to receive equal recognition with her brother, William. This poem illustrates Rich's shift from a masculine muse—her "fierce half-brother," Orion—to a demonic female muse, an aspect of the poet's creativity with which she can more readily come to terms. In "Planetarium," Rich explains, "at last the woman in the poem and the woman writing the poem become the same person."[46] Like Caroline Herschel, a "monster" in an age in which "thinking women" were considered anomalies, Rich's potent female persona may well be labeled "harpy, shrew and whore."[47] However, this is a risk she is now willing to take.

In fact, it is a risk she welcomes. The skies are full of monsters, Rich declares, celebrating the demonic power that accompanies woman's foray into the galactic unknown,

> encountering the NOVA
>
> every impulse of light exploding
> from the core
> as life flies out of us.

The monstrous women who populate the galaxies, "doing penance for impetuousness," are exploding old worlds, creating strange new planets, rich female vistas: "What we see, we see / And seeing is changing." Most important, the woman who re-members Caroline Herschel can imagine herself an architect of the universe, an interpreter of light:

> I am bombarded yet   I stand
>
> I have been standing all my life in the
> direct path of a battery of signals
> the most accurately transmitted most
> untranslatable language in the universe
> I am a galactic cloud so deep   so invo-
> luted that a light wave could take 15
> years to travel through me   And has
> taken   I am an instrument in the shape
> of a woman trying to translate pulsations
> into images   for the relief of the body
> and the reconstruction of the mind.[48]

By invoking Herschel as a demonic female muse, the poet renames herself a "galactic cloud," an "instrument in the shape of a woman." In so doing, she casts off her former identities as "a woman in the shape of a monster / a monster in the shape of a woman." Instead, she re-visions herself as an autonomous creator, a translator of "pulsations into images," in an act at once physical ("for the relief of the body") and intellectual ("and the reconstruction of the mind"). It "could take 15 years" for this female power to "travel through me," the poet asserts—"and has taken." But once this energy takes hold, its pulsating force becomes that of its translator. "The blood jet is poetry," Sylvia Plath declares. "There is no stopping it."[49]

How did the carefully masked, "objective" poet of "Aunt Jennifer's Tigers" give way to the galactic translator of "Planetarium"? Or, in the literary scholar Helen Vendler's rather melodramatic words,

> what has happened to the girl of 1951, that girl who wanted everything suffused by the delicate and the decorative, who questioned her passivity even while exhorting herself to that virtue, who mourned change and yet sensed its coming . . . — what has become of her?[50]

She has begun to confront and celebrate what Denise Levertov has called, "what, woman, / and who, myself, / I am."[51] For Rich, as for many women poets, naming the self once evoked both doubt and guilt, especially when it demanded a confrontation with the demon within. In her journal from the late 1950s and early 1960s, she laments the fragmentation she experiences in trying to balance her life and her art. But she despairs of attempting to change her situation,

> paralyzed by the sense that there exists a mesh of relationships—e.g., between my anger at the children, my sensual life, pacifism, sex . . . —an interconnectedness which, if I could see it, make it valid, would give me back myself, make it possible to function lucidly and passionately. Yet I grope in and out among these dark webs.[52]

This admission of conflict was recorded while she was writing "Snapshots of a Daughter-in-Law," a poem Rich considers central in her transition from a male to a female consciousness and voice. "It was an extraordinary relief to write that poem," she later declares.[53] From that work emerges Rich's first woman-centered inspiration and identification.

A scrapbook comprising ten separate yet intimately related "snapshots," the poem chronicles the efforts of a daughter-in-law—a woman defined by society according to her relationship to her husband and his family—to forge an autonomous identity. Ironically, it is her mother-in-law, her mind "moldering like wedding-cake, / heavy with useless experience," who inspires the daughter to challenge this family album; the daughter's matrophobia subjects her to "chiding angels" that pervade her consciousness daily. In section one, the narrator addresses this older woman, "once a belle," now "rich / with suspicion, rumor, fantasy / crumbling to pieces under the knife-edge / of mere fact. In the prime of [her] life." Angry at the "uselessness" of the mother-in-law yet simultaneously moved by her, the speaker goes on to describe the daughter's "crumbling to pieces." "*Have no patience*," demonic voices exhort her. "*Be insatiable. . . . Save yourself; others you cannot save.*" These demons are "probably angels," the frightened daughter tells herself in a futile effort to deny her vulnerability. "Nothing hurts her anymore," the narrator says ironically, "except / each morning's grit blowing into her eyes."[54]

In section three of "Snapshots," Rich confronts poetically what she will later call "the terrible negative power of the lie in the relationships between women."[55] Often, the poet recognizes, the "power of the lie" takes the form of self-directed anger. "A thinking woman sleeps with monsters," Rich's narrator in "Snapshots" declares. "The beak that grips her, she becomes." Women's anger rarely explodes against its actual sources, Rich implies; instead, it appears in "the argument *ad feminam*":

> Two handsome women, gripped in argument,
> each proud, acute, subtle, I hear scream
> across the cut glass and majolica
> like Furies cornered from their prey:
> The argument *ad feminam*, all the old knives
> that have rusted in my back, I drive in yours,
> *ma semblable, ma soeur*!

The adjectives of line two lend a special irony to Rich's portrait of women turned against themselves and one another. Pride and intelligence, characteristics long denied women, have been subverted by the "subtle" demon of fierce rivalry. These women are "handsome," not stereotypically beautiful; the household items over which they scream are expensive, exotic, tasteful: "cut glass and majolica." As "Furies cornered from their prey," the speaker concludes, such women drive into one another with a vengeance the "old knives" that the patriarchy has driven into them. The first demon the woman poet must exorcise, this section implies, is an impulse to undermine "*ma semblable, ma soeur*."

Rich goes on to catalog other "monsters" with whom "thinking women" have slept. Suppressed anger can at times be transformed into creative energy, section four suggests (Dickinson was "writing *My Life had stood—a Loaded Gun*" while "waiting / for the iron to heat").[56] But such rage can also quell the artistic impulse. The poet's subsequent image of Dickinson—"iron-eyed and beaked and purposed as a bird, / dusting everything on the whatnot every day of life"—reveals the conflicts this woman poet must have experienced as she defied daily monotony in order to write.[57] Yet another demon is female beauty, the frequent source of woman's cultural powerlessness: "*Dulce ridens, dulce loquens*, / she shaves her legs until they gleam / like petrified mammoth-tusk." Women have long been defined as "petrified" objects, the poet implies.

Finally, Rich decries the destructive nature of the traditional female muse, the passive, objectified "sister of the mirage and echo" immortalized through the courtly tradition. "When to her lute Corinna sings / neither words nor music are her own," the speaker mourns. Subsequent sections of "Snapshots" reveal an alternative to the traditional muse, a "new woman" by whom the poet is inspired. She is first represented by the pioneer feminist Mary Wollstonecraft, a woman "partly brave and partly good" rather than idealized, like the muses men invoke. But this inspirational source emerges ultimately as a revisionary goddess imbued with extraordinary creative energy:

>   Well,
> she's long about her coming, who must be
> more merciless to herself than history.

Her mind full to the wind, I see her plunge
breasted and glancing through the currents,
taking the light upon her
at least as beautiful as any boy
or helicopter,
                    poised, still coming,
her fine blades making the air wince

but her cargo
no promise then:
delivered
palpable
ours.[58]

This description of the new-age female muse recalls Simone de Beauvoir's stunning portrait in *The Second Sex* of the ancient matriarchal earth goddess, revisioned for our time:

> She comes down from the remoteness of ages, from Thebes, from Crete, from Chichen-Itza; and she is also the totem set deep in the African jungle; she is a helicopter and she is a bird; and there is this, the greatest wonder of all: under her tinted hair the forest murmur becomes a thought, and words issue from the breasts.[59]

Her ability to transform forest noises into potent female language identifies this goddess as a revised Orpheus, one who stills and awes nature by her rejuvenating song. As the Rich scholar Wendy Martin notes, this powerful woman whom both Rich and de Beauvoir celebrate is "the child of the furies, sharing their knowledge of the mysteries of blood and birth; yet resilent and articulate, she ushers in the future."[60]

Other poems from this middle period reveal Rich's preoccupation with woman as demonic force, a purveyor of powers either debilitating or transformative, depending upon how they are used. In "The Corpse-Plant" Rich uses the shadowy flower, "white as death," as a metaphor for the woman poet's descent into "the cratered night of female memory."[61] Prefacing the poem with a quotation from Whitman—"*How can an obedient man, or a sick man, / dare to write poems?*"—the speaker pronounces herself "neither obedient nor sick" and thus claims the right to write. But this assertion of creative identity, made in a moment of summer bliss, brings with it unseasonal thoughts, as the speaker confronts "winters of mind, of flesh, / sickness of the rot-smell of leaves / turned silt-black, heavy as tarpaulin." Despite the horror of such visions, they fade as the poet exerts her female power—a power that she as woman artist claims "by choice."[62]

For Rich as for many women poets, the archetype of woman as demonic is closely linked to her maternity. In "Night-Pieces: For a Child" the poet perceives herself from the vantage point of her infant, wrenched by nightmare. As the mother bends over the crib to check on her sleeping child,

You blurt a cry. Your eyes
spring open, still filmed in a dream.
Wider, they fix me—
—death's head, sphinx, medusa?
You scream.
Tears lick my cheeks, my knees
droop at your fear.
Mother I no more am,
but woman, and nightmare.

This vision of herself invokes the mother's own nightmares, fears fed by patriarchal evils: the horror of Hiroshima, the glint of murderers' knives. Mercifully, her dreams give way to the early sounds of the waking child. Heavy-hearted, the mother reflects upon both the power and the terror of the mother-child bond:

But you and I—
swaddled in a dumb dark
old as sickheartedness,
modern as pure annihilation—

we drift in ignorance.
If I could hear you now
mutter some gentle animal sound!
If milk flowed from my breast again. . . .[63]

On one level, this poem expresses Rich's guilt and ambivalence toward her maternity, her "sickheartedness" at the weight of the mother-child bond and her fears of inadequacy. But Rich is also talking about the woman poet's creativity, the "dumb dark" that results when the child whom she both loves and resents goes away, when her milk stops flowing. Like recent French feminists, Rich images female creativity in terms of mother's milk, the white ink of the powerful and nurturant breast.[64] When this ink ceases to flow, the poet implies, the creative woman is no longer whole. Linking artistic and biological creativity, Rich explores with ambivalence what May Sarton has called "the full motherhood, the full monsterhood" at the heart of those who attempt as writers to be "something more and something less than women."[65]

Rich's efforts to effect a truce with a demonic female Other who is at once the self can be seen in "Women," from *Leaflets*. Here the poet invokes three aspects of the female psyche, the "weird sisters" of folklore who alternately reveal, conceal, and transform the woman's self-perceptions:

My three sisters are sitting
on rocks of black obsidian.
For the first time, in this light, I can see who they are.

My first sister is sewing her costume for the procession.
She is going as the Transparent Lady
and all her nerves will be visible.

My second sister is also sewing,
at the seam over her heart which has never healed entirely.
At last, she hopes, this tightness in her chest will ease.

My third sister is gazing
at a dark-red crust spreading westward far out on the sea.
Her stockings are torn but she is beautiful.[66]

The sisters in stanzas two and three wear masks that the poet wishes to reject: the "Transparent Lady," whose "costume" exposes every nerve; the heartbroken woman who tries to ease the "tightness in her chest" by covering her scars. Although the poet sympathizes with the first two sisters, it is the third whose vision she seems to share—the vision of a survivor. "Her stockings are torn but she is beautiful," Rich says of the third sister, a description that recalls Denise Levertov's "turbulent moon-ridden girl," dressed in "torn taffeta" and singing "strange songs."[67] Despite her tatters, this shadow represents for both Rich and Levertov a potent, mystical aspect of the female self.

In these poems from the 1960s, Rich examines woman as freak, monster—so perceived by society and, at times, by herself. Frequently such poems reveal anger, but rarely is anger the work's dominant force. In *The Will to Change* (1971), however, Rich gives full vent to her rage, using the female demonic to inflict apocalyptic fury upon the patriarchy. Women's anger, she asserts, is both necessary and transformative:

> Both the victimization and the anger experienced by women are real, and have real sources, everywhere in the environment, built into society, language, the structures of thought. They will go on being tapped and explored by poets, among others. We can neither deny them, nor will we rest there.[68]

"I Dream I'm the Death of Orpheus" best illustrates Rich's use of rage as a form of female creative power. In Jean Cocteau's powerful motion picture *Orpheé*, to which this poem responds, Orpheus is flanked by Hell's Angels and driven through Hades by Death, personified as a woman in a black Rolls-Royce. To emerge unscathed from the underworld, this film Orpheus must pass through a mirror. In Rich's version, however, the focus switches from Orpheus' plight to that of the woman, Death, a "woman in the prime of life" with powers "severely limited / by authorities whose faces I rarely see." Despite these authorities and their implicit threats, the woman is determined to persevere. She will become a female Orpheus, driving through the streets of Hades in an act of defiance, inspired not by the song of the legendary singer but by herself:

I am a woman in the prime of life
driving her dead poet in a black Rolls-Royce
through a landscape of twilight and thorns.
A woman with a certain mission
which if obeyed to the letter will leave her intact.

A woman with the nerves of a panther
a woman with contacts among Hell's Angels
a woman feeling the fullness of her powers
at the precise moment when she must not use them
a woman sworn to lucidity
who sees through the mayhem, the smoky fires
of these underground streets
her dead poet learning to walk backward against the wind
on the wrong side of the mirror.[69]

Albert Gelpi argues that in this poem Rich "depicts herself as a woman whose animus is the archetypal poet. . . . The animus-poet comes alive again within the psyche, and his return is a sign of, and a measure of, her ability to 'see through' and move forward on her 'mission.' . . . Orpheus revives within her 'on the wrong side of the mirror,' 'learning to walk backward against the wind.' "[70] Although Gelpi's reading is feasible given Rich's earlier invocations of a male Other, the poem's title suggests instead a projection of the anima, the female self, as Orpheus. Or, more specifically, it projects a Jungian shadow, a same-sex figure with demonic powers.[71] The struggle to claim a female creative voice is fraught with difficulty, Rich acknowledges; the woman here is limited in her powers and her ability to act upon them. Yet in reconstructing Orpheus as female, Rich frees herself from the confines of patriarchal myth. She refuses to obey her mission "to the letter," because emerging "intact" cannot be her first priority. Instead, she will reintegrate and rejuvenate herself by "learning to walk backward against the wind / on the wrong side of the mirror."

As these poems illustrate, Rich has long been fascinated with the woman poet's relationship to the demonic—to the epithets of demon hurled at her throughout history, and to the "demons" within, forces of doubt and fear that she must transform into creative power. Once such transformations are under way, Rich turns her attention to modes of healing; hence in her next volume, *Diving into the Wreck*, she shifts from the demonic muse to a new metaphor for female creativity and wholeness, the androgyne.

"I AM SHE: I AM HE": THE ANDROGYNOUS MUSE

Her hands bled onto the sill.

. . . .

She's a shot hero. A dying poet.
Even now, if we went for her—
but they've gone with rags and putty to fix the pane.
She stays in with her mirrors and anger.

. . . .

Tell me how to bear myself,
how it's done, the light kiss falling
accurately
on the cracked palm.[72]

Discovering "how to bear myself" provides the central motif of *Diving into the Wreck*, Rich's effort to construct poetically a female *bildungsroman*, a mythos of the woman poet exploring her fragmented psyche and somehow emerging whole. In *The Will to Change*, Rich focuses on social, political, and sexual oppression—the "rubbish" that history under the patriarchy has become, the "squatters in their shacks" in American cities, the "permissible fibs" and the "knots of lies" between men and women. In *Diving into the Wreck*, in contrast, her attention shifts from an exterior to an interior landscape, the creative psyche the woman poet must reconstruct.[73]

Rich's emphasis in this volume on "making herself whole" is not a burgeoning solipsism. Instead, her efforts at re-vision and rejuvenation move toward a "shared subjectivity" that represents the heart of her "feminist ethics." As Marilyn R. Farwell has noted, Rich's desire for wholeness is part of her attempt to "relate ethics and language, text and artist, creation and relation, and ultimately art and life." In Rich's view, Farwell explains, patriarchal society has polarized the male principle, which Rich defines as separation and objectivity, and the female principle, which she images in terms of relationship and subjectivity. The result of such polarization is a "terrifying dissociation of sensibility," a dissociation evidenced, Farwell suggests, in "the divorce of the human being from the environment, the objectification of others and the separation of the conscious and unconscious sides of the self."[74] If society is to be re-visioned and the individual reconstructed, Rich believes, the female principle must be accorded the power and centrality it once held in matriarchal societies, whether actual or imagined. "We can no longer afford to keep the female principle enclosed within the confines of the tight little postindustrial family, or within any male-induced notion of where the female principle is valid and where it is not."[75]

As a metaphor of wholeness, Rich turns in *Diving into the Wreck* to androgyny. *Signs* editor Barbara Charlesworth Gelpi has defined androgyny as "a psychic unity, either potential or actual, conceived as existing in all individuals."[76] Ideally, androgyny would suggest a redefinition of what it means to be male and female, an openness to the forces of opposition within the self. A dynamic rather than a static concept, androgyny thus defined offers the woman poet a valuable paradigm—or so Adrienne Rich believed in the early 1970s.

A re-vision of female creativity through the androgyne is offered in "The Stranger":

> Looking as I've looked before, straight down the heart
> of the street to the river
> walking the rivers of the avenues
> feeling the shudder of the caves beneath the asphalt
> watching the lights turn on in the towers
> walking as I've walked before
> like a man, like a woman, in the city
> my visionary anger cleansing my sight

and the detailed perceptions of mercy
flowering from that anger

if I come into a room out of the sharp misty light
and hear them talking a dead language
if they ask me my identity
what can I say but
I am the androgyne
I am the living mind you fail to describe
in your dead language
the lost noun, the verb surviving
only in the infinitive
the letters of my name are written under the lids
of the newborn child.[77]

The poet's capacity to think and feel "like a man, like a woman" frees her from the restrictions that patriarchy attempts to impose upon women, who cannot safely walk alone at night in the modern city. As the female protagonist travels through this urban landscape, "straight down the heart / of the street to the river" of consciousness, she sees as she has never seen before, "my visionary anger cleansing my sight." From this "visionary anger" stem "detailed perceptions of mercy," the healing insights of the androgyne.

In the second part of the poem, Rich addresses the source of the androgyne's anger, the "dead language" of the patriarchy, long used as a weapon against the powerless. Despite patriarchal efforts to deny her speech, the woman poet will not be silenced, Rich asserts, for hers is the power of creation and maternity. Like Mary Daly, Rich perceives male-dominated language as nominal, dominated by static nouns.[78] The androgynous potential, in contrast, emerges in "the verb surviving / only in the infinitive." Female creativity, Rich implies, is inseparable from female fecundity, from the power "to be" and to cause others "to be." Hence the child as androgyne, as new mortal, becomes both a source and a manifestation of woman's gift of language, of her creative potency.

In the title poem, "Diving into the Wreck," the androgyne appears as a redeemer who, in the aftermath of patriarchal destruction, seeks psychological and spiritual regeneration. Armed with a book of myths, Rich's female quester descends into the life-giving, maternal sea to determine what has separated her from herself. The woman carries the proper equipment for such a journey: a loaded camera to capture reality, a sharp knife to cut through illusion, armor and a mask to disguise her vulnerability. It is important that the explorer travel alone, taking reasonable precautions yet descending the ladder in solitude and apprehension. She is bold in her undertaking yet unsure what the next step will bring—"there is no one / to tell me when the ocean / will begin." Drawing sustenance from the sea is an awesome task, since it holds both promise and distractions, "and besides / you breathe differently down here." But once she becomes familiar with her new environs, learns how to "breathe," the explorer affirms her journey's purpose:

I came to explore the wreck.
The words are purposes.
The words are maps.
I came to see the damage that was done
and the treasures that prevail.

Language, the act of creating in words, serves as a guide to both the damage and the treasures of civilization. Words let the speaker discover "the thing I came for: / the wreck and not the story of the wreck / the thing itself and not the myth."

In the last three stanzas Rich explicitly re-visions the "I" of the poem as an androgynous figure, a force that may reintegrate all that the wreck destroyed:

This is the place.
And I am here, the mermaid whose dark hair
streams black, the merman in his armored body
We circle silently
about the wreck
we dive into the hold.
I am she: I am he

whose drowned face sleeps with open eyes
whose breasts still bear the stress
whose silver, copper, vermeil cargo lies
obscurely inside barrels
half-wedged and left to rot.

The quester becomes not "I" but "we," as she assumes the identities of both merman and mermaid, the "half-destroyed instruments" of a psyche and of a culture divided against itself. The final stanza further reinforces the power of the androgyne to "rewrite" civilization and self:

We are, I am, you are
by cowardice or courage
the one who find our way
back to this scene
carrying a knife, a camera
a book of myths
in which
our names do not appear.[79]

By intermingling singular and plural, first and second person pronouns, Rich connects poet and reader, who ideally achieve a balance like that of the androgyne. Old myths and words are no longer valid, Rich suggests; an androgynous vision lets women transcend the limitations imposed by patriarchal dictates.

As Rich later recognizes, however, using androgyny to symbolize female creativity causes problems. Both Cynthia Secor and Marilyn R. Farwell note that what androgyny often amounts to is a subsuming of the feminine principle into the masculine. Farwell labels such a merger "fusion" and its opposite "balance," a state in which male and female unite as complementary forces, equal and equally valued. In other words, instead of "male plus female equals androgyne," androgyny has typically been construed as "male plus female equals male."[80] Because of the tenacity and invidiousness of this patriarchal reading, Rich ultimately abandons the term. In *Of Woman Born* she complains of its amorphousness: androgyny implies "many things to many people, from bisexuality to a vague freedom from imposed sexual roles." But she objects even more strongly to the inequity inherent in the word's "very structure," which replicates the sexual dichotomy and priority of *andros* (male) over *gyne* (female). "In a truly postandrogynous society the term 'androgyne' would have no meaning."[81]

The images of creativity and inspiration that replace androgyny can be seen in "Natural Resources," a poem from *The Dream of a Common Language*. Here the woman poet appears as a miner, "the core of the strong hill." "The miner is no metaphor," Rich insists. "She goes / into the cage like the rest, is flung / downward by gravity like them." Like the androgynous quester of "Diving into the Wreck," who descends in search of "a book of myths in which our names do not appear," the miner of "Natural Resources" goes down into the earth seeking new female vistas: "It is only she who sees: who was trained to see." What the miner sees, Rich continues, is the "passivity we mistake / —in the desperation of our search— / for gentleness": the woman's willingness to acquiesce, to be subsumed under the banner of male-oriented terms like androgyny. "Gentleness is active," the poet asserts, ". . . the refusal to be a victim."

Rich goes on to reject androgyny as a metaphor for female creativity:

> There are words I cannot choose again:
> *humanism androgyny*
>
> Such words have no shame in them, no diffidence
> before the raging stoic grandmothers:
>
> their glint is too shallow, like a dye
> that does not permeate
>
> the fibers of actual life
> as we live it, now.

In search of androgyny, after all, Rich as a younger poet had turned to a masculine muse, a half-brother imaged in the figure of Orion,

> the phantom of the man-who-would-understand,
> the lost brother, the twin—
>
> for him did we leave our mothers,
> deny our sisters, over and over?[82]

Like the archetype of the demon as masculine, the androgynous muse for Rich is no longer an adequate means of imaging female power. Instead, she invokes as muses her mothers and sisters, her "selves."

"HOMESICK FOR MYSELF, FOR HER": THE MATERNAL MUSE

> The cathexis between mother and daughter—essential, distorted, misused—is the great unwritten story. Probably there is nothing in human nature more resonant with charges than the flow of energy between two biologically alike bodies, one of which has lain in amniotic bliss inside the other, one of which has labored to give birth to the other.[83]

In *Of Woman Born* Rich explores the literal and metaphoric connections between the woman who gives life and the daughter to whom that life is given. Her own first muse, the poet admits, was her mother:

> My mother's very name had a kind of magic for me as a child: Helen. I still think it one of the most beautiful of names. Reading Greek mythology, while very young, I somehow identified Helen my mother with Helen of Troy; or perhaps even more with Poe's "Helen," which my father liked to quote. . . . She was, Helen my mother, *my* native shore of course; I think in that poem I first heard my own longings, the longings of the female child, expressed by a male poet, in the voice of a man—my father.[84]

Like H.D., whose mother's name was also Helen and likewise was associated with both Helen of Troy and Poe's Helen, Rich acknowledges her mother as an early wellspring of her own sexuality and creativity. "The mother is the Muse, the Creator, and in my case especially, as my mother's name was Helen," H.D. claims, in words that could as well be Rich's.[85] From this "profound matrilineal bequest," Rich explains, come two types of knowledge: "a knowledge that is subliminal, subversive, preverbal: the knowledge flowing between two like bodies, one of which has spent nine months inside the other," and that of woman's language and wisdom, "the verbally transmitted lore of female survival."[86]

Motherhood also offers two types of power: "the biological potential or capacity to bear and nourish human life, and the magical power invested in women by men, whether in the form of Goddess-worship or the fear of being controlled and overwhelmed by women."[87] Biological power is of particular interest to Rich, who uses it as an analogue for female creativity. In "The Antifeminist Woman" she calls for "a radical reinterpretation of the concept of motherhood" as a means of determining "more about the physical capacity for gestation and nourishment of infants and how it relates to psychological gestation and nurture as an intellectual and creative force." She goes on to emphasize the importance for women to "think connectedly" about the links between embryology and sexuality, between the human body rhythms and natural cycles, between woman's physiological and psychological patterns.[88] Such connections are especially important to the woman poet, Rich implies, for she must also investigate the relationship of her physical self to her female creativity:

> I am convinced that "there are ways of thinking that we don't yet know about." . . . I am really asking whether women cannot begin, at last, to *think through the body*, to connect what has been so cruelly disorganized—our great mental capacities, hardly used; our highly developed tactile sense; our genius for close observation; our complicated, pain-enduring, multipleasured physicality.[89]

The uncharted minds of women, their transformative touch, their physiological complexity represent for Rich vital sources of creative energy. Hence biological motherhood, expanded and reinterpreted, becomes a potent metaphor for the woman poet's relationship to her art.

The other "magical" power, that of woman as goddess, suggests a second important facet of female creativity. While man fears the power of the goddess, Rich implies, woman draws upon that power. As a model for the creative woman, she offers prepatriarchal woman, whose "physiology was the original source of her . . . power, both in making her the source of life itself, and in associating her more deeply than man with natural cycles and processes." Commenting on the anthropological work of Helen Diner and Elizabeth Gould Davis, both of whom argue the reality of a matriarchal era in prehistory, Rich acknowledges the importance of ancient woman as "head of family, and as deity—the Great Goddess who appears throughout early mythology, as Tiamat, Rhea, Ishtar, Astarte, Cybele, Demeter, Diana of Epheus, and by many other names: the eternal giver of life and embodiment of the natural order, including death." Whether or not one accepts the historical verity of matriarchies, Rich concludes, "there is an inescapable correlation between the idea of motherhood and the idea of power."[90]

This link between motherhood and power is epitomized for Rich in the story of Demeter and Kore and the reclamation of the "lost" daughter. For the woman poet this recovery of creative energy occurs through the power and inspiration of the maternal muse. "Each daughter . . . must have longed for a mother whose love for her and whose power were so great as to undo rape and bring her back from death. And every mother must have longed for the power of Demeter, the efficacy of her anger, the reconciliation with her lost self."[91] As "daughter" of the muse and "mother" to her art, the creative woman longs for both maternal love and maternal strength. By invoking the mother as muse figure, she becomes a modern Kore, connected to the transformative energy of the potent Demeter. And by expressing her own procreative capacities, creating new life through the powerful medium of language, she becomes Demeter herself, a vital source of human nourishment and sustenance. Especially in *The Dream of a Common Language*, therefore, Rich uses motherhood as a metaphor for the woman poet's relationship to her creative powers. Her poems on motherhood fall into three general categories: those that explore the political issues of motherhood; those that depict maternal sexuality and physicality, the mother as mirrored by the female lover; and those that portray female artistic creativity, the woman poet as mother to herself and her art.

Mothering as a political force can be seen in "Mother-Right," as Rich portrays women's and children's right to be together, to redefine the boundaries of the patriarchy:

> Woman and child running
> in a field A man planted
> on the horizon
>
> Two hands one long, slim one
> small, starlike clasped
> in the razor wind
>
> Her hair cut short for faster travel
> the child's curls grazing his shoulders
> the hawk-winged cloud over their heads
>
> The man is walking boundaries
> measuring He believes in what is his
> the grass the waters underneath the air
> the air through which child and mother
> are running the boy singing
> the woman eyes sharpened in the light
> heart stumbling making for the open.[92]

A poem about patriarchal versus matriarchal authority, about possession versus freedom, "Mother-Right" presents a sharp contrast between the man staking out "his" territory and the woman and child running, "making for the open." Rich conveys the urgency of her vision by the poem's staccato rhythm, its pauses between key words; the woman and child, this rhythm suggests, *must* make it. Significantly, the child is a boy unscathed by the patriarch who dominates the landscape. The mother and child bond evoked here parallels the relationship between poet and poem, which must also be freed from its patriarchal trappings. In asserting the predominance of "mother-right," Rich is "re-forming the crystal" of patriarchal poetics as well as law.

Rich also celebrates motherhood as a symbol of female sexuality and physicality. In her physiological multiplicity, Rich believes, lies woman's capacity to "think through the body" and hence to transform radically what it means to be sexual, to "create." Closely related to sexual transformation is the woman poet's linguistic re-vision of such patriarchal terms as *love, pain, separation, relation*— her efforts toward what Luce Irigaray terms *parler femme*.[93] In "Splittings," for example, the poet decries "myths of separation" perpetuated by heterosexual conventions. As the poem begins, the female speaker acknowledges her suffering in the absence of her lover: "I am not with her I have been waking off and on / all night to that pain." But the woman stops herself, refusing sorrow and insisting instead that she "think connectedly." Thus pain speaks to her and she learns to listen:

> Yet if I could instruct
> myself, if we could learn to learn from pain
> even as it grasps us . . .
> . . . .
> the mind could begin to speak to pain
> and pain would have to answer:
> . . . .
> *I am the pain of division creators of divisions*
> *it is I who blot your lover from you*
> *and not the time-zones nor the miles*
> . . . .
> *I have no existence apart from you.*

In stanza two, the poet elaborates her choice "not to suffer uselessly yet still to feel," using as an analogue the bond between mother and infant. Perhaps the child feels the mother's absence and responds to it instinctively:

> Does the infant memorize the body of the mother
> and create her in absence? or simply cry
> primordial loneliness? does the bed of the stream
> once diverted mourning remember wetness?

"I will not be divided from her or from myself / by myths of separation," the poet declares emphatically. She refuses to see love in traditional terms, as powerlessness or selflessness:

> I want to crawl into her for refuge lay my head
> in the space between her breast and shoulder
> abnegating power for love
> as women have done or hiding
> from power in her love like a man
> I refuse these givens the splitting
> between love and action I am choosing
> not to suffer uselessly and not to use her
> I choose to love this time for once
> with all my intelligence.[94]

In choosing "to love this time for once / with all my intelligence," the poet redefines maternal and sexual love and re-visions love poetry. Her lover is a muse, but not one to be idealized or in whom to seek refuge. Instead, the poet claims the right to act *and* to love, to be "intelligent."

Rich's use of motherhood as a metaphor for poetic creativity can be seen in many poems from earlier volumes, in which she depicts woman giving birth to herself through her art. A powerful image of this sort occurs at the end of "The Mirror in Which Two Are Seen as One":

> In this mirror, who are you?
> . . . .
> Dreams of your sister's birth
> your mother dying in childbirth over and over
> not knowing how to stop
> bearing you over and over
>
> your mother dead and you unborn
> your two hands grasping your head
> drawing it down against the blade of life
> your nerves the nerves of a midwife
> learning her trade.[95]

As "a midwife learning her trade," Rich suggests, the woman poet must transform maternal fecundity into female creativity, relying for this rebirth not on her mother but on herself. This imagery of the artist as her own midwife is continued in *The Dream of a Common Language*, in which the woman poet often gives suckle to herself, feeds on the milk of her words. In "Cartographies of Silence," for example, Rich rejects traditional language in favor of a new form of communication as intense as an infant's gropings for her mother's breast:

> Let me have this dust,
> these pale clouds dourly lingering, these words
>
> moving with ferocious accuracy
> like the blind child's fingers
>
> or the newborn infant's mouth
> violent with hunger.[96]

In another poem, the artist Paula Becker says to her friend Clara Westhoff, "sometimes I feel / it is myself that kicks inside me, / myself I must give suck to, love . . ."[97] In each of these poems, the creative woman becomes her own mother-muse.

Rich expands this metaphor of woman bearing herself in "Transcendental Etude." As women, she suggests, we have been told "nothing, nothing / of origins, nothing we needed / to know, nothing that could re-member us." Instead, we are told

> Only: that it is unnatural,
> the homesickness for a woman, for ourselves,
> for that acute joy at the shadow her head and arms
> cast on a wall, her heavy or slender
> thighs on which we lay, flesh against flesh,
> eyes steady on the face of love; smell of her milk, her sweat,
> terror of her disappearance, all fused in this hunger

for the element they have called most dangerous, to be
lifted breathtaken on her breast, to rock within her
—even if beaten back, stranded again, to apprehend
in a sudden brine-clear thought
trembling like the tiny, orbed, endangered
egg-sac of a new world:
This is what she was to me, and this
is how I can love myself—
as only a woman can love me.

Erotic and maternal elements fuse here, as Rich contrasts what women are told with what they come to know by their own apprehension: that mother, lover, and daughter are wrapped in one strand of longing, that each is mirrored in the other. She further connects this re-vision of the self to poetic creativity:

Homesick for myself, for her—
. . . .
I am the lover and the loved,
home and wanderer, she who splits
firewood and she who knocks, a stranger
in the storm, two women, eye to eye
measuring each other's spirit, each other's
limitless desire,
a whole new poetry beginning here.[98]

It is the bonding of mother, lover, and poet, Rich suggests, that makes her poems breathe.

As these works illustrate, Rich frequently uses motherhood as a metaphor for female creativity. Understanding our relationships to the maternal muse, Rich believes, helps us as women understand and re-create ourselves, one another, and our art. "Before sisterhood there was the knowledge—transitory, fragmented, perhaps, but original and crucial—of mother-and-daughterhood."[99]

"*WITH WHOM DO YOU BELIEVE YOUR LOT IS CAST?*": *THE COMMUNAL MUSE*

This question reverberates throughout "The Spirit of Place," perhaps the most powerful poem in *A Wild Patience Has Taken Me This Far*:

it was not enough to name ourselves anew
when the spirit of the masters
calls the freedwoman to forget the slave

With whom do you believe your lot is cast?
if there's a conscience in these hills
it hurls that question
. . . .

no human figures now in sight
(with whom do you believe your lot is cast?)[100]

This haunting refrain recalls an earlier passage from "Natural Resources":

> I have to cast my lot with those
> who age after age, perversely,
>
> with no extraordinary power,
> reconstitute the world.[101]

Casting her lot with women is hardly new for Rich; for many years her poems have celebrated women as sources of inspiration. In "Halfway," a poem from the mid-1960s, for example, the poet gleans creative nourishment from her grandmother: "To sit by the fire is to become another woman, / red hair charring to grey, / . . . My days lie open, listening, grandmother."[102] In "For a Russian Poet," Rich "casts her lot" with Natalya Gorbanevskaya, the Russian poet imprisoned for the radicalism of her art: "I'm a ghost at your table / touching poems in a script I can't read / we'll meet each other later."[103] In "The Observer" a woman scientist "darkhaired, in stained jeans / sleeps in central Africa," the poet "envying the pale gorilla-scented dawn / she wakes into."[104] In "The Blue Ghazals" the poet draws sustenance from the African woman whom her art allows her to become: "An Ashanti woman tilts the flattened basin on her head / to let the water slide downward: I am that woman / and that water."[105] In "Blood-Sister," the poet speaks with her sister of "destruction and creation," as together they wait for summer in the desert, "where survival / takes naked and fiery forms."[106] Finally, "From an Old House in America" contains what is perhaps Rich's strongest early statement about female common identity: "Any woman's death diminishes me."[107]

In her more recent poetry Rich has invoked with renewed vigor and commitment a muse of commonality—a vision for, by, and about women. In "Phantasia for Elvira Shatayev," for example, she pays tribute to the members of a women's climbing team who died on Lenin Peak in the USSR in 1974. Spoken by their leader, Shatayev, this poem resonates with the power of a woman risktaker—poet or climber—who names herself and other women:

> If in this sleep I speak
> it's with a voice no longer personal
> (I want to say *with voices*)
> When the wind tore our breath from us at last
> we had no need of words
>
> . . . .
>
> What we were to learn was simply what we had
> up here as out of all words that *yes* gathered
> its forces fused itself and only just in time
> to meet a *No* of no degrees
> the black hole sucking the world in.

The "*yes*" that Shatayev and her companions discover affirms not only their readiness for the climb but also their respect and love for one another, for the "unbegun, / the possible." Significantly, Shatayev has left behind a diary, the recorded legacy of a woman writing about, to, and for women:

> In the diary I wrote: *Now we are ready*
> *and each of us knows it I have never loved*
> *like this I have never seen*
> *my own forces so taken up and shared*
> *and given back*
>
> . . . .
>
> *What does love mean*
> *what does it mean "to survive"*
> *A cable of blue fire ropes our bodies*
> *burning together in the snow We will not live*
> *to settle for less We have dreamed of this*
> *all of our lives.*[108]

Exploring love and survival in terms of women's bonds with one another, the woman poet contemplates what Rich elsewhere calls "the true nature of poetry. The drive / to connect. The dream of a common language."[109]

In *A Wild Patience Has Taken Me This Far*, Rich explores with even greater intensity the need for women to "inspirit each other."[110] Embodied in the phrase "*nothing but myself? . . . my selves*," Rich's collective female and feminist voice informs nearly every poem in this volume. Here she challenges women's "amnesia"—their fearful denial of prototypical power by glorifying, sentimentalizing, whiting out the "true" experience of their foremothers and themselves.[111] One effort at avoiding amnesia can be seen in "Grandmothers," as the poet tries to describe the persons her grandmothers *were*, not what she would have liked them to be:

> Easier to encapsulate your lives
> in a slide-show of impressions given and taken,
> . . . .
> than to write in words in which you might have found
> yourselves, looked up at me and said
> "Yes, I was like that; but I was something more . . ."[112]

In "Heroines," Rich also invokes "as they were" her nineteenth-century literary foremothers, to whom she owes both tribute and restitution, yet toward whom she feels ambivalent:

> how can I give you
>   all your due
>   take courage from your courage
> honor your exact
>   legacy as it is
> recognizing
>   as well
>   that it is not enough?[113]

In "The Spirit of Place," she comes to terms with Emily Dickinson, thrice a muse, here approached in a powerful new way. "This is my third and last address to you," Rich tells Dickinson, and she goes on to describe the network of connections through which women serve one another as sources of inspiration:

> with the hands of a daughter I would cover you
> from all intrusion   even my own
> saying   rest to your ghost
>
> with the hands of a sister I would leave your hands
> open or closed as they prefer to lie
> and ask no more of who or why or wherefore
>
> with the hands of a mother I would close the door
> on the room you've left behind
> and silently pick up my fallen work.[114]

In *Women Writers and Poetic Identity*, Margaret Homans objects to those images in Rich's poems that she considers an inadvertent return to "female passivity."[115] Especially troublesome to Homans is Rich's image of a woman sheathed in silence, going quietly about her household work. As Joanne Feit Diehl has suggested, however, Rich uses such images to "convert ordinariness into mythos," to assert a gentle power, for "gentleness is active." Figures like the woman at the end of "The Spirit of Place," "silently [picking] up my fallen work," epitomize for her a new mythos of creative woman, quiet and potent in her chosen environs.[116]

The last poem sequence in *A Wild Patience*, "Turning the Wheel," brings together numerous images of women's community and inspiration. The "selves-consciousness" of women who "hear each other into speech" represents the woman poet's greatest source of creative power, Rich suggests; yet this consciousness of ourselves in other women must not negate their particularity, for from such amnesia could emerge a false history.[117] In "Burden Baskets" Rich acknowledges the dangers of invoking and mythologizing the ordinary woman according to one's own singular vision, which may be extraordinary, racist, or simply wrong. She also reveals her mistrust of the poet's tool, language; her doubts as to its potential for re-visioning; her awareness of its dangerous dual power—for concealing, for revealing:

> False history gets written every day
> and by some who should know better:
> the lesbian archaeologist watches herself
> sifting her own life out from the shards she's piecing,
> asking the clay all questions but her own.
> Yet suddenly for once the standard version
> splits open to something shocking, unintentional.
> . . . .
>   behind glass, without notation
> in the anthropologist's typewritten text
> which like a patient voice tired of explaining
> goes on to explain a different method of weaving.[118]

Imaging herself as a "lesbian archaeologist," an "anthropologist" trying to "explain a different method of weaving," Rich struggles to interpret texts that paradoxically both evade the truths of women's experience and attempt to assert those truths. Nostalgic recollection of women's pasts is inadequate, Rich continues; it is "only amnesia turned around." To speak for other women is a task fraught with potential danger and dishonesty.

Rich overcomes this dishonesty and suggests a model by which women poets can avoid the danger of amnesia by invoking two key female muse figures: the "desert-shamaness," who appears in part three of "Turning the Wheel" and recurs in parts five and six, and Mary Jane Colter, the woman architect who speaks in part seven. The shamaness, Rich explains in "Holokam," is a Hopi or a Navaho woman, one of "those who have ceased," according to placards in the Southwest Museum. But Rich refuses to let the shamaness "cease," even though to call her forth after years of non-entity is both risky and difficult:

> I try to imagine a desert-shamaness
> bringing water to fields of squash, maize and cotton
> but where the desert herself is half-eroded
> half-flooded by a million jets of spray
> to conjure a rich white man's paradise
> the shamaness could well have withdrawn her ghost.[119]

This muse "could well have withdrawn," Rich realizes, but instead she hovers still within the range of pursuit. Yet if she is to be pursued, Rich cautions, she must be acknowledged not as an archetype but as a prototype: an original, model form. As prototype, she will be "open to transformation," offering "similar patterns of experiencing *to* others, rather than imposing these patterns *on* others."[120] As a metaphor for female inspiration and vision, the shamaness will become a vital source of energy for the woman poet.

For further inspiration Rich turns to Mary Jane Colter, an American architect at the turn of the century who designed eight buildings at the Grand Canyon, all of which are still standing. The woman architect, Rich implies, does what the archaeologist and the anthropologist find difficult: she creates totally new structures, not ignoring the old but neither relying upon them. Colter reveals her goals in a letter written to her mother and sister:

> I have been asked
> to design a building in the Hopi style
> at the Grand Canyon. . . .
> I am here already, trying to make a start.
> I cannot tell you with what elation
> this commission has filled me. I regret to say
> it will mean I cannot come home to St. Paul
> as I hoped this spring. I am hoping this may lead
> to other projects here, of equal grandeur,
> (Do you understand? I want this glory,

I want to place my own conception
and that of the Indians whose land this was
at the edge of this incommensurable thing.)
. . . .

You will never lack
for what I can give you.[121]

As Diehl has noted, Rich often explores "the conventional aspects of language close to speech, in which secrets are laid open and wishes too long silent, find their voice."[122] Mary Jane Colter is hardly ordinary in one sense; her accomplishments were extraordinary for her day or for any age. But in her deep feeling and direct expression, she serves as both muse and mouthpiece for a poet asserting a mythology of ordinariness, a "shared mythology."

In part eight of "Turning the Wheel," Rich comes full circle on her journey "to the female core of a continent." On the road to the Grand Canyon, the poet imagines herself as "travelling to the edge to meet the face / of annihilating and impersonal time / stained in the colors of a woman's genitals." But Rich refuses annihilation, impersonality. Instead, she "turns the wheel," embracing a new course of feminist action and re-creation.[123] As she explains in "Conditions for Work," women must now rely on one another if they are to attain and sustain creative power: "We can challenge and inspirit each other, throw light on one another's blind spots, stand by and give courage at the birth throes of one another's insights."[124] As part of this shared feminist enterprise, Rich has invoked in her poetry a re-visioned female muse: maternal, communal, our selves. And in so doing, she herself has become a muse for many women poets who have come after her.

"Sisters in Pain": The Warrior Muse of Audre Lorde

"*To whom do I owe the symbols of my survival*?" Audre Lorde asks at the beginning of *Zami*, her "biomythography"; "*to whom do I owe the woman I have become*?" Her answer pays tribute to the women who have inspired her—as mothers, sisters, lovers, goddesses, muses. "Images of women flaming like torches adorn and define the borders of my journey, stand like dykes between me and the chaos. It is the images of women, kind and cruel, that lead me home"—home to what Lorde calls "the journeywoman pieces of myself."[1]

This struggle to name the female self as a "black lesbian feminist warrior poet" forms the core of Audre Lorde's poetry and poetics. As she explains in an interview with the writer Claudia Tate, her creative energy comes from being outspoken about these diverse parts of herself:

> With respect to myself specifically, I feel that not to be open about any of the different "people" within my identity, particularly the "mes" who are challenged by a status quo, is to invite myself and other women, by my example, to live a lie. In other words, I would be giving in to a myth of sameness which I think can destroy us.[2]

Different aspects of one's self, differences between ourselves and other women, must be seen as an opportunity for dialogue, Lorde argues. "We need to use these differences in constructive ways, creative ways, rather than in ways to justify our destroying each other"—as black and white women have sometimes done, she continues, through an allegiance to patriarchal myths of sameness and separation. An affirmation of self and an understanding of other women, she concludes, are essential for survival, particularly for the black lesbian writer: "I learned to speak the truth by accepting many parts of myself and making them serve one another. This power fuels my life and my work."[3]

For Lorde, as for many women of color, this celebration and assertion of female identity has been a key survival technique, a way of combatting a subtle but potent enemy: silence. As Lorde tells us in *Zami*, she did not speak until she was five years old, and when she finally found a voice, she talked in poetry—first by reciting verses she had memorized, then "when I couldn't find the poems to express the things I was feeling, that's when I started writing poetry."[4] To Lorde, poetry represents a refusal of "dishonesty by silence"; her foremost goal as a black woman poet then becomes "the transformation of silence into language and action"—a transformation essential if women are to overcome what Adrienne Rich has called "the terrible negative power of the lie" among them. Silence is a destructive quality, Lorde asserts, because "it's the nameless. As Adrienne has said, 'what remains nameless eventually becomes unspeakable, what remains unspoken becomes unspeakable.' "[5] To speak the unspeakable is thus a key task for Lorde as for Rich, to re-vision herself and other women.

In "A Song for Many Movements," Lorde explores poetically this issue of destructive silence transformed into constructive feminist action:

> Broken down gods survive
> in the crevasses and mudpots
> of every beleaguered city
> where it is obvious
> there are too many bodies
> to cart to the ovens
> or gallows
> and our uses have become
> more important than our silence
> after the fall
> too many empty cases
> of blood to bury or burn
> there will be no body left
> to listen
> and our labor
> has become more important
> than our silence.
> Our labor has become
> more important
> than our silence.[6]

For writers like H.D. and Louise Bogan—early modern poets and white women—silence is potentially an aesthetic stance from which, paradoxically, to speak. But for Lorde and other women of color, silence can signify only powerlessness, oppression, that which must be vanquished by "our uses . . . our labor." Of course, for such women, speech can be dangerous, as Lorde reveals in "Coal." Although some words "open like a diamond / on glass windows," others "live in my throat / breeding like adders"—they "bedevil me." Yet silence is not an alternative, the poet implies, for it conceals, entraps. Speech, in contrast, is always open and may be brilliant, like a jewel:

As the diamond comes into a knot of flame
I am Black because I come from the earth's inside
Now take my word for jewel in the open light.[7]

Only through words, then, is self-definition possible, the poet's labor useful.

Lorde's reliance in "A Song for Many Movements" on the plural pronoun—"our labor" / "our silence"—further reflects her emphasis on women's community. Like Rich, she perceives her voice as multifaceted, her self as "our selves." "I write for myself," she explains to Tate, but also

> for as many people as possible who can read me, who need to hear what I have to say—who need to use what I know. When I say myself, I mean not only the Audre who inhabits my body but all those feisty, incorrigible black women who insist on standing up and saying "I *am* and you cannot wipe me out, no matter how irritating I am, how much you fear what I might represent." I write for these women for whom a voice has not yet existed, or whose voices have been silenced. I don't have the only voice or all of their voices, but they are a part of my voice, and I am a part of theirs.

Men have had many spokespersons, Lorde continues, but "there are very few voices for women and particularly very few voices for black women, speaking from the center of consciousness, from the *I am* out to the *we are* and then out to the *we can*."[8] Silence thus revitalized as communal language and political action becomes a key source of female energy and power.

The role of poetry in such an endeavor is for Lorde essential, for poetry is "not a luxury":

> Poetry is an absolute necessity of our living because it delineates . . . is the beginning of that process by which we insure the future because we know so much more than we understand. . . . We have been taught how to understand, and in terms that will insure not creativity but the status quo. If we are looking for something which is new and something which is vital, we must look first into the chaos within ourselves.[9]

Often, she asserts, getting in touch with the chaos inside is the first step in asserting a feminist voice and vision. For Lorde, art is not possible without such vision; there is no "art for art's sake":

> I see protest as a genuine means of encouraging someone to feel the inconsistencies, the horror of the lives we are living. . . . What I saw was wrong, and I had to speak up. I loved poetry, and I loved words. But what was beautiful had to serve the purpose of changing my life, or I would have died. If I cannot air this pain and alter it, I will surely die of it. That's the beginning of social protest.[10]

Always, Lorde believes, the political begins with the personal, the need to recognize and confront what is "intolerable" in our lives, and poetry is one major means of such confrontation. Initiating this crucial dialogue with one's self and with others, she insists, "is the way in which the philosopher-queen, the poet-warrior leads."[11]

Another primary aspect of the "poet-warrior's" task is paying tribute to the women from whom she gleans her power, "recreating in words the women who helped give me substance."[12] In Lorde's writing of the last twenty-five years, we find four main sources of creative inspiration, all female. First, she celebrates as muses the women who make up her own family: her mother, her mother's West Indian female relatives, and her sisters, literal or figurative. Second, she pays homage to the women lovers who have "helped sustain" her, and to her own erotic power, which she considers a vital creative force. Third, she seeks sustenance from African goddesses, mythological women whose names and legends survive in black cultures as tributes to a strong matriarchal legacy: Yemanja, Mawulisa, Seboulisa, the "Women of Dan," her African warrior sisters. Finally, Lorde names as muses and acts as a mouthpiece for those women who have been victims of a racist, sexist, homophobic society—her "sisters in pain." Many such women have been violated, murdered, silenced, yet it is for and by them that the poet-warrior is empowered to speak. If women, black or white, are to survive, Lorde insists in "Meet," they must bring to bear on behalf of one another their passionate convictions, their powerful eroticism, their terrible anguish, their fluid and mutual identities:

When we meet again
will you put your hands upon me
will I ride you over our lands
will we sleep beneath trees in the rain?
You shall get young as I lick your stomach
hot and at rest before we move off again
you will be white fury in my navel
I will be sweeping night
Mawulisa foretells our bodies
as our hands touch and learn
from each others hurt.
Taste my milk in the ditches of Chile and Ouagadougou
in Tema's bright port while the priestess of Larteh
protects us
in the high meat stalls of Palmyra and Abomey-Calavi
now you are my child and my mother
we have always been sisters in pain.[13]

The first muse figure whom Lorde recognizes is the mother—her biological mother, Linda Belmar Lorde, and what she calls "the black mother who is the poet in every one of us." In her interview with Hammond, Lorde identifies her parents, but especially her mother, as powerful forces of inspiration, even though their teachings were sometimes "blind and terrible," "distorted":

> They kept me alive and that in *itself*, as I say in "Outside," is vital—that they did so against such terrific odds and gave me enough strength to seek my own language is their primary lesson—one of survival. Poetry was something I learned from my mother's strangenesses and from my father's silences. I learned from my mother's passion.[14]

The poem to which Lorde refers, "Outside" from *The Black Unicorn*, reveals her parents' strong influence on her life and art. "I grew up in a genuine confusion," Lorde explains as the poem begins—over distinctions between "grass and weeds and flowers," over "what colored meant." Much of this confusion came, Lorde believes, from her parents' "very private furies," which the child could not comprehend. The adult, however, needs and seeks such understanding if she is to name herself as black, as woman, and as poet:

> Who shall I curse that I grew up
> believing in my mother's face
> or that I live in fear of potent darkness
> wearing my father's shape
> they have both marked me
> with their blind and terrible love
> and I am lustful now for my own name.

At the same time she remonstrates her parents for the fears she inherited, however, Lorde acknowledges the crucial nature of their legacy:

> Between the canyons of their mighty silences
> mother bright and father brown
> I seek my own shapes now
> for they never spoke of me
> except as theirs
> and the pieces I stumble and fall over
> I still record as proof
> that I am beautiful
> twice
> blessed with the images
> of who they were
> and who I thought them once to be.

The poem ends on an affirmative note, as the poet integrates her parents' versions of her and her own re-vision of self and selves:

> I am blessed within my selves
> who are come to make our shattered faces
> whole.[15]

For Lorde, then, as for H.D., Sarton, Rich, and numerous other women poets, her mother has been a key source of creative nurture. Even though "the rhythms of my mother's voice telling about West Indian fruit she never called poetry," Lorde's mother nonetheless had a special relationship to language, which she passed on to her poet-daughter. From her mother, Lorde explains in an interview with Rich, she learned "the important value of nonverbal communication, beneath language," as well as "a strange way with words": "if a word didn't serve her or wasn't strong enough, she'd just make up another word, and then that word would enter our family language forever, and woe betide any of us who forgot it."[16] Her mother was the first poet Lorde knew, the person from whom she learned the complexities of language and its passions: "*I am a reflection of my mother's secret poetry as well as of her hidden angers.*"[17]

Two early poems illustrate the poet's ambivalent but powerful creative link to her mother. "Story Books on a Kitchen Table" is an angry poem, blameful of the mother's "deceits," of her inability or unwillingness to provide her adolescent daughter with a potent black female model:

> Out of her womb of pain my mother spat me
> into her ill-fitting harness of despair
> into her deceits
> where anger re-conceived me
> piercing my eyes like arrows
> pointed by her nightmare
> of who I was not
> becoming.[18]

The mother here has been appropriated by the white patriarchy, Lorde implies; as a disempowered woman, she seeks to make her daughter whiter—and thus, for Lorde, weaker—than she. Like Sylvia Plath in "The Disquieting Muses," the mother's betrayal causes the poet-daughter to be attended by frightening, ghostly women—for Plath, "three ladies / Nodding by night around my bed, / Mouthless, eyeless, with stitched bald head"; for Lorde, "iron maidens," "white witches" who bring her nightmares during the day and feed her "the wrinkled milk of legend."[19] The black girl's need for racial and sexual affirmation, for a black mother's warmth rather than the cold distance of her horrifying white substitutes, is apparent in the poet's vivid rendering of her adolescent fantasy:

> . . . I wandered through the lonely rooms of afternoon
> wrapped in nightmares
> from the Orange and Red and Yellow
> Purple and Blue and Green
> Fairy Books
> where white witches ruled
> over the empty kitchen table
> and never wept
> or offered gold
> nor any kind enchantment
> for the vanished mother
> of a Black girl.[20]

A slightly later poem, "Black Mother Woman," offers a more sympathetic tribute to Lorde's mother, whose "heavy love" and "myths of little worth" have restricted the poet-daughter. The black mother is angry at the white culture, which devalues and abuses her, but she has no power base from which to fight back. Thus she turns her fury on her daughter, "binding her feet" and teaching her lies. As an adult, the daughter can recognize her mother's entrapment and refuse such victimization for herself. Her struggle to claim identity and voice is not without conflict, Lorde explains, but it is nourished by her mother's "core of love":

> But I have peeled away your anger
> down to the core of love
> and look mother
> I Am
> a dark temple where your true spirit rises
> beautiful
> and tough as chestnut
> stanchion against your nightmare of weakness
> and if my eyes conceal
> a squadron of conflicting rebellions
> I learned from you
> to define myself
> through your denials.[21]

Aware of the "true spirit" of her mother within her, the poet celebrates her blackness and her womanhood: "I Am / a dark temple." This act of empowerment would have been impossible without her mother's legacy, albeit a legacy of "denials." As Lorde says in "The Woman Thing," the daughter's understandings of herself—her affirmations and her negations—are grounded in the teachings of her mother:

> Meanwhile
> the woman thing my mother taught me
> bakes off its covering of snow
> like a rising blackening sun.[22]

Like Rich in *Of Woman Born*, Lorde argues that patriarchal society is responsible for much of the conflict women often feel toward their mothers. As women, she explains, "we were taught to suspect each other, and it begins between mother and daughter." For black women in particular, "this occurs in a situation of grave oppression where oppression comes not just because you're a woman so much as because you're Black, and because you are a Black Woman. It's triple jeopardy." Her mother's love continues to be a potent force in her life and art, Lorde admits, yet she wishes it could have been "a more gentle love, a love that my mother and I could have spoken across and gotten more comfort from."[23] Despite her ambivalence, however, Lorde admits that she even sounds like her mother, whether she wants to or not. Sometimes, she tells Hammond, "I open my mouth . . . and I hear coming out of my deepest heart's words my mother's voice and it beats the shit out of me." Yet when she speaks from her mother's voice, Lorde explains in *Zami*, she always listens:

> *When the strongest words for what I have to offer come out of me sounding like words I remember from my mother's mouth, then I either have to reassess the meaning of everything I have to say now, or re-examine the worth of her old words.*[24]

Such reexaminations, Lorde asserts in "Prologue," make her a more tolerant parent as well as a more honest poetic voice:

My mother survives now
through more than a chance or token.
Although she will read what I write with embarrassment
or anger
and a small understanding
my children do not need to relive my past
in strength nor in confusion
nor care that their holy fires
may destroy
more than my failures.

Through her own pained yet loving words, reminiscent often of her mother's, Lorde concludes, "I shall leave a dark print / of the me that I am / and who I am not / etched in a shadow of angry and remembered loving."[25]

Lorde is given creative energy not only by the words and memories of her mother, but also by the images she recalls of her mother's female relatives, the West Indian aunts and grandmothers and sisters whose names and stories have helped her to survive. The title of her biomythography, *Zami*, is a Carriacou word "for women who work together as friends and lovers"—women similar to those in the poet's own family. In *Zami*, Lorde pays homage to these Grenadian matriarchs and to other women who captured her youthful imagination:

> *Ma-Liz, Delois, Louise Briscoe, Aunt Anna, Linda, and Genevieve; MawuLisa, thunder, sky, sun, the great mother of us all; and Afrekete, her youngest daughter, the mischievous linguist, trickster, best-beloved, whom we must all become. . . .* Their names, selves, faces feed me like corn before labor. I live each of them as a piece of me, and I choose these words with the same grave concern with which I choose to push speech into poetry, the mattering core, the forward visions of all our lives.[26]

Through her matriarchal legacy, Lorde has learned to celebrate the centrality of the bonds among a family's women:

> *I have felt the age-old triangle of mother father and child, with the "I" at its eternal core, elongate and flatten out into the elegantly strong triad of grandmother mother daughter, with the "I" moving back and forth flowing in either or both directions as needed.*[27]

As is true for the mother-daughter bond, the connections between sisters can cause either great joy or great pain. Relationships between adult sisters, both Rich and Lorde tell us, are especially complex, for they were nurtured at the same woman's breast, grew up in that woman's household; thus they serve one another as powerful links to that infant past. Rich presents this connection poignantly and sensuously in "Sibling Mysteries":

Remind me how we loved our mother's body
our mouths drawing the first
thin sweetness from her nipples

Our faces dreaming hour on hour
in the salt smell of her lap Remind me
how her touch melted childgrief

. . . .

Tell me again because I need to hear.[28]

Lorde feels strong ambivalence toward her sister, largely because she reminds the poet of the pain of growing up a black girl in a racist society. In "A Family Resemblance," Lorde's sister mirrors her former self:

My sister has my hair my mouth my eyes
and I presume her trustless.
When she was young and open to any fever
wearing gold like a veil of fortune on her face
she waited through each rain a dream of light.
But the sun came up
burning our eyes like crystal
bleaching the sky of promise and
my sister stood
Black, unblessed and unbelieving
shivering in the first cold show of love.

Like the poet as a young woman, her sister was exposed to "cold" love, a love that devalued her black identity and "bleached" her strength. Now, Lorde laments, her sister's gold has "wandered from her bed"; refusing to embrace her blackness, through "echoes of denial / she walks a bleached side of reason." Sadly, the poet invokes this "double" only to reject her:

My sister has my tongue
and all my flesh
unanswered
and I presume her trustless
as a stone.[29]

Another sororal portrait appears in "Harriet," which celebrates the sisters' closeness before their fall from innocence but laments their inevitable separation at the hands of a racist society:

Harriet there was always somebody calling us crazy
or mean or stuck-up or evil or black
or black
and we were
nappy girls quick as cuttlefish
scurrying for cover
trying to speak trying to speak
trying to speak

the pain in each others mouths
until we learned
on the edge of a lash
or a tongue
on the edge of the other's betrayal
that respect
meant keeping our distance
in silence
averting our eyes
from each other's face in the street
from the beautiful dark mouth
and cautious familiar eyes
passing alone.

Before they learn to mistrust each other, the sisters band together against the outside, trying to form a mutually protective cocoon from which to withstand the insults hurled at them. But as they confront the pain of their own efforts to find voice—"trying to speak" is repeated three times—the sisters experience a new isolation. Unable to communicate in words except by multiple tongue lashings, the sisters come to define each other as a peculiarly familiar enemy. Lorde illustrates this tragic separation through her punctuation: "each others" has no apostrophe at first, as the sisters' "otherness" unites them, but once the "betrayal" begins, "others" (plural) gives way to "other's" (singular possessive): "the other's betrayal," "each other's face." Yet however strong the forces of division, Lorde concludes, they cannot negate totally the sister's familial and racial connections:

I remember you Harriet
before we were broken apart
we dreamed the crossed swords
of warrior queens
while we avoided each other's eyes
and we learned to know lonely
as the earth learns to know dead
Harriet Harriet
what name shall we call our selves now
our mother is gone? [30]

For Lorde, then, it is essential to invoke as muses women from her own life. "The relationships I have had," she explains to Tate, "in which people kept me alive, helped sustain me, were sustained by me, were particular relationships. They gave me my particular identity, which is the source of my energy. Not to deal with my life in my art is to cut out the fount of my strength."[31] In addition to honoring her mother and her female family members, Lorde also acknowledges the creative energy she has found in her women lovers and in her own eroticism. As she has indicated frequently in interviews, her series of essays entitled *Uses of the Erotic* was crucial in developing her understanding of the close link between her sexual and her poetic creativity. The most pivotal of these essays, "The Erotic as Power," reveals much about Lorde's re-visionist use of the term "erotic" and about her erotic manifestation of the muse. "The erotic is a resource within each of us," Lorde begins her essay, "that lies in a deeply female and spiritual plane, firmly rooted in the power of our unexpressed or unrecognized feeling." Despite this power, or more likely because of it, women have been taught to suppress their erotic sense, to define it exclusively in terms of the sexual. Instead, Lorde argues, women must experience the erotic not only during sexual union but "in all our endeavors." Through the erotic, she explains, "my work becomes a conscious decision—a longed-for bed which I enter gratefully and from which I rise up empowered." The erotic, then, is "an assertion of the life-force of women; of that creative energy empowered, the knowledge and use of which we are now reclaiming in our language, our history, our dancing, our loving, our work, our lives."[32]

An early poem that illustrates the link between female eroticism and creativity is "Love Poem," in which the poet-lover becomes an earth mother–creator on and in the body of her beloved. The poem begins with a prayer for richness and honey:

Speak earth and bless me with what is richest
make sky flow honey out of my hips
rigid as mountains
spread over a valley
carved out by the mouth of rain.

Through her union with her lover, the poet creates the sky from her hips, valleys from her mouth; she becomes "high wind in her forests hollow / fingers whispering sound." Heady with her procreative power, the poet celebrates her erotic connection to her lover and the universe:

Greedy as herring-gulls
or a child
I swing out over the earth
over and over
again.[33]

Several other poems illustrate Lorde's view of the power of the erotic. In "Woman," for example, the lover is imaged again as an earth mother by whom the poet is nourished, a foundation on which her female core comes to rest:

I dream of a place between your breasts
to build my house like a haven
where I plant crops
in your body
an endless harvest
where the commonest rock
is moonstone and ebony opal
giving milk to all of my hungers
and your night comes down upon me
like a nurturing rain.[34]

In another poem, "Walking Our Boundaries," the poet records a painful moment between lovers after an argument. Yet even in their sadness, their small voices "too tentative for women / so in love," the women are sustained by the home they share and the mutuality that empowers them:

> Our footsteps hold this place
> together
> as our place
> our joint decisions make the possible
> whole.[35]

And in "Meet," the lover promises to provide her beloved with light and heat, energy that both amazes and illuminates:

> Coming to rest
> in the open mirrors of your demanded body
> I will be black light as you lie against me
> I will be heavy as August over your hair
> our rivers flow from the same sea
> and I promise to leave you again
> full of amazement and our illuminations
> dealt through the short tongues of color
> or the taste of each other's skin as it hung
> from our childhood mouths.[36]

The poem that most closely establishes the interdependence of eroticism and creativity is "Recreation," in which the lovers transform bodily images and translate "word countries."

> Coming together
> it is easier to work
> after our bodies
> meet
> paper and pen
> neither care nor profit
> whether we write or not
> but as your body moves
> under my hands
> charged and waiting
> we cut the leash
> you create me against your thighs
> hilly with images
> moving through our word countries.

As the poet's words become flesh, so the lover's flesh becomes words:

> my body
> writes into your flesh
> the poem
> you make of me.[37]

Not all of Lorde's love poems are fully celebratory, however. In "From the Greenhouse," for instance, she suffers at the lover's muteness and remoteness even as she lies near:

My blood yells against
your sleeping shoulder
this is a poem of summer
my blood screams at your false safety
your mute body beside me
driving me closer and closer
you seek your own refuge
farther and farther away
in your dreaming.[38]

Similarly, in "Letter for Jan" she challenges her former lover's fear of eroticism and the form this fear takes: silence and mistrust.

No, I don't think you were chicken not to speak
I think you
afraid I was mama as laser
seeking to eat out or change your substance
Mawulisa bent on destruction by threat.[39]

Yet even these poems, for all their anger and despair, affirm the speaker's sexual and creative energy, her power to withstand and to renew. In "From the Greenhouse," neither the lover's silence nor the rain surging outside keeps the poet from seeking and finding intimacy: "I have moved as far as I can / now my blood merges / into your dreaming." In "Letter for Jan" the affirmation of the erotic self is directly related to poetic rejuvenation:

we touch each other in secret places
draw old signs and stories
upon each other's back and proofread
each other's ancient copy.

Ultimately rejected by the "Jan" of the poem, the speaker remains sad but undaunted; she continues to sing and to encourage her lover to find voice.

I would have loved you
speaking
being a woman full of loving
turned on
and a little bit raunchy
and heavy
with my own black song.[40]

Her references to her "own black song" and to Mawulisa, omnipotent creator of life for the Dahomey peoples of Western Africa, suggest a third type of muse that Lorde invokes: the Amazons and goddesses of Africa.[41] In "Scar," Lorde describes vividly a Dahomean Amazon in all her fierce erotic power:

This is a simple poem
sharing my head with dreams
of a big black woman with jewels in her eyes
she dances
her head in a golden helmet
arrogant
plumed
her name is Colossa
her thighs are like stanchions
of flayed hickory trees
embraced in armour
she dances
slow earth-shaking motions
that suddenly alter
and lighten
as she whirls laughing
the tooled metal over her hips
comes to an end
and at the shiny edge
an astonishment
of soft black curly hair.[42]

In this as in other poems from *The Black Unicorn*, Lorde presents an African goddess of and through whom she is empowered to speak. Lorde has refused to anthologize or divide this volume because she considers it "a sequence/conversation that cannot yet be breached," and indeed nearly every poem contributes to an essential dialogue with these sources of inspiration.[43] But Lorde began paying homage to goddesses before *The Black Unicorn* was published. In "When the Saints Come Marching In," for example, Lorde offers an ironic yet powerful tribute to the "god" through whom the poverty and waste of New York City might yet be redeemed. Since "plentiful sacrifice and believers in redemption" are all it takes for a new faith to emerge, she claims wryly, "any day now / I expect some new religion / to rise up like tear gas / from the streets of New York." But the "high priests" who lie in wait for such an event are in for a surprise, Lorde concludes; the new "god" will be "terrible"—elderly, preoccupied, and female:

I do not know the rituals
the exhaltations
nor what name of the god
the survivors will worship
I only know she will be terrible
and very busy
and very old.[44]

In turning to the myths of Africa, Lorde celebrates specifically those goddesses responsible for creation. In "The Winds of Orisha" lie the seeds of *The Black Unicorn*, as the poet proclaims her connection to Yemanja, goddess of oceans and mother of the Orisha, the divine personification of the Yoruba peoples of Western Nigeria.

> Impatient legends speak through my flesh
> changing this earths formation
> spreading
> I will become myself
> an incantation
> dark raucous many-shaped characters
> leaping back and forth across bland pages
> and Mother Yemanja raises her breasts to begin my labor
> near water
> the beautiful Oshun and I lie down together
> in the heat of her body truth my voice comes stronger.[45]

The poet seeks to "become myself" through "the incantation," the act of creating poetry, whose analogue here is a sexual interaction with Oshun, a sensual Yoruba river deity.[46] This ritual of female affirmation is overseen by "Mother Yemanja," who gives birth to the poet-daughter as she once did the Orisha. As the goddess must "labor" to bear her daughter, so the daughter will work to tell the forgotten tales of the Orisha's struggles:

> I will swell up from the pages of their daily heralds
> leaping out of the almanacs
> instead of an answer to their search for rain they will read me
> the dark cloud
> meaning something entire
> and different.
>
> When the winds of Orisha blow
> even the roots of grass
> quicken.[47]

As Lorde explains in her notes to *The Black Unicorn*, Yemanja is foremost among the Orisha, a "goddess of oceans" from whose breasts rivers flow and thus a powerful symbol of female creativity. Yemanja appears as a central figure in *The Black Unicorn*, at times merging with the poet's biological mother, at other times fusing with the speaker herself, a warrior goddess in communion with other Amazons. "From the House of Yemanja" illustrates this goddess's dual guise. Her own mother, the poet explains, "had two faces and a frying pot / where she cooked up her daughters / into girls / before she fixed our dinner." As the mother was plagued by an oppressive duality, so the daughter:

I bear two women upon my back
one dark and rich and hidden
in the ivory hungers of the other
mother
pale as a witch
yet steady and familiar
brings me bread and terror
in my sleep
her breasts are huge exciting anchors
in the midnight storm.

Frightened yet aroused by the double image before her, the dark mother and the pale witch, the poet asks Yemanja to help her assert her black female identity:

Mother I need
mother I need
mother I need your blackness now
as the august earth needs rain.

The haunting repetition emphasizes the desperation of the daughter's plight. With her mother's blackness, the blackness of Yemanja, the poet will "rise up empowered," become whole. But without the mother's aid, Lorde concludes, she will remain

the sun and moon and forever hungry
the sharpened edge
where day and night shall meet
and not be
one.[48]

In several poems Yemanja is replaced by Seboulisa, mother-goddess of Abomey, legendary capital of the ancient kingdom of Dahomey and home of the famed Panther kings and Amazon queens. As "Mother of us all," Seboulisa (also called Mawulisa) offers a powerful model of female creation for the black woman poet. In "Dahomey," Lorde celebrates Seboulisa as a mother of both sorrow and magic, a sorceress who will help her daughter find a language from which to speak.

It was in Abomey that I felt
the full blood of my fathers' wars
and where I found my mother
Seboulisa
standing with outstretched palms hip high
one breast eaten away by worms of sorrow
magic stones resting upon her fingers
dry as a cough.[49]

Bereft of one breast yet nonetheless powerful and erotic, Seboulisa inspires the poet to become as Thunder, "a woman with braided hair," roaring her dangerous song for all who need to hear.[50]

> Bearing two drums on my head I speak
> whatever language is needed
> to sharpen the knives of my tongue
> the snake is aware although sleeping
> under my blood
> since I am a woman whether or not
> you are against me
> I will braid my hair
> even
> in the seasons of rain.[51]

According to Dahomean lore, Seboulisa rode in the mouth of her loyal snake, Aido Hwedo, as she created the world. Once her work was finished, the goddess, alarmed by the earth's heaviness, ordered the snake to crawl under the world and "hold up the weight of the earth so that it shall never fall."[52] Thus supported, Seboulisa could turn her attention to herself and her peoples.

Seboulisa is invoked again as muse in "125th Street and Abomey," a poem that, as the title suggests, fuses the ancient Dahomean capital with an ambivalent but familiar American landscape. As the poem opens, the speaker celebrates Seboulisa, present in the "foreign" territory of Manhattan:

> Head bent, walking through snow
> I see you Seboulisa
> printed inside the back of my head
> like marks of the newly wrapped akai
> that kept my sleep fruitful in Dahomey
> and I poured on the red earth in your honor
> those ancient parts of me
> most precious and least needed
> my well-guarded past
> the energy-eating secrets
> I surrender to you as libation,
> mother.

In the past, the poet tells us, she has been frightened, silent, reluctant "to whistle in the night." But encountering the mother-goddess on her own turf lets her speak. Claiming now her selves as "my warrior sisters / who rode in defense of your queendom," the poet calls upon Seboulisa to "give me the woman strength / of tongue in this cold season." Without the goddess's blessing, she implies, silence will reign in the city and bloodshed will perhaps loom eminent. But through the mother-goddess's strength, Lorde learns not only to speak—forcefully, vitally—but also to laugh:

Seboulisa mother goddess with one breast
eaten away by worms of sorrow and loss
see me now
your severed daughter
laughing our name into echo
all the world shall remember.[53]

Like Seboulisa, the poet is black, one-breasted, creative, incorrigible. Despite conflicts and losses, mother and daughter echo one another, laughing together and thereby re-membering themselves.

The female creative quest also provides the subject for "The Women of Dan Dance with Swords in Their Hands to Mark the Time When They Were Warriors." As Karla Hammond has noted, Lorde's poems are filled with images of women warriors: "warrior queens" ("Harriet"); "like a warrior woman" ("Chorus"); "like my warrior sisters" ("125th Street and Abomey"); "Assata my sister warrior" ("For Assata"). At times the epithet "warrior" becomes an emblem of hope for the future generations of women: "I bless your child with the mother she has / with a future of warriors and growing fire" ("Dear Toni Instead of a Letter").[54] In celebrating the women warriors of Dan, an ancient name for Dahomey, Lorde enacts a particularly strong re-visionist impulse, for she insists that these warriors be not "secret" but open, vulnerable. "I come as a woman," Lorde proclaims repeatedly, no longer a "secret warrior / with an unsheathed sword in my mouth / hidden behind my tongue / slicing my throat to ribbons." Instead, her weapons are erotic heat and poetic words, a combination vital for continued growth and vision:

I come like a woman
who I am
spreading out through nights
laughter and promise
and dark heat
warming whatever I touch
that is living
consuming
only what is already dead.[55]

Like Mawulisa, the peace-loving Dahomean goddess, Lorde resists war in its traditional sense. She refuses to be hidden or to fight unnecessarily, to be silent or to silence. Thus the female warrior-poet redefines herself through a passionate, ritualistic celebration with her sisters of Dan.

In several poems, however, Lorde invokes a black goddess whose message to the world is somber, even ominous. The first two poems of *The Black Unicorn* resound with such quiet anger, with implicit warning. In the title poem, Lorde's self-portrait is that of a "greedy" and "impatient" unicorn—not the white, idealized, mystical figure of European mythology but a potent, subversive creature, black and female, not to be mistaken for a "shadow / or symbol" and not be denied. The black unicorn's energy, Lorde suggests, emanates from the core of her female self: "It is not on her lap where the horn rests / but deep in her moonpit / growing." No longer confined to the tapestries at Cluny or the medieval gardens of the imaginative or the privileged, this unicorn wanders about and speaks loudly, fiercely. She is "restless," "unrelenting," "not / free."[56]

In the second poem, "A Woman Speaks," Lorde again asserts the subversive nature of her mission. She has been peaceful enough up to now, but she is nonetheless "treacherous." "Still seeking / my sisters / Witches in Dahomey," the poet feeds on their inspiration and acknowledges the conflict within her. She is woman and she is black, and that, Lorde suggests, is an explosive combination:

I have been woman
for a long time
beware my smile
I am treacherous with old magic
and the noon's new fury
with all your wide futures
promised
I am
woman
and not white.[57]

Other poems in *The Black Unicorn* reveal the warrior-poet's will to vengeance, but Lorde recognizes this impulse as dangerous. "Power," for example, was recorded first as a journal entry, on the day Lorde heard that the white policeman who had murdered ten-year-old Clifford Glover in New York had been acquitted. "The difference between poetry and rhetoric," Lorde asserts, "is being / ready to kill / yourself / instead of your children." Images of dying black children populate the poet's dreams, making it difficult to "make power out of hatred and destruction," to "heal my dying son with kisses." Fraught with anguish, the poet acknowledges her desire for revenge. Unless she can distinguish poetry from rhetoric, her power will grow poisonous:

. . . one day I will take my teenaged plug
and connect it to the nearest socket
raping an 85-year-old white woman
who is somebody's mother
and as I beat her senseless and set a torch to her bed
a greek chorus will be singing in 3/4 time
"Poor thing. She never hurt a soul. What beasts they are."[58]

Lorde uses a Greek chorus, an emblem of classical tradition, to speak for the status quo in this modern tragic saga, and to provide a dramatic contrast to her own persona as a black teenaged rapist-murderer. Her point is painful, volatile, brutally honest: if the wasteful, unrequited murders of black children continue, she as a black woman may be driven to seek retribution, even if such vengeance makes her power "run corrupt as poisonous mold." Yet Lorde passionately resists this self-destructive retaliation, preferring instead "to learn to use / the difference between poetry and rhetoric." As a black woman poet in a racist, antifeminist society, she must somehow claim her poetic gift as a constructive force, re-visioning words as tools for halting violence, not for perpetuating it.

In the final poem in *The Black Unicorn*, "Solstice," the poet sheds those encumbrances that would link her to a dying and destructive patriarchal civilization: "borrowed meat," roofs of houses, drinking pots, even "our skin." This ritualistic divesting of human properties signals the speaker's return to "our mothers / who are waiting for us by the river," her movement toward a primal state of being:

I will eat the last signs of my weakness
remove the scars of old childhood wars
and dare to enter the forest whistling
like a snake that has fed the chameleon
for changes
I shall be forever.

She now welcomes the chance to do what she once found difficult: to "whistle in the night," and to "enter the forest" thus empowered. As a final supplication for safe passage, Lorde invokes the blessing and guidance of the mother-goddess-self:

May I never remember reasons
for my spirit's safety
may I never forget
the warning of my woman's flesh
weeping at the new moon
may I never lose
that terror
that keeps me brave
May I owe nothing
that I cannot repay.[59]

The strength and safety Lorde gleans by re-membering herself have not blessed all women, and no one is more aware of the tragedy of lost female voices than Lorde herself. "As women," she argues in "The Erotic as Power," "we need to examine the ways in which our world can be truly different." One crucial task of the black woman poet who would change the world is "hearing into speech" women not able to name themselves:

> I write for those women who do not speak, for those who do not have a voice because they/we were so terrified, because we are taught to respect fear more than ourselves. We've been taught that silence would save us, but it won't. We *must* learn to respect ourselves and our needs more than the fear of our differences and we must learn to share ourselves with each other.[60]

To better represent those women who have succumbed to silence, out of fear of the patriarchy or out of violence at its hands, Lorde includes herself among them—"they" gives way to "they/we." This assumption of a communal voice is well illustrated by "A Litany for Survival," in which Lorde speaks "for those of us who live at the shoreline / standing upon the constant edges of decision / crucial and alone"; "for those of us / who were imprinted with fear / like a faint line in the center of our foreheads." Throughout the day and the night, she continues, "we are afraid":

> when our stomachs are full we are afraid
> of indigestion
> when our stomachs are empty we are afraid
> we may never eat again
> when we are loved we are afraid
> love will vanish
> when we are alone we are afraid
> love will never return
> and when we speak we are afraid
> our words will not be heard
> nor welcomed
> but when we are silent
> we are still afraid.

Given the nature and extent of women's fear, Lorde concludes, "it is better to speak / remembering / we were never meant to survive."[61]

Lorde's words are paradoxical, however, for at the same time women "were never meant to survive," they must struggle to ensure precisely that: their own and their sisters' survivals. "I have died too many deaths / that were not mine," Lorde exclaims in "Sequelae," a line that echoes an earlier question in "Change of Season": "Am I to be cursed forever with becoming / somebody else on the way to myself?"[62] The answer is apparently affirmative, but by invoking a communal muse and voice, the poet conceives this "curse" as a blessing—a celebrating chorus of women moving from the "*I am* out to the *we are* and then out to the *we can*."[63] Three poems illustrate particularly well the power and poignancy of Lorde's communal voice: "Chain," in which she is moved to speak by and for two teenaged incest victims; "Afterimages," in which the image of a desperate Southern white woman blends painfully with that of a mutilated black boy; and "Need: A Choral of Women's Voices," in which a group of murdered black women are resurrected to tell their own stories.

The fifteen- and sixteen-year-old incest victims in "Chain" are described as "skeleton children / advancing against us," seeking sanity and love and female identity:

> we will find womanhood
> in their eyes
> as they cry
> which of you bore me

will love me
will claim my blindness as yours
and which of you marches to battle
from between my legs?

Such haunting questions have no answers, Lorde implies; the poet feels helpless, forced to watch this crime of incest and abandonment assert itself again and again. "On the porch outside my door / girls are lying / like felled maples in the path of my feet / I cannot step past them nor over them." All the poet can do, what she indeed *must* do, is to hear and give voice to their cries, to recreate and so avenge them in her art. Thus Lorde becomes both their mother and their "sister in pain," while they serve her as voices of anguish and inspiration:

One begs me to hold her between my breasts
Oh write me a poem mother
here, over my flesh
get your words upon me
as he got this child upon me
our father lover
thief in the night
do not be so angry with us. We told him
your bed was wider
but he said if we did it then
we would be his
good children if we did it
then he would love us
oh make us a poem mother
that will tell us his name
in your language.

No poem, of course, could begin to heal the daughter's pain; no mother could respond coherently to such plaintive queries: "Do you know me better than I knew him / or myself? / Am I his daughter or girlfriend / am I your child or your rival?" The only hope in this tragically enmeshed web of relations, Lorde concludes, is the "chain" of connectedness among women, that "woman-force" capable sometimes of transforming sexual rivals into secret sharers. The daughters' final questions resonate with such possibility, however tentative:

Here is your granddaughter mother
give us your blessing before I sleep
what other secrets
do you have to tell me
how do I learn to love her
as you have loved me?[64]

The possibility of bonding between disparate humans—here a white Southern woman, a murdered black boy, and a black woman poet—provides the subject of "Afterimages," as the poet responds first with rage but finally with compassion to a poverty-stricken white woman whose few possessions have been destroyed in a Mississippi flood. Having "inherited Jackson, Mississippi" twenty-four years earlier, when fifteen-year-old Emmett Till was murdered and dismembered there by local white men for whistling at a white girl, Lorde initially can muster little sympathy for the flood victim. "Despair weighs down her voice like Pearl River mud," the poet declares, until "a man with ham-like hands pulls her aside / snarling 'She ain't got nothing more to say!' " "That lie," the poet tells us, "hangs in his mouth / like a shred of rotting meat."

Another lie permeates the poet's consciousness, however, as images of a white woman "bereft and empty" fuse with those of "a black boy hacked into a murderous lesson":

> His broken body is the afterimage of my 21st year
> when I walked through a northern summer
> my eyes averted
> from each corner's photographies
> newspapers protest posters magazines
> Police Story, Confidential, True
> the avid insistence of detail
> pretending insight or information
> the length of gash across the dead boy's loins
> his grieving mother's lamentation
> the severed lips, how many burns
> his gouged out eyes
> sewed shut upon the screaming covers
> louder than life.

As she must speak for victimized women, the poet implies, so must she remember black children who have been violated: Emmett Till's "black broken flesh" lies on the sidewalk "like a raped woman's face." To avenge the ghost of Till, Lorde first decides to "withhold my pity and my bread" from the pathetic white woman, "surveying her crumpled future." But the horrible afterimages continue to haunt her, until she realizes that creating a hierarchy of victims will not resolve the pain and rage she feels: "I wade through summer ghosts / betrayed by vision / hers and my own." As the poem ends, the black boy, the white woman, and the poet herself are imaged together as forces bound in the struggle against poverty and racism:

> A woman measures her life's damage
> my eyes are caves, chunks of etched rock
> tied to the ghost of a black boy
> whistling
> crying and frightened
> her tow-headed children cluster
> like little mirrors of despair
> their father's hands upon them
> and soundlessly
> a woman begins to weep.[65]

"Need: A Choral of Black Women's Voices" is actually verse-drama, as Lorde empowers with speech two murdered black woman, Patricia Cowan and Bobbie Jean Graham, and is empowered by them. As the "I" of the poem, its connecting and universalizing life-force, Lorde begins this dialogue on behalf of "the hundreds of other black women whose nightmares inform them my words":

> This woman is Black
> so her blood is shed into silence
> this woman is Black
> so her death falls to earth
> like the drippings of birds
> to be washed away with silence and rain.

But Lorde will not allow such silence, such "washing away"; instead, two particular murder victims must return, and Lorde must reveal their stories. The first speaker, Cowan, took her young child with her to answer an ad in the paper for a black actress, and so became the recipient of an anonymous, vicious misogyny: "He put a hammer through my head." Graham's story is equally horrifying, or perhaps even more so, since the public dismisses it euphemistically as a "crime of passion" when "your boyfriend methodically beats you to death."

> . . . I still died
> of a lacerated liver
> and a man's heel
> imprinted upon my chest.

These two speakers' statements are muted, ghostly, but the poet's wrath quickly explodes into vehement song: "Dead Black women haunt the black maled streets, / paying the cities' secret and familiar tithe of blood." There is method to this madness, Lorde as prosecuting witness reveals to her readers, offering tortured homage to the blood of child rape victims, sodomized grandmothers, strangers. "As women," she continues, "we were meant to bleed / but not this useless blood."

In section two of the poem, Cowan and Graham add their particular questions to Lorde's universal one: Why my blood? Why our blood? Decrying both the black men who have betrayed them and the white patriarchs who downplay or dismiss such acts of violence, the three women catalog the horrors of misogyny, a hatred ironically masked in the guise of idealization:

> Borrowed hymns veil the misplaced hatred
> saying you need me you need me you need me
> like a broken drum
> calling me black goddess black hope black strength
> black mother
> you touch me
> and I die in the alleys of Boston
> with a stomach stomped through the small of my back

a hammered-in skull in Detroit
a ceremonial knife through my grandmother's used vagina
my burned body hacked to convenience in a vacant lot
I lie in midnight blood like a rebel city
bombed into false submission
and our enemies still sit in power
and judgment
over us all.

In the poem's final section, Lorde passionately denounces the lie of black male "need" for black women. "I am wary of need / that tastes like destruction," she cries; what you tell us is the message of the enemy, not that of the lover. In stark contrast to such deceit is the clear and absolute truth of the women's voices, a truth that Lorde calls upon her readers to see and live within:

The simplest part of this poem
is the truth in each one of us
to which it is speaking.
How much of this truth can I bear to see
and still live
unblinded?
How much of this pain
can I use?[66]

The poem's final line, chanted twice by all the women, is taken from the writing of the antinuclear activist Barbara Deming: "*We cannot live without our lives.*" Wanton crime against black women on the streets of America (Lorde reminds us in her notes that twelve black women were murdered in a three-month period in Boston in 1979) is in itself a holocaust.

These poems by Lorde reveal with particular clarity her impulse toward a "woman-identified literature" born out of a "female tradition, a female consciousness which I think does exist." Matriarchy has not endured, Lorde explains, and patriarchy has failed:

> Now we're moving into a third kind of living—the shape of which we're in the process of defining. I call it a "queendom" because I see it in terms of a great deal more power for women on all levels. We will deal with female power in a realist sense. It will be power different from what has been displayed before because it will function for all human beings.[67]

The lesbian feminist's contribution to this new way of living is a commitment to create her art out of what Lorde has termed a "lesbian consciousness," what Rich calls a "lesbian continuum." According to Rich, "it is the lesbian in us who drives us to feel imaginatively, render, in language, grasp, the full connection between woman and woman. It is the lesbian in us who is creative, for the dutiful daughter of the fathers in us is only a hack."[68] Lorde defines "lesbian consciousness" in a similar manner, as that of "strongly women-identified women where love between women is open and possible, beyond physical in every way. . . . The true feminist deals out of a lesbian consciousness whether or not she ever sleeps with women." All black women are in essence lesbians, Lorde declares, because "we were raised in the remnants of a basically matriarchal society no matter how oppressed we may have been by patriarchy."[69] The black lesbian writer's task, therefore, is to integrate this consciousness into all facets of her writing.

For Lorde, such an integration requires that she "get in touch with all of the people that I am: *warrior, poet, lesbian, mother*," and that she work fiercely to counter and ultimately to destroy all forms of "human blindness."[70] One key way to do this is to speak by, of, and for the diverse women who have inspired her—ordinary women who through their quiet strength have become extraordinary, mythic women who share the poet's quest as "outriders for a queendom not yet assured." Mothers, sisters, lovers, muses, these women blend their voices with the poet's in invoking and celebrating a potent black goddess, a woman-identified woman, a legendary figure fast coming into her own:

> Seboulisa, mother of power
> keeper of birds
> fat and beautiful
> give me the strength of your eyes
> to remember
> what I have learned
> help me to attend with passion
> these tasks at my hand for doing.[71]

7

"Unlearning to Not Speak": New Sources of Women's Inspiration

It is the imitation of male poetry that causes the false ring in the work of almost all women poets. A woman who concerns herself with poetry should, I believe, either be a silent Muse and inspire the poets by her womanly presence, as Queen Elizabeth and the Countess of Derby did, or she should be the Muse in a complete sense: she should be in turn Arianrhod, Blodeuwedd and the Old Sow of Maenawr Penardd who eats her farrow, and should write in each of these capacities with antique authority. She should be the visible moon: impartial, loving, severe, wise.

—Robert Graves, *The White Goddess*

Everything will be changed once woman gives woman to the other woman. There is hidden and always ready in woman the source; the locus for the other. The mother, too, is a metaphor. . . . Text: my body—shot through with streams of song; I don't mean the overbearing, clutchy "mother" but, rather, what touches you, the equivoice that affects you, fills your breast with an urge to come to language and launches your force; the rhythm that laughs you; the intimate recipient who makes all metaphors possible and desirable; body (body? bodies?), no more describable than god, the soul, or the Other; that part of you that leaves a space between yourself and urges you to inscribe in language your woman's style.

—Hélène Cixous, "The Laugh of the Medusa"

Find the muse within you. The voice that lies buried under you, dig it up. Do not fake it, try to sell it for a handclap or your name in print.

—Gloria Anzaldúa, "Speaking in Tongues: A Letter to Third World Women Writers"[1]

The quotation from Robert Graves reveals what the male poet traditionally has wanted woman to be: never a poet, ever a muse. At her best, she is a catalyst for his poetry, the mute presence behind man's song. If she must concern herself at all with poetry, declares Graves—an enormous *if*—she should be "a silent Muse and inspire the poets by her womanly presence." Interestingly, Graves offers as a model for such a woman Queen Elizabeth, merely the most powerful ruler England has known and herself a poet of no small talent, as "On Monsieur's Departure" and "The Doubt of Future Foes" reveal.[2]

But Graves suggests also a subversive alternative to the silent muse, although he does so with ambivalence and indeed with trepidation. If woman refuses solely to inspire, she then should be "the Muse in a complete sense," as were, we presume, the ancient Celtic women Arianrhod, Blodeuwedd, and the Old Sow of Maenawr Penardd. As one learns from *The White Goddess*, Arianrhod was a "wicked woman" whose primary act of rebellion was to claim the right to name her illegitimate son. "I lay this destiny upon him," Arianrhod declares, "that he shall never have a name until he receives one from me." Blodeuwedd, who subsequently marries Arianrhod's son, is a Clytaemnestra figure who murders her husband in his bath; for her crime she is turned into an owl and, significantly, forced to keep her own name for all time: "and thou shalt not lose thy name but shalt be always called Blodeuwedd." The Old Sow, a Celtic Kali, spews forth and then devours countless young, feasting on corpses of her own making.[3] If woman involves herself actively with poetry, Graves warns, she becomes a potent, perverse Triple Goddess, unleashing her evil words with "antique authority."

Although Graves' assertions are eccentric, they are by no means unique. In *The Anxiety of Influence*, a Freudian analysis of the male poet as contemporary "ephebe," Harold Bloom argues that to achieve poetic identity the young ephebe must destroy his "father," the male precursor, by dallying with the mother-lover-muse. Citing the Italian philosopher Vico's esoteric views of the muse as one who sings "in the sense in which the Latin verbs *camere* and *cantare* mean 'foretell,' " Bloom discusses the "dark implications" of such a muse. The poet, Bloom suggests, must recognize that "his muse has whored with many before him," that he is new to the struggle of which she has always been a part. Although he thinks he loves her, and indeed does long for divination, the ephebe truly "loves himself in the Muse, and fears that she hates herself in him." In the male poet's imagination, Bloom concludes,

> the Muse is mother and harlot at once, for the largest phantasmagoria most of us weave from our necessarily egoistic interests is the family romance, which might be called the only poem that even unpoetical natures continue to compose.[4]

Bloom continues to speak as a contemporary blend of Graves and Freud in *A Map of Misreading*, where he turns to the issue of the woman poet. It is her fault, Bloom reveals grimly, that the muses are no more with us:

> Nor are there Muses, nymphs who *know*, still available to tell us the secrets of continuity, for the nymphs certainly are departing. I prophesy though that the first

> true break with literary continuity will be brought about in generations to come, if the burgeoning religion of Liberated Woman spreads from its clusters of enthusiasts to dominate the West. Homer will cease to be the inevitable precursor, and the rhetoric and forms of our literature then may break at last from tradition.[5]

Precisely. The modern woman poet, I would argue, has begun to take Graves' second piece of advice, to write with "antique authority." But as Bloom fears, it is not the authority of Homer, nor are her rhetoric and forms usually those of male tradition. Instead, modern woman insists, like Arianrhod, on her right to name that which is her own; like Blodeuwedd, on her right to retain her *own* "name," her strong identity as a poet; and like the Old Sow, on the right to taste with pleasure the fruits of her creative efforts. For help in these endeavors, she turns to a re-mythologized muse—neither Graves' passive sister nor Bloom's mother-whore, but a potent mother-goddess-sister-self of her own invention and design.

Denise Levertov's "Song for Ishtar" illustrates well the powerful dynamic between woman poet and female muse:

> The moon is a sow
> and grunts in my throat
> Her great shining shines through me
> so the mud of my hollow gleams
> and breaks in silver bubbles
>
> She is a sow
> and I a pig and a poet
>
> When she opens her white
> lips to devour me I bite back
> and laughter rocks the moon
>
> In the black of desire
> we rock and grunt, grunt and
> shine.[6]

Levertov flatters neither herself nor her muse: "she is a sow / and I a pig and a poet." Yet in her honest and intoxicating invocation, she exhibits neither the naïveté that Margaret Homans suggests permeates the poetry of modern women who advocate truth-telling, nor the isolation that leads the critic Pamela DiPesa to argue that the woman poet is inspired by "no one."[7] Instead, the poet and her female muse "rock and grunt, grunt and / shine," laughing at and wielding the power and pleasure they share.

The image of two equally powerful women sharing artistic stimulation and energy raises further questions about the modern woman poet's reclamation of her creative identity. "Everything will be changed once woman gives woman to the other woman," asserts the French feminist Hélène Cixous. "There is hidden and always ready in woman the source; the locus for the other." What does it mean for one woman to serve as "locus for the other," to "give woman" to her sister poet? How do women writers inspire one another to "inscribe in language" their "woman's style"? In what ways, finally, are literary women muses for one another? Such questions parallel those raised by the writer Ruth Perry in her study of "mothering the mind," that complex psychological webbing through which one person fosters creativity in another. "Such relationships are more central to the creative process than we had hitherto imagined," Perry asserts. ". . . The most propitious conditions for writing, for playing with versions of reality, might include the presence of another—someone who bears a complicated relationship to that initial presence in which the self came into being." Men *can* mother, as the bond between G. H. Lewes and George Eliot reveals, but often it is women who *do*. "A mother . . . might call forth certain qualities that are central to the work, qualities that seem to press for externalization in the texts—or she might embody them." Whatever the specific dynamic, Perry and her contributors agree that to understand the nature of literary artistry, we must investigate more fully "the combination of response, encouragement, expectation, and utter detachment, that helps to catalyze creative work."[8]

A further examination of the poets on whom this book has focused reveals that complex poetic reciprocities exist. In fact, the three fascinating muse relationships that emerge—those of Bogan and Sarton, H.D. and Rich, and Rich and Lorde—suggest a contemporary creative matrix among women who inhabit poetic space collaboratively. For May Sarton, Louise Bogan served as a crucial source of artistic inspiration and personal sustenance for the thirty years in which they were "poet-friends" and correspondents. "I have few masters and they are mostly French," Sarton wrote to Bogan in 1940, some years before the writers actually met. "But you in America have been always a source of humility and joy, a pure standard to me."[9] In a similar vein, Adrienne Rich relied on her foremother H.D. as inspiration for what many feminist critics consider her most fully realized volume of poetry. "About the importance of H.D.'s epic poems to me in the period when I was writing *The Dream of a Common Language*," Rich explains, "there is no question."[10] Finally, as lesbian-feminist poets committed to "the transformation of silence into language and action," Adrienne Rich and Audre Lorde offer an important paradigm of female creative interdependence.[11] These poets dedicate poems to each other, publish joint interviews, quote from and respond to each other's work. Each expands the other's vision through the crystalline lens of her own.

BOGAN AND SARTON

"Long before I ever saw her face to face," May Sarton explains, "Louise Bogan, both as poet and critic, had been a key figure for me. I bought *The Sleeping Fury* in 1937 when I was twenty-five and my first book had just appeared. I can still remember the shock and exhilaration it meant, how I pondered the poems—those strict spare lines, where emotion was so often disciplined by irony."[12] For Sarton, feelings of "shock" and "exhilaration" are associated most often with the presence of the muse, before whom the poet is "seized and shaken" with awe, through whose catalytic influence an artistic dialogue begins. "In the presence of the Muse," Sarton claims in *Mrs. Stevens Hears the Mermaids Singing*, "the sources of poetry boil, the faculty of language itself ferments."[13] Discouraged by a poetic climate unfavorable to the lyric poetry she was attempting to write, Sarton turned to Bogan, an older and more experienced writer, for creative nurture. In 1940, at twenty-eight years of age, with two published volumes of poetry, Sarton confided to Bogan her professional doubts and fears. "What can be done concerning the general distrust and even hatred shown toward lyric poetry, so prevalent now, I can't think. Nothing, I suppose," Bogan replied with characteristic forthrightness. Nonetheless, she encouraged Sarton to persevere. "These turns of the wheel of taste always happen; the distrust of form and emotion is always present, in every generation. . . . The only thing to do is: do what one can, and not sell out."[14]

Despite efforts on Sarton's part, their first meeting did not take place until the fall of 1953, when Bogan invited the younger poet to visit her New York apartment. For Sarton, the encounter was "momentous . . . deeply [moving], more than I dared show." Bogan's home, "as intimate and revealing as a self-portrait," captured Sarton's imagination: "Perhaps it was partly that one sensed an intense inner life at work. It was an apartment where a poet lived alone, a woman lived alone. It breathed an air of achieved calm."[15] As Sarton admits in her book *A World of Light*, her admiration for Bogan's lyrical verse and solitary environment eventually gave way to her desire for an "*amitie amoreuse*," a desire Bogan did not share. Yet because Bogan always treated her "with the utmost tact, generosity, and respect," Sarton willingly accepted instead a deep friendship that she describes as "stable and joyful and lasting." Bogan's letters to Sarton during that time attest to the strength of their bond as well as her sensitivity to her friend's complex emotional attachment. "Be happy, dear May," she exhorts in a letter in February 1954, "and remember that I proffer you all that I can proffer any human being. Which isn't, I suppose, v. much; but all of it is fresh and real and non-*patterned*."[16]

The primary bond between the two women, however, was creative. Because she considered Bogan's writing "the epitome of lyric art," Sarton took seriously both her praise and her criticism. "Louise used to say to me, 'You keep the Hell out of your work,'" Sarton reflects in *Journal of a Solitude*. "I have thought much about this. I have felt that the work of art (I am thinking especially of poetry), a kind of dialogue between me and God, must present resolution rather than conflict. The conflict is there, all right, but it is worked through by means of writing the poem."[17] As Elizabeth Frank notes in her recent biography of Bogan, Sarton learned from the elder poet that anger, grief, and despair were at the heart of lyric poetry. "Get all the *bear* into your work!" Bogan advised. "Get all the bitterness, too. That's the place for it." Ironically, Bogan praised Sarton's poems most highly when they took risks she herself was often unwilling to take—when they took a "troubled turn toward those frightening figures (symbols) of the subconscious, that are so difficult to touch, and to use." Inclined toward reticence, Bogan admired that work of Sarton that "marched; proceeded; opened out."[18]

Their growing friendship and mutual respect led Bogan and Sarton in 1956 to collaborate on a translation of Valéry, a project both women apparently enjoyed even though the press that originally had funded the work decided not to publish it. Sarton remembers biweekly meetings in New York in which she, the better French scholar, would present her verse adaptations to Bogan, the "flat" translator and more rigorous critic, for "scrutiny." Laughter would abound "at certain absurdities we (or I) had perpetrated." For Sarton, this collaborative relationship was "life-enhancing." Working with Bogan, she could appreciate "above all her sense of what poetry is, her poetic wisdom."[19]

Bogan served, then, as teacher and mentor as well as muse for Sarton. As Elizabeth Frank points out, she "patiently bestowed what creative wisdom she herself had won through long practice and hard experience upon a younger writer eager for technical and emotional guidance"—much as she had done for younger male poets like Theodore Roethke and William Maxwell.[20] But Sarton and Bogan experienced a unique bond as *women* poets, what Frank calls "the special solitude and discipline of the woman who lived for her work."[21] They also shared a profound dread of poetic stasis, which they openly admitted and often analyzed. Together they discussed, for example, Brewster Ghiselin's anthology *The Creative Process*; Bogan was especially intrigued by Henri Poincaré's emphasis on the "preliminary conscious" work that preceded an artistic epiphany. "I guess it's the *preliminary conscious* task that I side-step at present," she acknowledged during a time of severe writer's block. "*Bless you*," she concluded a letter to Sarton from this period; "keep feeling and working. For the work is really, for us, the important thing. The channels must be kept open so that it may live and grow."[22] For Sarton, furthermore, Bogan was a woman of creative genius who defended the unpopular causes of lyric poetry and female sensibility. "For women to abandon their contact with, and their expression of, deep and powerful emotional streams, because of contemporary pressures on mistaken self consciousness, would result in an impoverishment not only of their inner resources but of mankind's at large," Bogan wrote in her 1947 essay "The Heart and the Lyre." "Certainly . . . women are capable of perfect and poignant song."[23] As a female lyric poet struggling against double odds, Sarton fed upon these rejuvenating words.

One can find common themes in Bogan's and Sarton's poetry. Both women were fascinated with the demonic muse, struggled to redefine the "monster" within as a source of creative nurture. "The Sleeping Fury," one of the first

Bogan poems that Sarton read, examines the process by which a raging Other, "my scourge, my sister," casts off her vengeful mask, "sly, with slits at the eyes," and turns instead to silence and repose.

> . . . And now I may look upon you,
> Having once met your eyes. You lie in sleep and forget me.
> Alone and strong in my peace, I look upon you in yours.[24]

An early Sarton poem, "The Furies," seems to be a dialogue with Bogan about the difficulty of laying to rest this "monstrous" aspect of the self. "How then to recognize / The hard unseeing eyes, / or woman tell from ghost?" the poet wonders. She also warns. "Never look straight at one, / For then your self is gone." In a later poem, however, she offers both "the angels and the furies" as forces who help the writer keep her balance, find "the light of understanding."

> Who has ever reached it
> Who has not met the furies again and again?
> Who has reached it without
> Those sudden acts of grace?[25]

Sarton's "The Muse as Medusa" may be seen as an expansion of Bogan's earlier "Medusa." In her work Bogan again confronts directly a fury in the legendary person of Medusa: ". . . the bare eyes were before me / And the hissing hair." Rather than a debilitating experience, the poet's encounter with Medusa is empowering.

> And I shall stand here like a shadow
> Under the great balanced day,
> My eyes on the yellow dust, that was lifting in the wind,
> And does not drift away.[26]

Although Bogan's voice emerges from the "dead scene," the silent aftermath of her confrontation with Medusa, it does so quietly, tentatively. Sarton's response to Medusa, in contrast, is an active and celebratory identification with the demon.

> I turn your face around! It is my face.
> That frozen rage is what I must explore—
> Oh secret, self-enclosed, and ravaged place!
> This is the gift I thank Medusa for.[27]

Both Bogan and Sarton have spoken often of "ravaged places," and of the masks and secrets and self-enclosures that conceal and contain them. Both have relied heavily on silence and solitude for creative sustenance. "It is silence which comes from us," Bogan claims in one poem about poetry-making; in another, "the loud sound and pure silence fall as one."[28] For Sarton, "silence opens the world that I explore"; the poem "rises / In an unbroken wave and topples to silence."[29] Both poets believe, in Sarton's words, that "prose is earned and poetry given"—that poetic inspiration can occur anytime, anywhere (even on a street corner, Bogan told Sarton of her poem "The Daemon") but that it cannot be willed.[30] Each woman, therefore, earned her living by writing prose but learned to be and know herself by writing poetry.

The personal and literary relationship of Bogan and Sarton was often filled with anger and anxiety, as several letters from the 1950s and 1960s reveal. Bogan at times resisted the role of muse. "Dear May, how I wish that I could set you *carolling*. But I am not the Muse; and one must wait and pray for grace."[31] She also objected to Sarton's experimentation with the sonnet sequence, which she believed could not be written "with any hope of effectiveness"; thus, she argued imperiously, "*women* should not write them, any more!"[32] Especially off-putting to Bogan were Sarton's "A Divorce of Lovers" sonnets in *Cloud, Stone, Sun, Vine*, because they not only relied on what Bogan considered the outmoded sequential form, but they also mourned in fairly explicit terms the loss of a particular lover. "On the whole, you have a *metaphysical* bent," Bogan wrote in 1961; "you desire the universal behind the apparent; you have a passion for the *transcendent*. That is why I am perturbed when you seem in the sonnets to put so much spiritual capital in the *temporal*: in a *person*." On this issue, as on many, the two poets finally agreed to disagree. "I well understand . . . your theory," Sarton wrote on Bogan's fifty-seventh birthday, "that at a certain point of maturity relying on personal emotion, on relationships for motor power would mean going backward rather than forward, or—a better image—not going down one level deeper, which is what you want of course. On the other hand life *is* relationship and the going deeper . . . may be simply in the wisdom one can bring to them, not on avoiding them, not feeling less, but feeling more and differently."[33]

Sarton today admits that she never knew, finally, what Bogan thought of her work and that this uncertainty created tension between the two. Bogan praised Sarton's *The Land of Silence*, on the one hand, for its naturalness: "you have come into yourself and are able to render your mature feelings in your own way." Yet she critiqued numerous poems from the same volume, which she believed emerged from "*an impulse toward literature*" instead of "direct impulsions from life."[34] Later she would challenge Sarton to be more emotionally honest: "It should be clear that your sonnets are written to a woman. This is not clear."[35] Another time she accused Sarton of "writing *around* your travel experience," of failing to be fully present to her poems.[36] Bogan's honest acknowledgement of her own creative struggle softened her otherwise harsh assessments of Sarton's work; she discussed openly, for instance, her debilitating depression: "Thank God very little of it got into the poems. . . . Except for a certain saving *humor*, I should have indeed been a full *monster*."[37] Despite Bogan's confessions, however, a breach developed. Especially hurtful to Sarton was Bogan's failure to recognize her poetry in *The New Yorker*, where Bogan was poetry critic for many years. Once, after promising to review *The Land of Silence*, Bogan gave it only a few sentences at the end of an essay on Edith Sitwell. A 1960 letter from Bogan to Ruth Limmer suggested that she was not, in fact, totally open with Sarton: "if only she [Sarton] would stop writing sentimental poems! I had her take out two mentions of 'kittens,' from one poem. 'Cats,' yes, 'kittens,' no."[38] By August of 1962, Sarton had apparently confronted Bogan with her distress. "I am, of course, very sorry indeed that my professional critic side has come to bulk so large in your view," Bogan replied stiffly. "This will not always be the case, I feel, and we shall be poet-friends (or just human friends) once again."[39]

Despite "violent disagreements and tensions," however, Bogan has continued to be a primary source of inspiration and sustenance for Sarton: "I can re-read no letter from her without realizing freshly how much she taught me." Each woman encouraged the other to seek harmony and balance, in her poetry and in her life. "It all comes back to poise," Sarton claims, "poise of the soul when it is in true balance." With Bogan, Sarton explains, she felt "at home in my inner self."[40] Without Bogan, she felt bereft. "How shall we live without her ironies / That kept her crystal clear and made us wise?" she wonders in her "Elegy for Louise Bogan," written on the day of the poet's death in 1970. As collaborator, instructor, friend, and muse, Bogan would be long remembered.

> Deprived, distraught, often despairing,
> You kneaded a celestial bread for sharing.
>
> I have not wept a tear, nor shall I do,
> Stripped to this naked praise that shines for you.[41]

H.D. AND RICH

In an essay entitled "Adrienne Rich and H.D.: An Intertextual Study," Susan Stanford Friedman has traced the deep literary connections between H.D.'s epic poetry and Rich's feminist re-visions.[42] That H.D. has inspired Rich is evident from the epigraph of *The Dream of a Common Language*, a passage from H.D.'s *Trilogy* on the power of love:

> I go where I love and where I am loved,
> into the snow;
>
> I go to the things I love
> with no thought of duty or pity.[43]

As Friedman notes, Rich pays tribute to many literary foremothers in her search to understand and validate women's influence on one another, a key means of transcending those barriers among women dictated and reinforced by patriarchy. Anne Bradstreet, Emily Dickinson, and Charlotte Brontë are subjects of extended essays by Rich, and figures from Susan B. Anthony to Sojourner Truth to Virginia Woolf frequently appear in her poetry. But H.D. has been particularly significant, Friedman argues persuasively, as "a rich presence nourishing the evolution of the younger woman's poetic vision toward the woman-identified, gynocentric feminism of *The Dream of a Common Language*."[44] Before Rich, after all, H.D. offered "a complex critique of the violence at the core of the patriarchy, a quest for the personal and mythic maternal principle to counter the patriarchy, and the exploration of rich bonds between women as friends and lovers to feed their emotional, intellectual, and erotic lives."[45] Clearly H.D. and Rich are, in H.D.'s words, "born of one mother, / companions / of the flame."[46]

Friedman explores four areas in which H.D. has profoundly influenced Rich. First, she anticipated Rich's emphasis on a "passion for survival," the desire and rebellion that Rich finds characteristic of contemporary women's poetry. Early in the century H.D. recognized the uselessness of attempting to build a better, more "female" world on the faltering foundations of patriarchy. As Rich explains, H.D. "insisted that the poet-as-woman should stop pouring her energies into a ground left sterile by the power-mongers and death-cultists: '*Let us leave / the place-of-a-skull / to them that have made it.*' "[47] Both *Trilogy* and *Dream* begin with walks through violence-ridden cities, with a surveillance of the torn walls and pornographic images that "culture" has produced. For both poets, hope for salvation from such destruction emerges only in a matriarchal or woman-centered alternative vision, which each places at the heart of her work. Thus *Trilogy* centers on H.D.'s invocation of "Our Lady," a "new Eve" who carries a book containing "the blank pages / of the unwritten volume of the new"; while at the core of *Dream* lie Rich's "Twenty-one Love Poems," explicit rejections of patriarchal values in favor of female creativity, eroticism, culture.

Furthermore, Friedman continues, both H.D. and Rich consider the mother relationship, literally and symbolically, "an essential element in their reconstruction of an authentic female principle."[48] Both writers had mothers named Helen by whom they were greatly influenced and whom they associated with Poe's Helen, as distant yet inspiring female spirits. In *Trilogy*, H.D. celebrates the alchemical process by which the "great-mother" must be rejuvenated for the modern age:

> now polish the crucible
> and set the jet of flame
>
> under, till *marah-mar*
> are melted, fuse and join
>
> and change and alter,
> mer, mere, mère, mater, Maia, Mary
>
> Star of the Sea,
> Mother.[49]

Similarly, Rich claims in *Of Woman Born* that "the cathexis between mother and daughter . . . is the great unwritten story"; and in "Sibling Mysteries," she argues powerfully that "the daughters never were / true brides of the father / the daughters were to begin with / brides of the mother / then brides of each other / under a different law / Let me hold and tell you."[50] For both writers, a re-mythologizing of the maternal muse was vital to their creative identity.

Finally, Friedman discusses the extent to which Rich has been moved by her understanding of H.D.'s closeness to Bryher, her female companion for most of her adult life. "Working together as women," Rich asserts,

> . . . we can confront the problems of women's relationships, the mothers we came from, the sisters with whom we were forced to divide the world, the daughters we love and fear. We can challenge and inspirit each other . . . stand by and give courage at the birth throes of one another's insights. I think of the poet H.D.'s account of the vision she had on the island of Corfu, in the *Tribute to Freud*.[51]

As Friedman points out, H.D. credits Bryher with both sharing and encouraging her psychic-creative experience of "writing-on-the-wall," for "without her," H.D. insists, "admittedly, I could not have gone on."[52] For Rich, as for H.D., women's intimate bonds, especially their erotic connections, help to make their creative lives possible.

In her response to Friedman's article, Rich has affirmed that her work of the 1970s was indeed informed by a "silent dialogue" with H.D., whose later poetry was crucial "to me, and to other lesbian-feminist poets, including Judy Grahn, Marilyn Hacker, and Susan Sherman." Rich agrees with Friedman's assertion that H.D. pursued early the theme of patriarchal violence, a theme Rich addresses most directly in "Natural Resources": "it is absolutely true that her poetry—and her spirit—were with me when I was writing that poem." But Rich urges Friedman to carry her study further to Rich's later work, specifically to *A Wild Patience Has Taken Me This Far*, which the poet believes in many ways continues and extends the analysis of patriarchal violence *Dream* began, but in other ways challenges it. Despite H.D.'s influence, she concludes, "I was writing, as H.D. was not, out of a movement that has described and analyzed male violence politically."[53]

While I agree with Friedman that H.D.'s influence on Rich is most pronounced in *The Dream of a Common Language* and her prose writing from the mid-1970s, I find echoes of H.D. also in *A Wild Patience*, the volume Rich asks Friedman to examine. There Rich herself struggles and encourages her readers to move from the ideal, the archetypal in our portrayals of women's experiences, to the real, the concrete, the particulars of our lives—those daily activities that may distinguish us from one another and yet also unite us. In pursuing this direction, I would argue, Rich refines and expands her earlier dialogue with H.D., especially with H.D.'s vision as revealed through "Our Lady" in *Trilogy*.

Challenging H.D. as well as herself not to take refuge in the abstractions of mythical and mystical idealization, Rich envisions new and bolder ways of "turning the wheel," the title of her culminating poetic sequence in *A Wild Patience.*[54]

In *Trilogy* H.D. celebrates the arrival of Our Lady but warns her audience not to identify this figure with male images of female divinity. "We have seen her / the world over," the poet explains ironically, "Our Lady of the Goldfinch, / Our Lady of the Candelabra, / . . . We have seen her head bowed down / with the weight of a domed crown." Yet none of these namings suffice, H.D. insists, "none of these / suggest her as I saw her."[55] She goes on to stress that the lady "is no rune nor symbol," that she is "not awe-inspiring like a Spirit."[56] At moments, however, H.D. ignores her own warning, idealizing her lady even as she cautions her readers not to. She names her "Our Lady of the Snow" because of her white veils, and although she refuses to make her the bride or mother of Christ, the Lady nonetheless is envisioned as married and maternal: "We are her bridegroom and lamb."[57] H.D.'s rendering of Our Lady as a poetic muse, "one of us," and as the carrier of "the unwritten volume of the new" is important, but its association with Judeo-Christian and patriarchal imagery may limit its paradigmatic value for contemporary feminists.

What Rich proposes in "Turning the Wheel," I believe, is "Our Lady" re-visioned and particularized. Early in the poem she warns the reader of "the dangers of false history," the importance of "a different method of weaving": "there is no room for nostalgia." In contrast to Our Lady, or perhaps as a new-age complement to her, Rich calls forth a figure from Native American culture, a "desert-shamaness," who might well have already withdrawn in disgust from these remnants of patriarchal culture but will perhaps reappear. Unlike H.D.'s rhapsodic imagining of her Lady, however, Rich's invocation is halting, for she realizes the hubris of asserting cultural authority, the need to confront our tunnel vision and historical limitations. "Unborn sisters," she pleads, "look back on us in mercy where we failed ourselves, / see us not one-dimensional but with / the past as your steadying and corrective lens."[58]

With this apologia, Rich pays homage to the shamaness in all her "Particularity":

> In search of the desert witch, the shamaness
> forget the archetypes, forget the dark
> and lithic profile, do not scan the clouds
> massed on the horizon, violet and green,
> for her icon, do not pursue
> the ready-made abstraction, do not peer for symbols.

We must acknowledge and accept this woman's ordinary, visceral qualities, Rich insists.

So long as you want her faceless, without smell
or voice, so long as she does not squat
to urinate, or scratch herself . . .
she is kept helpless and conventional
her true power routed backward
into the past.[59]

Only by daring to witness her female physicality, and hence her essential humanity, can we hope to touch or name her. Not that such a naming is necessarily easy or even appropriate, Rich continues in a companion piece, "Apparition." If the shamaness should appear "ringed with rings you dreamed about" or "wearing shawls of undyed fiber" or "skirted like a Christian," she warns, beware of assuming that you recognize her. "Look at her closely if you dare," the poet concludes, "do not assume you know those cheekbones / or those eyesockets; or that still-bristling hair."[60]

Rich continues her dialogue with H.D. in *A Wild Patience* by delineating, as the older poet had, a redemptive goddess-muse through whom she and her sisters can seek creative sustenance. Yet in her wariness, her impassioned insistence that this muse be consistently scrutinized and particularized—that she be *prototypical* rather than *archetypal*, in Rachel Blau DuPlessis' terms[61]—Rich expands her predecessor's feminist epistemology. At the end of her essay in response to Friedman, Rich juxtaposes her own words against those of H.D. to stress the necessity of process among feminists rather than stasis:

> Feminism really means the end of that world in which any poet or critic can draw safe lines within which we will evoke what is already familiar. "She carries a book but it is not / the book of the ancient wisdom." What I said in a speech in 1977, I still believe: "The meaning of our love for women is what we have constantly to expand."[62]

Rich concludes *A Wild Patience* similarly, "turning the wheel" in order to drive full circle, beyond the "female core / of a continent," to return to her lover and their vital dialogue. And in so doing, she turns another page in H.D.'s Lady's book, "the unwritten volume of the new."

RICH AND LORDE

Adrienne Rich:
I wish we could explore this [issue of female choice] more—about you and me, but also in general. I think it needs to be talked about, written about: the differences in alternatives or choices we are offered as black and white women. There is always a danger of seeing it in an all-or-nothing way. I think it's a very complex thing. White women are constantly offered choices, or the appearance of choices. But also real choices that are undeniable. We don't always perceive the difference between the two.

> *Audre Lorde:*
> Adrienne, in my journals I have a lot of pieces of conversations that I'm having with you in my head. I'll be having a conversation with you and I'll put it in my journal because stereotypically or symbolically these conversations occur in a space of black woman/white woman, where it's beyond Adrienne and Audre, almost as if we're two voices. . . . This piece, I think, is one of these—about the different pitfalls.[63]

This interview with Audre Lorde by Adrienne Rich, published in *Signs* in 1980, illustrates well the ongoing public and private dialogue between two committed lesbian-feminist writers who feed and feed upon each other. As their joint signatures suggest, this is less a traditional interview than a seminar or forum. From a rhetorical perspective, it is interesting to note how often Rich anticipates Lorde's responses; Lorde's most frequent replies to Rich's queries are "Yes" and "That's right." In an interview with Lorde by Karla Hammond published in the same year, the dynamic between interviewer and interviewee differs; Lorde often takes issue with or kindly corrects Hammond's suppositions: "that quotation isn't really about myths," or "that's what we've been talking about," or "that's a very seductive but misleading question."[64] Rich and Lorde, in contrast, complement and echo each other's words.

> *AL:*
> The one thread I feel coming through over and over in my life is the battle to preserve my perceptions, the battle to win through and to keep them—pleasant or unpleasant, painful or whatever—
>
> *AR:*
> And however much they were denied.
>
> *AL:*
> And however much they were denied.[65]

Crucial to Audre Lorde's literary and feminist vision is Adrienne Rich, and crucial to Adrienne Rich's is Audre Lorde. The common language they share employs a consistent vocabulary couched in the continual present, the syntax of process; key words and concepts include *surviving, breaking silence, naming, particularizing, redefining power.* "Re-vision," Rich explains, "—the act of looking back, of seeing with fresh eyes, of entering an old text from a new critical direction—is for women more than a chapter in cultural history: it is an act of survival."[66] The passion to survive, she asserts elsewhere, is the driving impulse of women's poetry today. Audre Lorde agrees, and in her analysis of the black woman's complex struggle to persevere, she both clarifies and expands Rich's meaning. "I write not only for my peers but for those who will come after me. . . . I write for those women who do not speak, for those who do not have a voice because they/we were so terrified. . . . Survive and teach; that's what we've got to do and to do it with joy."[67]

In order to survive, Lorde and Rich insist, black and white women must first learn to speak. "Writing is re-naming," Rich claims; thus women who would find voice must reexamine "how our language has trapped as well as liberated us, how the very act of naming has been till now a male prerogative, and how we can begin to see and name—and therefore live—afresh."[68] The patriarchy is invested in women's silence, she implies in "Frame"; it does not intend for women to tell the tales of one another's oppressions: "it is meant to be in silence that this happens."[69] Refusing muteness is also vital to Lorde's feminist vision, for "our uses have become more important than our silence."[70] Women must recognize "the distortions silence commits us to," Lorde argues; and on this point as on many she cites the work of Rich.[71] "As Adrienne has said, what remains nameless eventually becomes unspeakable." As black women, Lorde insists, "we must constantly name ourselves."[72]

Both poets celebrate and scrutinize woman and woman identification through the careful lens of the particular, the concrete—not the universal or the abstract, but our "common differences." Rich's poem "Particularity" urges us not to pursue "the ready-made abstraction," not to "peer for symbols," but instead to defy both conventional power and myths of female helplessness by seeking our strength in the ordinary, as we scratch, grimace, snore.[73] Lorde also recognizes the danger of efforts to universalize (or, for her, to "whitewash") experience—as males, heterosexuals, whites so often have claimed to do, while in reality privileging their own visions. She rejects this illusion of universality in favor of an empowering honesty and specificity: "The poem happens when I, Audre Lorde, poet, deal with the particular instead of the 'UNIVERSAL.' My power as a person, as a poet, comes from who I am. I am a particular person. The relationships I have had, in which people kept me alive, helped sustain me, were particular relationships. They help give me my particular identity, which is the source of my energy."[74]

Finally, both poets are committed to exploring and redefining power from a lesbian-feminist perspective. Each has written a poem entitled "Power," and though the poems appear at first to be quite different, they share common themes: the pain and destruction caused by denial, the entrapment experienced by women who inhabit a patriarchal desert, the need to transform anger and self-destructiveness into energy and affirmation of self and selves. Rich's "Power" purports to be about Marie Curie, who

> must have known she suffered   from radiation sickness
> her body bombarded for years   by the element
> she had purified.

But the poem also speaks to and of each woman who insists upon "denying / her wounds," who fails to see that "her wounds came from the same source as her power."[75] Lorde's poem "Power" has especially influenced Rich; she quotes from it at the beginning of "Disloyal to Civilization," her essay on "feminism, racism, and gynephobia," asks Lorde during her interview to explain what it means, and echoes its language in several poems from *A Wild Patience*.[76] Like Rich, Lorde examines the interrelatedness of "wounds" and "power":

> I have not been able to touch the destruction within me.
> But unless I learn to use
> the difference between poetry and rhetoric
> my power too will run corrupt as poisonous mold
> or lie limp and useless as an unconnected wire.[77]

These poets agree that for women today, as Rich has said, "the commonest words are having to be sifted through, rejected, laid aside for a long time, or turned to the light for new colors and flashes of meaning."[78] At the head of this list of words, for both writers, is *power*.

Lorde and Rich pay tribute to each other as collaborator and inspirer at many points in their work. In her preface to *Zami*, Lorde expresses gratitude to her sister poet, "who insisted the language could match and believed that it would."[79] In an angry speech directed primarily to white feminists, Lorde credits Rich for being one of the few white women to acknowledge and challenge racism in the women's movement. "As Adrienne Rich pointed out in a recent talk, white feminists have educated themselves about such an enormous amount over the past ten years, how come you haven't also educated yourselves about black women and the differences between us—white and black—when it is key to our survival as a movement?"[80] In 1977, when Lorde had first been diagnosed as having breast cancer, she was scheduled along with Rich to be part of a conference panel entitled "The Transformation of Silence into Language and Action." After deciding not to go, Lorde changed her mind because of Rich's inspirational vision:

> You said, why don't you tell them about what you've just been through? That's what you said. And I started saying, now that doesn't have anything to do with the panel. And as I said that I felt the words "silence." "Transformation." I hadn't spoken about this experience. . . . This is silence. . . . Can I transform this? Is there any connection? Most of all, how do I share it? And that's how a setting down became clear on paper, as if the connections became clear in the setting down.[81]

Clearly Rich "mothered the mind" of Lorde during this crisis in her life, just as she mothered her friend in body and spirit while Lorde was in the hospital recovering from her eventual mastectomy.[82]

Rich gives homage to Lorde at many moments in her writing, but nowhere is her gratitude expressed more powerfully than in the poem from *The Dream of a Common Language* that she dedicates to Lorde. In stanza one of "Hunger," Rich images herself as a woman split in two, acknowledging the limitations of her "Western vision" yet suffering anger and agony as she confronts the widespread starvation and neglect of Third World children:

> . . . I'm wondering
> whether we even have what we think we have—
> lighted windows signifying shelter,
> a film of domesticity
> over fragile roofs. I know I'm partly somewhere else—
> hats strung across a drought-stretched land
> not mine, dried breasts, mine and not mine, a mother
> watching my children shrink with hunger.
> I live in my Western skin,
> my Western vision, torn
> and flung to what I can't control or even fathom.

Moved by Lorde's many poems about the horrors of starvation, Rich goes on to challenge the male hierarchy that "rules the world," the "male god that acts on us and on our children / till our brains are blunted by malnutrition, / yet sharpened by the passion for survival." Yet the "male god" does not bear sole responsibility for such suffering, she realizes; Western women, white women, also have shunned the power they might have wielded:

> Quantify suffering? My guilt at least is open,
> I stand convicted by all my convictions—
> you, too. We shrink from touching
> our power, we shrink away, we starve ourselves
> and each other, we're scared shitless
> of what it could be to take and use our love,
> . . . .
> like the terrible mothers we long and dread to be.

As "terrible mothers" of the world, contemporary Demeters, women have both the power and the duty to "take and use our love," to claim responsibility for the mothers and the children of Third World civilization. "The decision to feed the world / is the real decision," Rich insists; "no revolution / has chosen it." Instead, it must be chosen by revolutionary women of all colors, women "alive to want more than life, / want it for others starving and unborn." Rich's final lines portray an impoverished mother's persistent will to survive:

> Swathed in exhaustion, on the trampled newsprint,
> a woman shields a dead child from the camera.
> The passion to be inscribes her body.
> Until we find each other, we are alone.[83]

In addition to its feminist political vision, this poem also makes a statement about female creativity in its broadest and most vital sense. "The passion to be" recalls Lorde's assertion that women of all colors and experience "*must* learn to respect ourselves and our needs more than the fear of our difference, and we must learn to share ourselves with each other."[84] To refuse to "quantify suffering" is "to be" present to one another as women in the fullest possible way: to be concerned, to be angry, to suffer together, to be politically responsible, to be transformative. Such responsibility falls especially to the woman poet, Lorde and Rich imply, as one privileged to articulate in language cries of need and pain and hunger. "Until we find each other, we are alone," then, is an affirmation of the creative woman's profound commitment to "reconstitute the world," a commitment Lorde and Rich share.

As was true for Bogan and Sarton, or for that matter for any creative women sustaining each other personally as well as artistically, Rich and Lorde have experienced tensions in their relationship.

> *Audre Lorde*:
> I've never forgotten the impatience in your voice that time on the telephone—when you said, "It's not enough to say to me that you intuit it." Do you remember? I will never forget that. Even at the same time that I understood what you meant, I felt a total wipeout of my modus, my way of perceiving and formulating.
>
> *Adrienne Rich*:
> Yes, but it's not a wipeout of your modus. Because I don't think my modus is unintuitive, right? And one of the crosses I've borne all my life is being told that I'm rational, logical, cool—I am not cool, and I'm not rational and logical in that icy sense. But there's a way in which, trying to translate from your experience into mine, I do need to hear chapter and verse from time to time. . . . If I ask for documentation, it's because I take seriously the spaces between us that difference has created, that racism has created. There are times when I simply cannot assume that I know what you know, unless you show me what you mean.[85]

In addition to revealing here their own vulnerabilities, the two poets acknowledge the risks of dialogue between women of different races. By feeding each other's imaginations and intellects, however, Rich and Lorde move beyond differences to commonality, even when that commonality is couched in fear. "I've had great resistance to some of your perceptions," Rich admits to Lorde. "They can be very painful to me. Perceptions about what goes on between us, what goes on between black and white people, what goes on between black and white women. . . . But I don't want to deny them. I know I can't afford to." To this admission, Lorde responds with conflicted yet healing lines from one of her own poems. "How much of this truth can I bear to see / and still live / unblinded? How much of this pain / Can I use?"[86] Remarkably, any tension produced by their dialogue ultimately gives way to a clarifying and loving respect. "I'm not rejecting your need for documentation," Lorde concludes gently. And Rich responds in kind: "And in fact, I feel you've been giving it to me, in your poems always, and most recently in the long prose piece you've been writing, and in talks we've been having. I don't feel the absence of it now."[87]

Lorde and Rich are struggling side by side to create what Rich calls a "common language," to rename the world, and in so doing they serve as muses and mouthpieces for each other. Their commitment is to truth-telling, however horrible or painful that truth might be; to exploring woman identification in all its richness and diversity:

> woman-to-woman relationships: mothers and daughters, sister-siblings, lover and lover, friendships, and the spirit-sisters of a collective past and future. . . . The necessity for women to find each other, both for pure survival and for the transformation of all social institutions.[88]

As lesbian-feminist survivors, transformers, and creators, Adrienne Rich and Audre Lorde "hear each other into speech."[89] Together they give new resonance to Rich's words from "Hunger": "Until we find each other, we are alone."

Robert Graves claimed that women must be their own muses, and ironically, many modern women poets writing in English agree. "Find the muse within you," Gloria Anzaldúa urges her Chicana sisters. "The voice that lies buried under you, dig it up." Creative women are responsible to and for their own visions, finally, and formulating such visions can be joyful and empowering. Maya Angelou, for instance, revels in her *jouissance*, her "inner mystery":

> It's in the arch of my back,
> The sun of my smile,
> The ride of my breasts,
> The grace of my style.
> I'm a woman
> Phenomenally.
> Phenomenal woman,
> That's me.[90]

Nikki Giovanni's "Ego Tripping" likewise reveals a gleeful act of self-affirmation:

> I am so perfect so ethereal so surreal
> I cannot be comprehended
>   except by my permission.[91]

Judy Grahn also claims to be divine, a "knitter of the sacred," and she challenges the traditional paradigm of woman as "maker" of poetry for man. Rather, she is maker of herself and her work, *for* herself:

> The good weef is both
> weaver and wife, those old
> words meant the woman-as-a-maker,
> not especially bonded
> to one husband,
> but to the Spider Woman of life,
> the one with ties that bind,
> knitter of the sacred, magic knots,
> who with her scissors or her knife,
> is tie-breaking life-taker,
> queen of what is not.

This "wife and weef and weaver," Grahn continues, was once criticized as a "fishwife" of "stinking reputation," who had, men said with "a certain sneer," a "certain smell." That woman's smell, Grahn declares, "is / of queens." As the poem ends, Grahn asserts her own creative authority:

> . . . The midwife stands midway
> between the laboring weaver and her weaving
> and the world, easing the way to life.
> I am please to call myself a wife too,
> a word-wyfe.[92]

As Grahn's poem illustrates, women poets are increasingly reluctant to listen to what Emerson called "the courtly Muses of Europe," for these muses and the tradition from which they emanate do not speak for them. Instead, such women affirm what Cixous calls "that part of you that leaves a space between yourself and urges you to inscribe in language your woman's style." That such inscriptions can be tinged with doubt for the woman who would claim the self as muse can be seen in this poem by the Puerto Rican poet Julia de Burgos:

> The people are saying that I am your enemy,
> That in poetry I give you to the world.
> They lie, Julia de Burgos. They lie, Julia de Burgos.
> The voice that rises in my verses is not your voice:
>   it is my voice;
> For you are clothing and I am the essence.
> . . . .
>
> I am life. I am strength. I am woman.[93]

Despite her initial uncertainties—"the people say"—De Burgos voices her own right to name, to create. The following dialogue between Gloria Anzaldúa and her pen reveals a less conflicted impulse to assert self as potent inspirer of self:

> Pen, I feel right at home in your ink doing a pirouette, stirring the cobwebs, leaving my signature on the window pane. Pen, how could I ever have feared you. You're quite house-broken but it's your wildness I am in love with. I'll have to get rid of you when you start being predictable, when you stop chasing dustdevils. The more you outwit me the more I love you. It's when I'm tired or have had too much caffeine or wine that you get past my defenses and you say more than what I had intended. You surprise me, shock me into knowing some part of me I'd kept secret even from myself.[94]

What Carol Gilligan calls "the different voice of women" is asserting itself in the poetry of modern women who reimagine the female muse.[95] "The voice that lies buried" they are digging up; "the intimate recipient who makes all metaphors possible and desirable," they are redefining and re-creating. Like Ntozake Shange's "colored girls," they are proclaiming their own "antique authority": "i found god in myself & i loved her / I loved her fiercely."[96] Like Marge Piercy's female quester, they are "unlearning to not speak" in a potent voice both singular and collective:

> She must learn again to speak
> starting with I
> starting with We
> starting as the infant does
> with her own true hunger
> and pleasure
> and rage.[97]

Notes

CHAPTER 1

1. The quotations in the epigraph are from Robert Graves, "In Dedication," prologue to *The White Goddess: A Historical Grammar of Poetic Myth* (1948; reprint ed., New York: Farrar, Straus and Giroux, 1975), p. 5; Luce Irigaray, "When Our Lips Speak Together," trans. Carolyn Burke, *Signs: Journal of Women in Culture and Society* 6 (Autumn 1980): 69; and Olga Broumas, "Triple Muse," in *Beginning with O* (New Haven: Yale University Press, 1977), pp. 9–10. The title quote, "a whole new psychic geography," is from Adrienne Rich, "When We Dead Awaken: Writing as Re-Vision," in *On Lies, Secrets, and Silence: Selected Prose, 1966–1978* (New York: Norton, 1979), p. 35.
2. Maud Bodkin, *Archetypal Patterns in Poetry: Psychological Studies of Imagination* (1934; reprint ed., London: Oxford University Press, 1971), p. 99.
3. The term "inspiring anima" and the definition that follows are from Erich Neumann, *The Great Mother: An Analysis of the Archetype*, trans. Ralph Manheim (1955; reprint ed., Princeton: Princeton University Press, 1972), pp. 295–296; the second quotation is from Bodkin, *Archetypal Patterns in Poetry*, p. 153.
4. Quoted in Adrienne Rich, "Poetry, Personality and Wholeness: A Response to Galway Kinnell," *Field: Contemporary Poetry and Poetics* 7 (Fall 1972): 14.
5. Plato, *Ion*, in *Criticism: Twenty Major Statements*, ed. Charles Kaplan (Scranton, Pa.: Chandler Publishing, n.d.), p. 18.
6. *The Second Sex*, ed. and trans. H. M. Parshley (1952; reprint ed., Vintage, 1974), p. 157.
7. Rich, "Poetry, Personality and Wholeness," p. 16.
8. Carolyn Heilbrun, *Reinventing Womanhood* (New York: Norton, 1979), p. 164.
9. See, for example, Margaret Homans, *Women Writers and Poetic Identity:*

Dorothy Wordsworth, Emily Brontë, and Emily Dickinson (Princeton: Princeton University Press, 1980); Adrienne Rich, "When We Dead Awaken"; and Mary Daly, *Beyond God the Father: Toward a Philosophy of Women's Liberation* (Boston: Beacon Press, 1973).

10. Rich, "Poetry, Personality and Wholeness," p. 15.
11. ———, "Vesuvius at Home: The Power of Emily Dickinson," in *On Lies*, p. 170.
12. Such reactions by Dickinson and Rossetti are documented in Joanne Feit Diehl, " 'Come Slowly—Eden': An Exploration of Women Poets and Their Muse," *Signs: Journal of Women in Culture and Society* 3 (Spring 1978): 572–587. In addition, Homans discusses these tendencies in Brontë and Dickinson in *Women Writers and Poetic Identity*, pp. 104–214.
13. Suzanne Juhasz, *Naked and Fiery Forms: Modern American Poetry by Women, a New Tradition* (New York: Harper & Row, 1976), pp. 1–5; and Sandra M. Gilbert, " 'My Name is Darkness': The Poetry of Self-Definition," *Contemporary Literature* 8 (August 1977): 448–449.
14. Catherine Smith, "Jane Lead: Mysticism and the 'Woman Cloathed with the Sun,' " *Shakespeare's Sisters: Feminist Essays on Women Poets*, ed. Sandra M. Gilbert and Susan Gubar (Bloomington: Indiana University Press, 1979), p. 18.
15. Carol Gilligan, *In a Different Voice: Psychological Theory and Women's Development* (Cambridge, Mass.: Harvard University Press, 1982), pp. 173–174.
16. Alice Walker, *In Search of Our Mothers' Gardens: Womanist Prose* (San Diego: Harcourt Brace Jovanovich, 1983); H.D., *End to Torment* (New York: New Directions, 1979), p. 41. The phrase "reconstitutes the world" appears in Adrienne Rich, "Natural Resources," in *The Dream of a Common Language: Poems, 1974–1977* (New York: Norton, 1978), p. 67. "After so long, this answer" is taken from Rich's poem "Integrity," in *A Wild Patience Has Taken Me This Far: Poems, 1978–1981* (New York: Norton, 1981), pp. 8–9.
17. Alexandra Grilikhes, *On Women Artists: Poems, 1975–1980* (Minneapolis: Cleis Press, 1981), p. 17.
18. Harold Bloom, *The Anxiety of Influence: A Theory of Poetry* (New York: Oxford University Press, 1973). For further discussion of the woman poet's affirmation of influence, see my introduction to the Women's Poetry Issue of *Poet and Critic* 14, no. 2 (1983): 1–5.
19. For a discussion of one woman poet's "intoxicating" (empowering/annihilating) effect on another, see Sandra M. Gilbert, "Sylvia Plath's Visions and Revisions," in *Poet and Critic* 14, no. 2 (1983): 12–15. I am indebted to Gilbert for these terms. Gilbert and Susan Gubar also discuss the nineteenth-century woman writer's "anxiety of authorship" in *The Madwoman in the Attic: The Woman Writer and the Nineteenth-century Literary*

Imagination (New Haven: Yale University Press, 1979). For insights into the struggles of modern women poets, see Alicia Ostriker, *Writing Like a Woman* (Ann Arbor: University of Michigan Press, 1983).

20. Bella Debrida, "Drawing from Mythology in Women's Quest for Selfhood," in *The Politics of Women's Spirituality: Essays on the Rise of Spiritual Power within the Feminist Movement* (New York: Doubleday, 1982), pp. 138–151.
21. Ovid, *The Metamorphoses*, trans. Horace Gregory (New York: Viking Press, 1958), pp. 146–147.
22. Graves, *The Greek Myths*, vol. 1 (1955; reprint ed. Baltimore: Penguin Books, 1957), p. 55.
23. Ibid., p. 79.
24. Ovid, *The Metamorphoses*, p. 273.
25. Ibid., p. 275.
26. Plato, *Phaedrus*, in *The Works of Plato*, ed. Irwin Edman (New York: Modern Library, 1930), p. 285.
27. ———, *Ion*, in *Criticism: Twenty Major Statements*, p. 16.
28. ———, *Republic*, Ibid., p. 14.
29. Aristotle, *The Generation of Animals*, trans. A. L. Peck (Cambridge, Mass.: Harvard University Press, 1953), pp. 103–104.
30. Cited in Maurice Valency, *In Praise of Love: An Introduction to the Love Poetry of the Renaissance* (1958; reprint ed., New York: Farrar, Straus and Giroux, 1975), p. 2.
31. Plato, *Republic*, in *Criticism: Twenty Major Statements*, p. 15.
32. Beauvoir, *Second Sex*, pp. 205–206.
33. Lu Emily Pearson, *Elizabethan Love Conventions* (Berkeley: University of California Press, 1933), p. 4. For further discussion of courtly conventions, see C. S. Lewis, *The Allegory of Love: A Study in Medieval Tradition* (Oxford: Clarendon Press, 1936).
34. Valency, *In Praise of Love*, p. 109.
35. Quoted in J. W. Lever, *The Elizabethan Love Sonnet* (1956; reprint ed., London: Methuen, 1966), pp. 1–2.
36. For an informative analysis of the woman's role in courtly tradition and of women troubadours, see Meg Bogin, *The Women Troubadours* (New York: Norton, 1976).
37. Petrarch, *Selected Sonnets, Odes and Letters*, ed. Thomas Goddard Bergin (New York: Appleton-Century-Crofts, 1966), p. 55.
38. Pearson, *Elizabethan Love Conventions*, p. 33.
39. Petrarch, *Selected Sonnets*, p. 64.
40. *Collected Poems of Sir Thomas Wyatt*, ed. Kenneth Muir and Patricia Thompson (Liverpool: Liverpool University Press, 1969), p. 227.
41. Philip Sidney, Sonnet LV, *Astrophel and Stella*, in *The Poems of Sir Philip Sidney*, ed. William A. Ringler, Jr. (Oxford University Press, 1962), p. 192.

42. Ibid., Sonnet XL, p. 184.
43. Edmund Spenser, Sonnet LXXXV, *Amoretti*, in *The Poetical Works of Edmund Spenser*, ed. J. C. Smith and E. de Selincourt (London: Oxford University Press, 1929), p. 576.
44. ———, Sonnet LXIV, Ibid., p. 573.
45. William Shakespeare, *Love's Labour's Lost*, act 4, sc. 3, lines 74–76. In *The Complete Works of William Shakespeare*, ed. Hardin Craig (Glenview, Ill.: Scott, Foresman, 1961), p. 116.
46. ———, Sonnet 78, Ibid., p. 484.
47. ———, Sonnet 100, Ibid., p. 488.
48. ———, Sonnet 101, Ibid.
49. ———, Sonnet 130, Ibid., pp. 492–493.
50. ———, Sonnet 138, Ibid., pp. 493–494.
51. Plato, *Symposium*, in *The Works of Plato*, pp. 367–379.
52. For further discussion of this topic, see Denis de Rougemont, *Love in the Western World* (Garden City, N.Y.: Doubleday, 1957), pp. 108–110.
53. Marianne Shapiro, *Woman Earthly and Divine in the Comedy of Dante* (Lexington: University of Kentucky Press, 1975), pp. 124–125.
54. Ibid., p. 125.
55. Irene Samuel, *Dante and Milton: The Commedia and Paradise Lost* (Ithaca: Cornell University Press, 1966), pp. 58–62.
56. John Milton, *Paradise Lost*, bk. 9, lines 21–25. In *The Poems of John Milton*, ed. James Holly Hanford (New York: The Ronald Press Co., 1936), p. 367.
57. For varying opinions on the gender and nature of Milton's muse, see Christopher Grose, *Milton's Epic Poems: Paradise Lost and Its Miltonic Background* (New Haven: Yale University Press, 1973), pp. 245–263; Joan Webber, *Milton and His Epic Tradition* (Seattle: University of Washington Press, 1979), p. 149; and John T. Shawcross, "The Metaphor of Inspiration in *Paradise Lost*," in *Th' Upright Heart and Pure*, ed. Amadeus P. Fiore (Pittsburgh: Duquesne University Press, 1967), p. 83.
58. William Wordsworth, "Prospectus" to *The Recluse*, in *The Poetical Works of William Wordsworth*, 7 vols., ed. Edward Dowden (London: George Bell and Sons, 1892), 1:25–30. For an excellent analysis of the Romantic poets and their female Others, see Harold Bloom, *The Visionary Company: A Reading of English Romantic Poetry* (Garden City, N.Y.: Doubleday, 1961).
59. Homans, *Women Writers and Poetic Identity*, p. 13.
60. Wordsworth, "Prospectus," 1:47–48.
61. ———, "Three years she grew in sun and shower," in *The Poetical Works of William Wordsworth*, Cambridge ed. (Boston: Houghton Mifflin, 1982), pp. 112–113.
62. Ibid., p. 298.

63. Percy Bysshe Shelley, *Selected Poetry*, ed. Neville Rogers (Boston: Houghton Mifflin, 1968). "Hymn to Intellectual Beauty," pp. 327–329; "Epipsychidion," pp. 242–256.
64. John Keats, "The Fall of Hyperion: A Dream," *Keats' Poetical Works*, ed. H. W. Garrod, 2nd ed. (Oxford: Clarendon Press, 1958), pp. 507–523.
65. Walt Whitman, "Song of Myself," section 24, line 497, in *Leaves of Grass*, ed. Harold W. Blodgett and Sculley Bradley (New York: Norton, 1968), p. 52.
66. Walt Whitman, "Out of the Cradle Endlessly Rocking," Ibid., p. 253.
67. Ralph Waldo Emerson, "The Poet," in *The Works of Ralph Waldo Emerson* (Boston and New York: Fireside, 1909), pp. 12, 26.
68. Ezra Pound, "Praise of Ysolt," in *Collected Early Poems of Ezra Pound*, ed. Michael John King, intro. Louis L. Martz (New York: New Directions, 1976), pp. 79–80.
69. Louis L. Martz, introduction to *Collected Early Poems of Ezra Pound*, p. xix.
70. Pound, "The Summons," in *Collected Early Poems*, pp. 262–263.
71. William Carlos Williams, "The Wanderer: A Rococo Study," in *The Collected Earlier Poems of William Carlos Williams* (New York: New Directions, 1951), pp. 3–12.
72. Pound, "Und Drang," in *Collected Early Poems*, pp. 167–174. The phrase "make it new" is also Pound's.
73. ———, "N.Y.," Ibid., p. 185.
74. Williams, "Sunday in the Park," in *Paterson* (New York: New Directions, 1963), p. 57.
75. ———, "The Library," Ibid., pp. 117–154.
76. T. S. Eliot, *The Waste Land*, in *The Complete Poems and Plays, 1909–1950* (New York: Harcourt, Brace and World, 1952), pp. 37–55. For a helpful discussion of Eliot's muses and mythic women, see Lillian Feder, *Ancient Myth in Modern Poetry* (Princeton: Princeton University Press, 1971).
77. Both poems by Auden are cited in Feder, pp. 265–267.
78. T. S. Eliot, "Ash Wednesday," in *Complete Poems and Plays*, pp. 60–67.
79. Wallace Stevens, "Sunday Morning," in *The Collected Poems of Wallace Stevens* (New York: Knopf, 1954), pp. 67–70.
80. ———, "The Idea of Order at Key West," Ibid., pp. 128–130.
81. Robert Creeley, "Air: 'The Love of a Woman,'" in *The Collected Poems, 1945–75* (Berkeley: University of California Press, 1983), p. 240.
82. James Merrill, "From the Cupola," in *Nights and Days* (New York: Atheneum, 1966), pp. 45–53.
83. Allen Ginsberg, "Kaddish," in *Collected Poems, 1947–1980* (New York: Harper & Row, 1984), p. 211.
84. Ibid., p. 223.
85. Ibid., p. 225.

86. John Berryman, *Homage to Mistress Bradstreet* (New York: Farrar, Straus and Cudahy, 1956), pp. 2–3.
87. Irving Feldman, "Teach Me, Dear Sister," in *Teach Me, Dear Sister* (New York: Viking Press, 1983), pp. 29–32.
88. Rich, "When We Dead Awaken," in *On Lies*, p. 39.
89. Denise Levertov, *Relearning the Alphabet* (New York: New Directions, 1970), p. 116.
90. Irigaray, "When Our Lips Speak Together," p. 73.
91. Anne Finch, "To Mr. F., now Earl of W.," in *The Poems of Anne Countess of Winchilsea*, ed. Myra Reynolds (Chicago: University of Chicago Press, 1903), pp. 20–23.
92. Catharine Stimpson, "Ad/d Feminam: Women, Literature, and Society," in *Literature and Society: Selected Papers from the English Institute, 1978*, ed. Edward Said (Baltimore: John Hopkins, 1980), p. 180.
93. Anne Bradstreet, "The Prologue," in *The World Split Open: Four Centuries of Women Poets in England and America, 1552–1950*, ed. Louise Bernikow (New York: Vintage, 1974), pp. 188–189.
94. Bell Gale Chevigny, *The Woman and the Myth: Margaret Fuller's Life and Writings* (Old Westbury, N.Y.: The Feminist Press, 1976), p. 263.
95. Rich quotes Griffin on the muse in "Conditions for Work," in *On Lies*, p. 210; her views on the traditional muse appear in "Poetry, Personality and Wholeness," pp. 14–16.
96. Diehl, "'Come Slowly—Eden,'" pp. 573–574.
97. Ibid., p. 578.
98. Rich, "Vesuvius at Home," in *On Lies*, p. 173.
99. Ibid., p. 166.
100. Lillian Faderman and Louise Bernikow, "Comments on Joanne Feit Diehl's "'Come Slowly—Eden': An Exploration of Women Poets and Their Muse," in *Signs: A Journal of Women in Culture and Society* 4 (Autumn 1978): 188–196. Dickinson's poem on witchcraft is cited in Bernikow's response in *Signs*, p. 194.
101. Homans, *Women Writers and Poetic Identity*, pp. 104–161.
102. Emily Brontë, Poem 176, in *The Complete Poems of Emily Jane Brontë*, ed. C. W. Hatfield (New York: Columbia University Press, 1941), pp. 208–209.
103. ———, Poem 154, Ibid., p. 178.
104. ———, Poem 85, Ibid., p. 86.
105. ———, Poem 174, Ibid., pp. 205–206.
106. This line is from a poem entitled "Often rebuked, yet always back returning," cited in *Complete Poems of Emily Jane Brontë*, pp. 255–256. Although Hatfield questions this poem's authorship, most subsequent critics, including the biographer Winifred Gérin, attribute it to Emily Brontë.

107. Rich, "Vesuvius at Home," in *On Lies*, p. 174.
108. Heilbrun, *Reinventing Womanhood*, p. 67.
109. Katherine Philips, "To my Excellent Lucasia, on our Friendship," in *The World Split Open*, p. 61.
110. Anne Killigrew, "Upon the Saying That My Verses Were Made by Another," Ibid., pp. 79–81.
111. Anna Akhmatova, "Muse," in *Way of All the Earth*, trans. D. M. Thomas (Athens: Ohio University Press, 1979), p. 59.
112. Broumas, "Triple Muse," in *Beginning with O*, p. 9.
113. Sylvia Plath, "The Disquieting Muses," in *The Collected Poems* (New York: Harper & Row, 1981), pp. 74–76.
114. Bella Akhmadulina, "Muteness," in *Three Russian Women Poets*, ed. and trans. Mary Maddock (Trumansburg, N.Y.: Crossing Press, 1983), p. 99.
115. Carolyn Kizer, "A Muse of Water," in *The Ungrateful Garden* (Bloomington: Indiana University Press, 1961), pp. 61–63.
116. Denise Levertov, "The Well," in *Poems, 1960–1967* (New York: New Directions, 1967), pp. 40–41.
117. M. L. von Franz, "The Process of Individuation," in *Man and His Symbols*, ed. C. G. Jung (New York: Dell, 1964), pp. 207–209.
118. Levertov, "In Mind," in *Poems, 1960–1967*, p. 143.
119. Neumann, *The Great Mother*, pp. 80–83.
120. For an illuminating discussion of modern women poets' mythic revisions, see Alicia Ostriker, "The Thieves of Language: Women Poets and Revisionist Mythmaking," in *Signs: Journal of Women in Culture and Society* 8 (Autumn 1982): 68–90. This essay also appears in Ostriker, *Stealing the Language: The Emergence of Women's Poetry in America* (Boston: Beacon Press, 1986).
121. May Sarton, "The Muse as Medusa," in *Collected Poems, 1930–1973* (New York: Norton, 1974), p. 332.
122. Muriel Rukeyser, "The Poem as Mask," in *The Collected Poems of Muriel Rukeyser* (New York: McGraw-Hill, 1978), p. 435.
123. Elizabeth Sewell, *The Orphic Voice: Poetry and Natural History* (New Haven: Yale University Press, 1960), p. 3.
124. H.D., "Eurydice," in *Collected Poems, 1912–1944*, ed. Louis L. Martz (New York: New Directions, 1983), pp. 51–55.
125. alta, "euridice," in *I Am Not A Practicing Angel* (Trumansburg, N.Y.: Crossing Press, 1975), p. 8.
126. Rachel Blau DuPlessis, "Eurydice," in *Wells* (New York: Montemora, 1980).
127. Gilligan, *In a Different Voice*, pp. 22–23.
128. C. G. Jung and Carl Kérenyi, *Essays on a Science of Mythology*, trans. R. F. C. Hull (1949; reprint ed. Princeton: Princeton University Press, 1973), p. 137. For further discussion of the Demeter myth in modern

poetry by women, see Susan Gubar, "Mother, Maiden and the Marriage of Death: Women Writers and an Ancient Myth," *Women's Studies* 6 (1979): 301–315.

129. Rich, *Of Woman Born: Motherhood as Experience and Institution* (New York: Norton, 1976), p. 225.
130. Dorothy Wellesley, "Demeter in Sicily," in *Early Light: The Collected Poems of Dorothy Wellesley* (London: Rupert Hart-Davis, 1955), p. 240.
131. Dorothy Wellesley to W. B. Yeats; cited in *The World Split Open*, p. 162.
132. H.D., "Demeter," in *Collected Poems*, pp. 111–115.
133. Robin Morgan, "Network of the Imaginary Mother," in *Lady of the Beasts* (New York: Random House, 1976), pp. 73–88.
134. "Maya Angelou," in *Black Women Writers at Work*, ed. Claudia Tate (New York: Continuum, 1983), pp. 1–2.
135. Mary Helen Washington, "Alice Walker: Her Mother's Gifts," *Ms*, June 1982, p. 38.
136. Cherrié Moraga, "For the Color of My Mother," in *This Bridge Called My Back: Writings by Radical Women of Color*, ed. Cherrié Moraga and Gloria Anzaldúa (Watertown, Mass.: Persephone Press, 1981), pp. 12–13.
137. Nellie Wong, "From a Heart of Rice Straw," in *Dreams of Harrison Railroad Park*; quoted in *This Bridge*, p. 202.
138. Maxine Hong Kingston, *The Woman Warrior: Memoirs of a Girlhood Among Ghosts* (New York: Random House, 1976), pp. 101–102.
139. Plath, "Medusa," in *The Collected Poems*, pp. 224–226.
140. Sarton, *Mrs. Stevens Hears the Mermaids Singing* (New York: Norton, 1965), p. 193.
141. Carolyn Kizer, "A Muse," in *Yin* (Brockport, N.Y.: BOA Editions, 1984), pp. 37–41.
142. Quoted in Rich, *Of Woman Born*, p. 250.
143. Anne Sexton, "Rapunzel," in *Transformations* (Boston: Houghton Mifflin, 1971), p. 35.
144. Audre Lorde, "Recreation," in *The Black Unicorn* (New York: Norton, 1978), p. 81.
145. Olga Broumas, *Caritas #2*, quoted in Mary J. Carruthers, "The Re-Vision of the Muse: Adrienne Rich, Audre Lorde, Judy Grahn, Olga Broumas," *Hudson Review* (Summer 1983), p. 310. Carruthers' essay provides an important analysis of the "lesbian muse" of these four poets.
146. Rich, "Twenty-one Love Poems," in *The Dream of a Common Language*, pp. 25–36.
147. Rich, "Natural Resources," Ibid., p. 67; "The Spirit of Place," in *A Wild Patience Has Taken Me This Far*, pp. 40–45.
148. Alice Walker, "Women," reprinted in "In Search of Our Mothers' Gardens," in *In Search of Our Mothers' Gardens*, pp. 242–243.

149. Lucille Clifton, "Miss Rosie," in *Good Times: Poems* (New York: Random House, 1967), p. 5.
150. Sandra M. Gilbert, *Emily's Bread: Poems* (New York: Norton, 1984), pp. 17–18.
151. Nellie Wong, "In Search of the Self as Hero: Confetti of Voices on a New Year's Night—A Letter to Myself," in *This Bridge*, p. 180.
152. Gilbert and Gubar, *Madwoman in the Attic*, p. 17.

CHAPTER 2

1. Louise Bogan, "What Makes a Writer?," lecture delivered at New York University, March 18, 1967; cited in Louise Bogan/Ruth Limmer, *Journey around My Room: The Autobiography of Louise Bogan* (New York: Viking Press, 1980), p. 119.
2. ———, "What the Women Said," lecture delivered at Bennington College, Bennington, VT , October 11, 1962; cited in *Journey around My Room*, p. 136.
3. ———, "Men Loved Wholly beyond Wisdom," in *The Blue Estuaries: Poems, 1923–1968* (New York: Ecco Press, 1977), p. 16. For an excellent discussion of Bogan's personal and aesthetic struggles, see Elizabeth Frank, *Louise Bogan: A Portrait* (New York: Knopf, 1985).
4. Bogan to Morton D. Zabel, August 10, 1936; cited in *What the Woman Lived: Selected Letters of Louise Bogan, 1920–1970*, ed. Ruth Limmer (New York: Harcourt Brace Jovanovich, 1973), p. 135.
5. For a discussion of the woman poet's double bind, see Suzanne Juhasz, *Naked and Fiery Forms: Modern American Poetry by Women, a New Tradition* (New York: Harper & Row, 1976), pp. 1–5.
6. The phrase "aesthetic of silence" is used by Jeanne Kammer, "The Art of Silence and the Forms of Women's Poetry," in *Shakespeare's Sisters: Feminist Essays on Women Poets*, ed. Sandra M. Gilbert and Susan Gubar (Bloomington: Indiana University Press, 1979), pp. 163–164. "My scourge, my sister" is taken from Bogan's "The Sleeping Fury," in *Blue Estuaries*, pp. 78–79.
7. Bogan, "The Heart and the Lyre," in *Selected Criticism: Poetry and Prose* (New York: Noonday Press, 1955), pp. 339–340.
8. The Louise Bogan Papers, Amherst College, Amherst, Mass.; undated; cited in *Journey around My Room*, p. 133.
9. Bogan, "Heart and Lyre," in *Selected Criticism*, p. 237.
10. ———, "No Poetesses Maudites: May Swenson, Anne Sexton" (1963), in

A Poet's Alphabet: Reflections on the Literary Art and Vocation, ed. Ruth Limmer and Robert Phelps (New York: McGraw-Hill, 1970), pp. 431–432.

11. Gloria Bowles, "Louise Bogan: To Be (Or Not to Be?) Woman Poet," *Women's Studies* 5 (1977): 131–132. For further insights into Bogan's aesthetic conflicts, see Bowles, *The Aesthetic of Limitation: Louise Bogan's Poetry* (Bloomington: Indiana University Press, forthcoming 1987).
12. Unaddressed letter, May 1, 1939; cited in *What the Woman Lived*, p. 190.
13. Bogan to Harriet Monroe, January 17, 1930; Ibid., p. 55.
14. Bogan to John Hall Wheelock, July 1, 1935; Ibid., p. 86.
15. Bowles, "Louise Bogan," p. 132.
16. Bogan, "Heart and Lyre," in *Selected Criticism*, p. 341.
17. Ibid.
18. Bogan, "Women," in *Blue Estuaries*, p. 19.
19. Bogan to Humphries, July 24, 1924; cited in *What the Woman Lived*, p. 9.
20. From "The Journals of a Poet," published posthumously in *The New Yorker*, January 30, 1978; cited in *Journey around My Room*, p. 50.
21. Quoted to Ruth Limmer, March 1959; cited in *Journey around My Room*, pp. 68–69.
22. Bogan, "The Springs of Poetry," *New Republic*, December 5, 1923; cited in *Journey around My Room*, p. 70.
23. ———, "Journals of a Poet," September 21, 1961; cited in *Journey around My Room*, p. 72.
24. ———, "Marianne Moore," in *Selected Criticism*, p. 253.
25. ———, "Journals of a Poet," undated; cited in *Journey around My Room*, p. 162.
26. Ibid., September 21, 1961; cited in *Journey around My Room*, p. 172.
27. Ibid., September 21, 1961; cited in *Journey around My Room*, p. 173.
28. The Louise Bogan Papers, 1940; cited in *Journey around My Room*, pp. 54–55.
29. Bogan, "Homunculus," in *Blue Estuaries*, p. 65.
30. ———, "The Daemon," Ibid., p. 114.
31. Bogan to Sarton, November 13, 1959; cited in *What the Woman Lived*, p. 317.
32. Bogan, "Single Sonnet," in *Blue Estuaries*, p. 66.
33. Bogan to Sarton, October 31, 1961; cited in *What the Woman Lived*, p. 333.
34. Bogan, "Short Summary," in *Blue Estuaries*, p. 73.
35. ———, "Poem in Prose," Ibid., p. 72.
36. Ihab Hassan, Introduction to *The Literature of Silence: Henry Miller and Samuel Beckett* (New York: Knopf, 1967), pp. 5 and 15.
37. Tillie Olsen, *Silences* (New York: Dell, 1979), p. 6.
38. Ibid., p. 145.

39. Ihab Hassan, introduction to *The Dismemberment of Orpheus: Toward Postmodern Literature* (New York: Oxford University Press, 1971), p. ix.
40. Jeanne Kammer, "The Art of Silence," p. 157.
41. Bogan, "Sonnet," in *Blue Estuaries*, p. 48.
42. Bogan to Morton D. Zabel, January 23, 1932; cited in *What the Woman Lived*, p. 61.
43. Bogan, "The Crossed Apple," in *Blue Estuaries*, pp. 45–46.
44. ———, "The Dream," in *Blue Estuaries*, p. 103.
45. Bogan to Sarton, August 14, 1954; cited in *What the Woman Lived*, p. 369, note 2.
46. Bogan describes her pride as "neurotic" and "pathological" in her journal of August 1933 (*Journey around My Room*, p. 78). Also, in a letter to John Hall Wheelock (April 11, 1931) she discusses her "stiff-necked pride" as a liability (*What the Woman Lived*, p. 57). And several years later, during the *Partisan Review* symposium, she claims to "fear . . . the self-satisfied proud. In them lies evil" (*Journey around My Room*, p. 58). Clearly the problem of excessive pride was of great concern to her.
47. Bogan to Sister Angela M., August 20, 1966; cited in *What the Woman Lived*, p. 368.
48. Bogan, "What the Women Said," lecture delivered at Bennington College; cited in *Journey around My Room*, pp. 137–138.
49. Hélène Cixous, "Sorties," in Catherine Clement and Hélène Cixous, *La Jeune Née* (Paris: Union d'Editions, 1975), pp. 114–246.
50. Bogan, "Sonnet," in *Blue Estuaries*, p. 26.
51. ———, "Cassandra," Ibid., p. 33.
52. According to Jeanne Kammer, the most appropriate descriptive model for the woman poet's voice is the oracle, not the bard; her chief poetic activity is "seeing, not singing." This model seems appropriate for describing Bogan's poetics. See Kammer, "The Art of Silence," in *Shakespeare's Sisters*, p. 164.
53. Bogan, "Medusa," in *Blue Estuaries*, p. 4.
54. ———, "A Tale," "March Twilight," and "Little Lobelia's Song," in *Blue Estuaries*, pp. 3, 127, and 132–133.
55. William Butler Yeats, "Leda and the Swan," *Selected Poems and Two Plays of William Butler Yeats*, ed. M. L. Rosenthal (New York: Macmillan, 1962), p. 114.
56. Bogan, "The Sleeping Fury," in *Blue Estuaries*, pp. 78–79.
57. ———, "Heart and Lyre," in *Selected Criticism*, p. 342.
58. ———, "Unofficial Poet Laureate," Ibid., p. 155.
59. T. S. Eliot, "Tradition and the Individual Talent," in *The Sacred Wood: Essays on Poetry and Criticism* (1920; reprint ed., London: Methuen, 1969), p. 54.

60. From "Did you ever seek God?," The Louise Bogan Papers, November 1930?; cited in *Journey around My Room*, p. 57.
61. Adrienne Rich, quotation from book jacket of *The Blue Estuaries* (New York: Ecco Press, 1977).

CHAPTER 3

1. H.D., *Hermetic Definition* (New York: New Directions, 1972), p. 7.
2. My italics. In his foreword to *Hermetic Definition*, Norman Holmes Pearson, H.D.'s friend and literary executor, identifies the "you" as Lionel Durand, chief of the Paris Bureau of *Newsweek*, whom she met during an interview in 1960. The quotation "fascinating . . . if you can stand its preciousness" comes from the *Newsweek* article on H.D. that subsequently appeared—though this article was *not* written by Durand, as H.D. had thought. For a discussion of the H.D.-Durand meeting and its consequences, see Barbara Guest, *Herself Defined: The Poet H.D. and Her World* (Garden City, N.Y.: Doubleday, 1984), pp. 318–327.
3. Erich Neumann, *The Great Mother: An Analysis of the Archetype*, trans. Ralph Manheim (1955; reprint ed., Princeton, N.J.: Princeton University Press, 1972), p. 22.
4. H.D.'s homages to Artemis and other Greek goddesses are documented in H.D., *Collected Poems, 1912–1944*, ed. Louis L. Martz (New York: New Directions, 1983).
5. This poem was first published in its entirety under the title "Amaranth" in *Contemporary Literature* 10 (Autumn 1969): 589–594. It is now reprinted in *Collected Poems*, pp. 310–315.
6. H.D., *Trilogy*, in *Collected Poems*, p. 570.
7. ———, *Helen in Egypt* (1961; reprint ed., New York: New Directions, 1974), p. 17.
8. ———, "Sagesse," in *Hermetic Definition*, p. 75.
9. ———, "Winter Love," Ibid., pp. 85–117.
10. Susan Stanford Friedman, *Psyche Reborn: The Emergence of H.D.* (Bloomington: Indiana University Press, 1981), pp. 271–272. I am indebted to Friedman for her compelling analysis of H.D.'s psychoanalysis with Sigmund Freud and her perceptive insights into H.D.'s search for female divinity.
11. H.D., *End to Torment* (New York: New Directions, 1979), p. 41.
12. ———, "Advent," in *Tribute to Freud* (1956; reprint ed. Boston: David R. Godine, 1974), p. 121.
13. ———, *Tribute to Freud* (New York: Pantheon Books, 1956), p. 104.
14. Ibid., p. 65.
15. H.D. to Bryher, March 23, 1933, unpublished letter, Beinecke Rare Book and Manuscript Library, Yale University, New Haven, Conn.

16. H.D., *Bid Me to Live (A Madrigal)* (New York: Grove Press, 1960), pp. 182–183. Both this work and *Hermione* (New York: New Directions, 1981) are "fictional" accounts of H.D.'s early experiences as an Imagist poet among male mentors.
17. ———, "Because One is Happy," in *The Gift*, unpublished manuscript, Beinecke Library, p. 10. A greatly abridged version of *The Gift* has been published by New Directions (New York, 1982).
18. ———, *Tribute to the Angels* in *Collected Poems*, p. 552.
19. ———, *The Walls Do Not Fall*, Ibid., p. 543.
20. ———, *Tribute to Freud*, p. 65.
21. ———, *The Walls Do Not Fall* in *Collected Poems*, pp. 521–522.
22. Jacques Derrida, "Living On: Border Lines," in *Deconstruction and Criticism*, trans. James Hulbert (New York: Seabury Press, 1979), pp. 96–101.
23. H.D., *Helen in Egypt*, pp. 22–23.
24. H.D. presents these relationships in *End to Torment, Hermione*, and *Bid Me to Live*.
25. Jeanne Kammer, "The Art of Silence and the Forms of Women's Poetry," in *Shakespeare's Sisters: Feminist Essays on Women Poets*, ed. Sandra M. Gilbert and Susan Gubar (Bloomington: Indiana University Press, 1979), pp. 156–157.
26. Joseph N. Riddel, "H.D. and the Poetics of 'Spiritual Realism,'" *Contemporary Literature* 10 (Autumn 1969): 449.
27. Adrienne Rich, "Vesuvius at Home: The Power of Emily Dickinson," in *On Lies, Secrets, and Silence: Selected Prose, 1966–1978* (New York: Norton, 1979), p. 170.
28. H.D., *Palimpsest* (Boston: Houghton Mifflin, 1926), p. 180.
29. ———, "Pygmalion," in *Collected Poems*, pp. 48–50.
30. ———, "Triplex," Ibid., p. 291.
31. This poem appears on p. 101 of the *Collected Poems* as the untitled introductory verse to *Hymen*, but according to Thomas Swann, it was once called "Pallas." *The Classical World of H.D.* (Lincoln: University of Nebraska Press, 1962), pp. 40–41.
32. H.D., "All Mountains," in *Collected Poems*, pp. 288–290.
33. ———, *Hippolytus Temporizes* (Boston: Houghton Mifflin, 1927), pp. 137–138.
34. ———, "Huntress," in *Collected Poems*, pp. 23–24.
35. ———, "Moonrise," Ibid., p. 56.
36. ———, *Hermione*, p. 175.
37. Susan Gubar, "The Echoing Spell of H.D.'s *Trilogy*," in *Shakespeare's Sisters*, p. 201. The passage quoted is from *The Hedgehog* (England: Breding, 1936), pp. 75–76; cited in Gubar, p. 201.
38. H.D., "Amaranth," in *Collected Poems*, pp. 310–315. For an interesting discussion of H.D.'s Artemis-Aphrodite conflict, see Alicia Ostriker's chap-

ter on H.D. in *Writing Like a Woman* (Ann Arbor: University of Michigan Press, 1983), pp. 7–26.

39. H.D., "Eurydice," in *Collected Poems*, pp. 51–55.
40. ———, *Bid Me to Live*, p. 51.
41. Rachel Blau DuPlessis, "Romantic Thralldom in H.D.," *Contemporary Literature* 20 (Spring 1979): 184–186. An expanded version of this essay appears in *Writing Beyond the Ending: Narrative Strategies of Twentieth-Century Women Writers* (Bloomington: Indiana University Press, 1985).
42. H.D., *Bid Me to Live*, pp. 76–77.
43. ———, *Tribute to Freud*, p. 70.
44. Ibid., p. 72.
45. H.D., "Heliodora," in *Collected Poems*, pp. 151–154.
46. ———, "Chance Meeting," in *Collected Poems*, pp. 231–236.
47. For a full account of each of these influences, see Friedman, *Psyche Reborn*.
48. H.D., *Tribute to Freud*, pp. 60–84.
49. Ibid., pp. 75–76.
50. Ibid., p. 60.
51. H.D., "The Master," in *Collected Poems*, pp. 451–461.
52. From an unpublished journal at Beinecke Library, dated March 10, 1933; cited in *Psyche Reborn*, p. 121.
53. H.D., *Tribute to Freud*, p. 25.
54. ———, *The Walls Do Not Fall*, in *Collected Poems*, p. 511.
55. Ibid.
56. Ibid.
57. Ibid., p. 512.
58. For an analysis of this female imagery, see Susan Gubar, "The Echoing Spell of H.D.'s *Trilogy*," pp. 203–204; and Susan Stanford Friedman, "Psyche Reborn: Tradition, Re-Vision and the Goddess as Mother-Symbol in H.D.'s Epic Poetry," *Women's Studies* 6 (1979): 155–156.
59. H.D., *The Walls Do Not Fall*, in *Collected Poems*, p. 523.
60. Ibid., p. 524.
61. Ibid., pp. 525, 529.
62. Ibid., p. 534.
63. Ibid., pp. 534–535.
64. Ibid., p. 536.
65. Ibid.
66. Riddel, "H.D. and the Poetics of 'Spiritual Realism,'" p. 407.
67. H.D., *Pilate's Wife*, unpublished historical novel, Beinecke Library; p. 25.
68. ———, *The Walls Do Not Fall*, in *Collected Poems*, p. 537.
69. Ibid., p. 540.
70. Ibid., p. 541.
71. Ibid., p. 543.
72. H.D., *Bid Me to Live*, p. 162.

73. ———, *Tribute to the Angels*, in *Collected Poems*, pp. 547–548.
74. Ibid., p. 552.
75. Ibid., pp. 553–554.
76. Ibid., p. 554.
77. Ibid., p. 563.
78. Ibid., pp. 564–566.
79. Ibid., p. 567.
80. Neumann, *Great Mother*, pp. 319–325.
81. H.D., *Tribute to the Angels*, in *Collected Poems*, p. 568.
82. Ibid., p. 569.
83. Ibid., p. 570.
84. Ibid.
85. Ibid., pp. 571–572.
86. H.D., *The Flowering of the Rod*, in *Collected Poems*, pp. 578–579.
87. Ibid., p. 590.
88. Ibid., p. 593.
89. Virginia Woolf, *A Room of One's Own* (1929; reprint ed., New York: Harcourt Brace, 1957), p. 79. The full quotation reads, "For we think back through our mothers if we are women. It is useless to go to the great men writers for help, however much one may go to them for pleasure."
90. H.D., *The Flowering of the Rod*, in *Collected Poems*, p. 596.
91. Ibid., p. 598.
92. Ibid., pp. 600–602.
93. Ibid., p. 603.
94. Gubar, "The Echoing Spell of H.D.'s *Trilogy*," p. 213.
95. For a thorough analysis of these family constructs, see Du Plessis, "Romantic Thralldom in H.D.," p. 189.
96. H.D., *The Flowering of the Rod*, in *Collected Poems*, p. 612.
97. ———, *Tribute to Freud*, p. 16.
98. ———, "Helen," in *Collected Poems*, pp. 154–155.
99. ———, *Helen in Egypt*, p. 2.
100. The comment on the mother as muse is from the introduction to *End to Torment*, p. 41; the quotation from Edgar Allan Poe's "Helen" appears in *Tribute to Freud*, p. 65.
101. H.D., *Tribute to Freud*, p. 55.
102. The phrase "herself/her selves" is a variation on Adrienne Rich's "*Nothing but myself? . . . my selves*," from "Integrity," *A Wild Patience Has Taken Me This Far: Poems, 1978–1981* (New York: Norton, 1981), p. 8. The second quotation is attributed to H.D. by Horace Gregory in his introduction to the New Directions edition of *Helen in Egypt*, p. ix.
103. Susan Stanford Friedman, "Creating a Women's Mythology: H.D.'s *Helen in Egypt*," *Women's Studies* 5 (1977); 167–168.
104. H.D., *Helen in Egypt*, p. 3.

105. Ibid., p. 2.
106. Ibid., p. 4.
107. Ibid., p. 7.
108. Ibid., p. 10.
109. Ibid., p. 13.
110. Ibid.
111. Ibid., p. 16.
112. Ibid., p. 17.
113. Ibid.
114. Ibid., pp. 22–23.
115. Ibid., p. 26.
116. Ibid., p. 28.
117. Ibid., pp. 37–38.
118. Ibid., p. 36.
119. Ibid., p. 47.
120. Ibid., p. 63.
121. Ibid., pp. 68–69.
122. Louise Bogan, "The Sleeping Fury," in *The Blue Estuaries: Poems, 1923–1968* (New York: Ecco Press, 1977), pp. 78–79.
123. H.D., *Helen in Egypt*, p. 69.
124. Ibid., pp. 72–73.
125. Ibid., p. 76.
126. Ibid., p. 72.
127. Ibid., p. 75.
128. Ibid., p. 85.
129. Ibid., p. 91.
130. Ibid.
131. Ibid., p. 97.
132. This point of view is best represented by Linda Welshimer Wagner, "*Helen in Egypt*: A Culmination," *Contemporary Literature* 10 (Autumn 1969): 530.
133. For a more detailed discussion of H.D.'s pacifism, see Friedman, "Creating a Women's Mythology," p. 180.
134. H.D., *Helen in Egypt*, pp. 93–94.
135. Ibid., p. 98.
136. Ibid., pp. 102–103.
137. Ibid., pp. 109–110.
138. Ibid., p. 175.
139. Ibid., p. 176.
140. Ibid., p. 177.
141. Ibid., pp. 178–179.
142. Ibid., p. 187.
143. Ibid., p. 190.

144. Ibid., p. 193.
145. Ibid., pp. 195–197.
146. Ibid., p. 205.
147. Ibid., p. 209.
148. Ibid., p. 240.
149. For an illuminating discussion of the resentment that accrues from male efforts at separation from the mother, see Dorothy Dinnerstein, *The Mermaid and the Minotaur: Sexual Arrangement and the Human Malaise* (New York: Harper & Row, 1976).
150. H.D:, *Helen in Egypt*, p. 256.
151. Ibid., pp. 227–228.
152. Friedman, "Creating a Women's Mythology," p. 182.
153. H.D., *Helen in Egypt*, p. 255.
154. Ibid., p. 264.
155. Ibid., p. 269.
156. Ibid., p. 271.
157. Ibid., p. 187.
158. H.D., *Tribute to Freud*, p. 108.
159. Ibid., p. 17.
160. H.D., "Hermetic Definition," in *Hermetic Definition*, p. 3.
161. Ibid., p. 4.
162. Ibid., p. 7.
163. Ibid., p. 8.
164. The quotation is from Norman Holmes Pearson's foreword to *Hermetic Definition*, but Vincent Quinn advances a similar argument in "H.D.'s 'Hermetic Definition': The Poet as Archetypal Mother," *Contemporary Literature* 18 (Winter 1977); 51–61.
165. H.D., "Hermetic Definition," in *Hermetic Definition*, pp. 22–23.
166. Ibid., p. 31.
167. Ibid., p. 33.
168. Ibid., p. 37.
169. Ibid., p. 44.
170. Pearson, foreword to *Hermetic Definition*.
171. H.D., "Hermetic Definition," in *Hermetic Definition*, p. 45.
172. Ibid., p. 49.
173. Ibid., p. 50.
174. Ibid., p. 54.
175. Ibid., p. 55.
176. H.D., "Sagesse," in *Hermetic Definition*, p. 59.
177. Ibid., p. 69.
178. Ibid., p. 73.
179. Ibid., p. 75.
180. Ibid., p. 82.

181. H.D., "Winter Love," in *Hermetic Definition*, p. 91.
182. Ibid., p. 92.
183. Ibid., pp. 104–108.
184. Ibid., p. 110.
185. Ibid., p. 111.
186. Ibid., p. 115.
187. Ibid., p. 116.
188. Ibid., p. 117.
189. Book LXV, *Vale Ave*, a "historical epic" poem, Beinecke Library; p. 57. Published in *New Directions* 44 (1982): pp. 18–166.

CHAPTER 4

1. May Sarton, *Plant Dreaming Deep* (New York: Norton, 1973), p. 151.
2. ———, "The Autumn Sonnets," in *Collected Poems, 1930–1973* (New York: Norton, 1974), p. 386.
3. Robert Graves, "In Dedication," prologue to *The White Goddess* (1948; reprint ed., New York: Farrar, Straus & Giroux, 1975), p. 5.
4. Quoted in Adrienne Rich, "Poetry, Personality and Wholeness: A Response to Galway Kinnell," *Field: Contemporary Poetry and Poetics* 7 (Fall 1972); 14.
5. Sarton, *Mrs. Stevens Hears the Mermaids Singing* (New York: Norton, 1965), p. 186.
6. ———, "Birthday on the Acropolis," in *Collected Poems*, pp. 251–253.
7. ———, *Mrs. Stevens*, p. 191.
8. Southey to Charlotte Brontë, March 1837. Cited by Winifred Gérin, *Charlotte Brontë: The Evolution of Genius* (Oxford: Oxford University Press, 1967), p. 110.
9. Sarton, *Mrs. Stevens*, p. 190.
10. Ibid., p. 47.
11. Aphra Behn, Preface to *The Lucky Chance*, in *The Works of Aphra Behn*, ed. Montague Summers (New York: Benjamine Blom, 1967), 6 vols., 3:187. Cited in Sandra M. Gilbert and Susan Gubar, *The Madwoman in the Attic: The Woman Writer and the Nineteenth-century Literary Imagination* (New Haven: Yale University Press, 1979), p. 66.
12. Sarton, *Mrs. Stevens*, p. 127.
13. Gilbert and Gubar, *Madwoman in the Attic*, pp. 49–50.
14. Sarton, *Mrs. Stevens*, p. 77.
15. Ibid., p. 190.
16. *World of Light: A Portrait of May Sarton*, Ishtar Films, 1979. In this chapter I use the title *World of Light* to identify the film and to distinguish it from Sarton's collection of biographical sketches, *A World of Light*.

17. Sarton, *Journal of a Solitude* (New York: Norton, 1973), p. 40.
18. *World of Light* (Ishtar).
19. Sarton, *Mrs. Stevens*, p. 181.
20. Ibid., pp. 185–186.
21. Ibid., p. 154.
22. Ibid., p. 83.
23. Ibid., p. 147.
24. Sarton, "The Invocation to Kali," in *Collected Poems*, p. 316.
25. Sarton, *Mrs. Stevens*, p. 193.
26. For a discussion of this mother-daughter link, see Dorothy Dinnerstein, *The Mermaid and the Minotaur: Sexual Arrangement and Human Malaise* (New York: Harper & Row, 1976); and Adrienne Rich, *Of Woman Born: Motherhood as Experience and Institution* (New York: Norton, 1976).
27. Sarton, *Plant Dreaming Deep*, p. 70.
28. ———, *Journal of a Solitude*, p. 16.
29. See, for example, Delores Shelley, "An Interview with May Sarton," *Women and Literature* 7 (Spring 1979): 33–41.
30. Sarton, *Mrs. Stevens*, p. 107.
31. Ibid., p. 108.
32. Ibid., p. 141.
33. Ibid., p. 146.
34. Ibid., p. 92.
35. Ibid., p. 16.
36. Ibid., pp. 161–162.
37. Ibid., p. 164.
38. Ibid., p. 169.
39. Ibid.
40. Ibid., p. 171.
41. Ibid., p. 170.
42. Ibid., p. 181.
43. Ibid., p. 64.
44. Ibid., pp. 192–193.
45. Sarton, *Journal of a Solitude*, pp. 12, 55.
46. ———, "My Sisters, O My Sisters," in *Collected Poems*, pp. 74–77.
47. ———, "Poets and the Rain," Ibid., p. 110.
48. Denise Levertov, "In Mind," in *Poems, 1960–1967* (New York: New Directions, 1967), p. 143; and Louise Bogan, "The Dream," in *The Blue Estuaries: Poems, 1923–1968* (New York: Ecco Press, 1977), p. 103.
49. Sarton, "Poets and the Rain," in *Collected Poems*, p. 111.
50. ———, "Journey Toward Poetry," Ibid., p. 151.
51. ———, *Mrs. Stevens*, p. 151.
52. Ibid., p. 185.
53. Shelley, "An Interview with May Sarton," pp. 38–39.

54. For a discussion of Aphrodite's link to dual-faceted Eastern goddesses, see Erich Neumann, *The Great Mother: An Analysis of the Archetype*, trans. Ralph Manheim (1955; reprint ed., Princeton: Princeton University Press, 1972), pp. 80–81, 273–275.
55. Sarton, "These Images Remain," in *Collected Poems*, pp. 144–147.
56. ———, *Mrs. Stevens*, p. 153.
57. ———, "The Return of Aphrodite," in *Collected Poems*, p. 367.
58. ———, "A Divorce of Lovers," Ibid., pp. 201–205.
59. See, for example, Bogan's "Poem in Prose," "My Voice Not Being Proud," and "Sub Contra," all in *Blue Estuaries*, pp. 72, 13, and 5, respectively.
60. Sarton, "A Divorce of Lovers," in *Collected Poems*, p. 207.
61. ———, *Letters from Maine* (New York: Norton, 1984), pp. 18–27.
62. ———, *Mrs. Stevens*, p. 92.
63. ———, "A Divorce of Lovers," in *Collected Poems*, p. 202.
64. Ibid., p. 205.
65. Ibid., p. 207.
66. Sarton, "Furies," in *Collected Poems*, p. 162.
67. ———, "A Storm of Angels," Ibid., p. 69.
68. ———, "Control," in *Halfway to Silence* (New York: Norton, 1980), p. 32.
69. ———, "After the Tiger," in *Collected Poems*, pp. 321–322.
70. Bogan, "The Sleeping Fury," in *Blue Estuaries*, pp. 78–79.
71. Sarton, "Godhead as Lynx," in *Collected Poems*, pp. 352–53.
72. ———, "The Muse as Medusa," Ibid., p. 332.
73. ———, *Mrs. Stevens*, p. 161.
74. Ibid., pp. 155–156.
75. Sarton, "She Shall Be Called Woman," in *Collected Poems*, pp. 20–26.
76. ———, "An Observation," in *Collected Poems*, p. 271.
77. Sarton discussed this poem and her difficulties in writing it in a speech entitled "Proteus: The Joys and Hazards of Being a Poet," St. Benedict's College, St. Joseph, Minn., November 24, 1980.
78. ———, *Mrs. Stevens*, p. 156.
79. ———, "The Invocation to Kali," in *Collected Poems*, pp. 316–317.
80. H.D., *End to Torment* (New York: New Directions, 1979), p. 35.
81. Sarton, "The Invocation to Kali," in *Collected Poems*, pp. 316–320.
82. Adrienne Rich, "Motherhood: The Contemporary Emergency and the Quantum Leap," in *On Lies, Secrets and Silence: Selected Prose, 1966–1978* (New York: Norton, 1979), p. 260.
83. Sarton, "Of the Muse," in *Halfway to Silence*, p. 62.
84. Rich, "Women and Honor: Some Notes on Lying," in *On Lies*, pp. 186–188.
85. Sarton, "Of the Muse," in *Halfway to Silence*, p. 62.

CHAPTER 5

1. Adrienne Rich, "Poetry, Personality and Wholeness: A Response to Galway Kinnell," *Field: Contemporary Poetry and Poetics* 7 (Fall 1972): 14–15.
2. ———, "Vesuvius at Home: The Power of Emily Dickinson," in *On Lies, Secrets, and Silence: Selected Prose, 1966–1978* (New York: Norton, 1979), pp. 165–166.
3. Ibid., p. 166.
4. Ibid., p. 173.
5. ———, "Power and Danger: Works of a Common Woman," in *On Lies*, p. 250.
6. ———, "When We Dead Awaken: Writing as Re-Vision," Ibid., p. 36.
7. ———, "Poetry, Personality and Wholeness," p. 12.
8. ———, "Integrity," in *A Wild Patience Has Taken Me This Far: Poems, 1978–1981* (New York: Norton, 1981), pp. 8–9.
9. Ibid., p. 9.
10. Rich, "When We Dead Awaken," in *On Lies*, p. 35.
11. This statement by Rich appeared in the original version of "When We Dead Awaken," in *College English* 24 (October 1972): 25.
12. ———, "Power and Danger," in *On Lies*, p. 248.
13. ———, "When We Dead Awaken," Ibid., p. 43.
14. ———, "Power and Danger," Ibid., p. 247.
15. Ibid., p. 248.
16. ———, "Natural Resources," in *The Dream of a Common Language: Poems, 1974–1977* (New York: Norton, 1978), p. 67.
17. Marilyn R. Farwell, "Adrienne Rich and an Organic Feminist Criticism," *College English* 39 (October 1977): 194. I am indebted to Farwell for her thorough and insightful work on Rich's poetic theory.
18. Rich, *Of Woman Born: Motherhood as Experience and Institution* (New York: Norton, 1976), p. 225.
19. ———, "Poetry and Experience: Statement at a Poetry Reading, 1964," in *Adrienne Rich's Poetry*, ed. Barbara Charlesworth Gelpi and Albert Gelpi (New York: Norton, 1975), p. 89.
20. ———, *Of Woman Born*, p. 16.
21. ———, "Vesuvius at Home," in *On Lies*, p. 181.
22. ———, Preface to "Women and Honor: Some Notes on Lying," Ibid., p. 185. Rich attributes the phrase "liberating ourselves from our secrets" to Beverly Tanenhaus.
23. Margaret Homans, *Women Writers and Poetic Identity: Dorothy Wordsworth, Emily Brontë, and Emily Dickinson* (Princeton: Princeton University Press, 1980), p. 217.
24. Rich, "Women and Honor," in *On Lies*, p. 188.

25. Ibid., p. 191.
26. Marilyn R. Farwell develops this theory further in "Adrienne Rich's Images of Female Creativity: Androgyne, Mother and Lesbian," a paper delivered at the Conference on Women Writing Poetry in America, Stanford University, April 1982.
27. "The Antifeminist Woman: Review Essay on *The New Chastity, and Other Arguments against Women's Liberation* by Midge Decter," *New York Review of Books* 19, no. 9 (November 30, 1972): 39–40. Interestingly, Rich deleted the quotation I have cited when the essay was reprinted in *On Lies*, pp. 69–84. In her preface to the reprinted version, Rich explains, "Rereading this text in 1978 I find opinions which I now question (*Is* there a 'ghostly woman' in all men? What did I mean by this anyway?)."
28. Rich, *Of Woman Born*, p. 284.
29. ———, "It is the Lesbian in Us," in *On Lies*, p. 201.
30. The first quote is from Rich, "Transcendental Etude," in *Dream*, p. 77; the second is from "When We Dead Awaken, in *On Lies*, p. 35.
31. W. H. Auden, foreword to *A Change of World*, in *Adrienne Rich's Poetry*, pp. 126–127.
32. T. S. Eliot, "Tradition and the Individual Talent," in *The Sacred Wood: Essays on Poetry and Criticism* (1920; reprint ed., London: Methuen, 1960), p. 54.
33. Albert Gelpi, "Adrienne Rich: The Poetics of Change," in *Adrienne Rich's Poetry*, p. 130.
34. Rich, "When We Dead Awaken," p. 39.
35. Randall Jarrell uses these adjectives to describe Rich and her early poetry in his review of *The Diamond Cutters and Other Poems*. Reprinted in *Adrienne Rich's Poetry*, pp. 127–129. Rich discusses her dissatisfaction with her early poetry and poetic strategies, especially her various distancing devices, in "When We Dead Awaken," pp. 44–48.
36. Rich, "Aunt Jennifer's Tigers," in *Poems: Selected and New, 1950–1974* (New York: Norton, 1975), p. 4.
37. ———, "When We Dead Awaken," in *On Lies*, p. 40.
38. ———, "The Loser," in *Poems: Selected and New*, pp. 45–46.
39. ———, "The Roofwalker," Ibid., pp. 63–64.
40. Homans, *Women Writers and Poetic Identity*, p. 104.
41. Rich, "Lucifer in the Train," in *Poems: Selected and New*, p. 18.
42. ———, "The Insomniacs," Ibid., pp. 27–29.
43. ———, "Orion," Ibid., pp. 95–96.
44. ———, "When We Dead Awaken," in *On Lies*, pp. 45–47.
45. ———, "Planetarium," in *Poems: Selected and New*, p. 147.
46. ———, "When We Dead Awaken," in *On Lies*, p. 47.
47. Rich explains in "Snapshots of a Daughter-in-Law" that these epithets were delivered against Mary Wollstonecraft. See *Poems: Selected and New*, p. 49.

48. Rich, "Planetarium," in *Poems: Selected and New*, pp. 147–148.
49. Sylvia Plath, "Kindness," in *The Collected Poems* (New York: Harper & Row, 1981), p. 270.
50. Helen Vendler, "Ghostlier Demarcations, Keener Sounds," in *Adrienne Rich's Poetry*, p. 163.
51. Denise Levertov, "Stepping Westward," in *The Sorrow Dance* (1963; reprint ed., New York: New Directions, 1966), p. 15.
52. Rich, "When We Dead Awaken," in *On Lies*, p. 44.
53. Ibid., pp. 44–45.
54. Rich, "Snapshots," in *Poems: Selected and New*, pp. 47–48.
55. ———, "Women and Honor," in *On Lies*, p. 185.
56. ———, "Snapshots," in *Poems: Selected and New*, p. 48.
57. For a different poetic picture of Dickinson as one who "chose to have it out on her own premises," see "I Am in Danger—Sir," written in 1964, four years after "Snapshots."
58. Rich, "Snapshots," in *Poems: Selected and New*, pp. 49–51.
59. The quotation from Beauvoir was originally cited by Rich in French. See note 19, *Adrienne Rich's Poetry*, p. 16.
60. Wendy Martin, "From Patriarchy to Female Principle: A Chronological Reading of Adrienne Rich's Poems," in *Adrienne Rich's Poetry*, p. 175.
61. The latter quote appears in Rich, "Re-forming the Crystal," in *Poems: Selected and New*, p. 228.
62. Rich, "The Corpse-Plant," Ibid., pp. 72–74.
63. ———, "Night-Pieces: For a Child," Ibid., pp. 81–82.
64. Hélène Cixous, "Sorties," in Catherine Clement and Hélène Cixous, *La Jeune Née* (Paris: Union d'Editions, 1975), pp. 114–246.
65. May Sarton, *Mrs. Stevens Hears the Mermaids Singing* (New York: Norton, 1965), p. 156.
66. Rich, "Women," in *Poems: Selected and New*, pp. 109–110.
67. Levertov, "In Mind," in *Poems, 1960–1967* (New York: New Directions, 1967), p. 143.
68. Rich, "When We Dead Awaken," in *On Lies*, p. 49.
69. ———, "I Dream I'm the Death of Orpheus," in *Poems: Selected and New*, pp. 151–152.
70. Albert Gelpi, "Adrienne Rich: The Poetics of Change," p. 147.
71. See M. L. von Franz, "The Process of Individuation," in *Man and His Symbols*, ed. C. G. Jung (New York: Dell, 1964), pp. 171–185.
72. Rich, "Letters: March 1969," in *Poems: Selected and New*, pp. 161–162.
73. ———, *Diving into the Wreck: Poems, 1971–1972* (New York: Norton, 1973).
74. Farwell, "Adrienne Rich and an Organic Feminist Criticism," pp. 193–194.
75. Rich, "The Antifeminist Woman," in *On Lies*, p. 84.
76. Barbara Charlesworth Gelpi, "The Politics of Androgyny," *Women's Studies*

2 (1974): 151. This entire issue is devoted to the topic of androgyny as a literary and psychological construct.

77. Rich, "The Stranger," in *Diving into the Wreck*, p. 18.
78. Mary Daly discusses androgyny as a potentially liberating concept in *Beyond God the Father: Towards a Philosophy of Women's Liberation* (Boston: Beacon Press, 1973). Like Rich, however, she later repudiates the term.
79. Rich, "Diving into the Wreck," in *Diving into the Wreck*, pp. 22–24.
80. See Marilyn R. Farwell, "Virginia Woolf and Androgyny," *Contemporary Literature* 16 (Autumn 1975): 433–451; and Cynthia Secor, "Androgyny: An Early Reappraisal," *Women's Studies* 2 (1974): 161–167.
81. Rich, *Of Woman Born*, pp. 76–77(fn).
82. ———, "Natural Resources," in *Dream*, pp. 60–67.
83. ———, *Of Woman Born*, pp. 225–226.
84. Ibid., pp. 219–220.
85. H.D., *End to Torment* (New York: New Directions, 1979), p. 41.
86. Rich, *Of Woman Born*, p. 220.
87. Ibid., p. 13.
88. Rich, "The Antifeminist Woman," in *On Lies*, pp. 77–78.
89. ———, *Of Woman Born*, pp. 283–284.
90. Ibid., p. 72.
91. Ibid., p. 240.
92. Rich, "Mother = Right," in *Dream*, p. 59.
93. For a cogent analysis of Irigaray's feminist theory, see Carolyn Burke, Introduction to Luce Irigaray, "When Our Lips Speak Together," *Signs: Journal of Women in Culture and Society* 6 (Autumn 1980): 67.
94. Rich, "Splittings," in *Dream*, pp. 10–11.
95. ———, "The Mirror in Which Two Are Seen as One," in *Poems, Selected and New*, pp. 194–195.
96. ———, "Cartographies of Silence," in *Dream*, pp. 16–20.
97. ———, "Paula Becker to Clara Westhoff," in *Dream*, p. 44.
98. ———, "Transcendental Etude," in *Dream*, pp. 72–77.
99. ———, *Of Woman Born*, p. 225.
100. ———, "The Spirit of Place," in *Wild Patience*, pp. 40–45.
101. ———, "Natural Resources," in *Dream*, p. 67.
102. ———, "Halfway," in *Poems: Selected and New*, p. 89.
103. ———, "For a Russian Poet," Ibid., p. 106.
104. ———, "The Observer," Ibid., pp. 112–113.
105. ———, "The Blue Ghazals," Ibid., p. 153.
106. ———, "Blood-Sister," Ibid., p. 223.
107. ———, "From an Old House in America," Ibid., p. 245.
108. ———, "Phantasia for Elvira Shatayev," in *Dream*, pp. 4–6.
109. Ibid., p. 7.

110. Rich, "Conditions for Work: The Common World of Women," in *On Lies*, p. 208.
111. Rich talked at length about her efforts to write a poetry free from "amnesia" during a reading at Reed College, Portland, Ore., February 3, 1982.
112. Rich, "Grandmothers," in *Wild Patience*, p. 112.
113. ———, "Heroines," Ibid., pp. 35–36.
114. ———, "The Spirit of Place," Ibid., pp. 40–45.
115. Homans, *Women Writers and Poetic Identity*, pp. 226–229.
116. Joanne Feit Diehl, " 'Cartographies of Silence': Rich's *Common Language* and the Woman Poet," *Feminist Studies* 6 (Fall 1980): 531–532.
117. Rich attributes the phrase "hearing each other into speech," to Nelle Morton. Introduction to "Women and Honor," in *On Lies*, p. 185.
118. Rich, "Burden Baskets," in *Wild Patience*, p. 53.
119. ———, "Hohokam," Ibid., p. 54.
120. For this distinction between *archetype* and *prototype*, I am grateful to Rachel Blau DuPlessis. See "The Critique of Consciousness in Levertov, Rich and Rukeyser," in *Shakespeare's Sisters*, p. 299. A later version of this chapter appears in her *Writing Beyond the Ending: Narrative Strategies of Twentieth-century Women Writers* (Bloomington: Indiana University Press, 1985).
121. Rich, "Mary Jane Colter, 1904," in *Wild Patience*, p. 58.
122. Diehl, " 'Cartographies of Silence': Rich's *Common Language* and the Woman Poet," p. 531.
123. Rich, "Turning the Wheel," in *Wild Patience*, p. 59.
124. ———, "Conditions for Work," in *On Lies*, pp. 208–209.

CHAPTER 6

1. Audre Lorde, *Zami: A New Spelling of My Name* (1982; reprint ed., Trumansburg, N.Y.: Crossing Press, 1983), pp. 3–5.
2. Claudia Tate, ed., *Black Women Writers at Work* (New York: Continuum, 1983), p. 102.
3. Ibid.
4. Ibid., p. 106.
5. The phrase "the transformation of silence into language and action," which first appeared in *Sinister Wisdom* 6, is quoted in Karla Hammond, "An Interview with Audre Lorde," *American Poetry Review*, March/April 1980, p. 18. Adrienne Rich's phrase appears in her preface to "Women and Honor: Some Notes on Lying," in *On Lies, Secrets, and Silence: Selected Prose, 1966–1978* (New York: Norton, 1979), p. 185.
6. Lorde, "A Song for Many Movements," in *The Black Unicorn: Poems* (New York: Norton, 1978), pp. 52–53.

7. ———, "Coal," in *Chosen Poems—Old and New* (New York: Norton, 1982), pp. 10–11.
8. Tate, *Black Women Writers*, p. 104.
9. Hammond, "Interview with Audre Lorde," p. 19.
10. Tate, *Black Women Writers*, p. 108.
11. Hammond, "Interview with Audre Lorde," p. 19.
12. Lorde, *Zami*, p. 255.
13. ———, "Meet," in *The Black Unicorn*, pp. 33–34.
14. Hammond, "Interview with Audre Lorde," p. 18.
15. Lorde, "Outside," in *The Black Unicorn*, pp. 61–62.
16. Audre Lorde and Adrienne Rich, "An Interview with Audre Lorde," *Signs: Journal of Women in Culture and Society* 6 (Summer 1981): 715.
17. Lorde, *Zami*, p. 32.
18. ———, "Story Books on a Kitchen Table," in *Chosen Poems*, p. 35.
19. Sylvia Plath, "The Disquieting Muses," in *The Collected Poems* (New York: Harper & Row, 1981), pp. 74–76.
20. Lorde, "Story Books on a Kitchen Table," in *Chosen Poems*, p. 35.
21. ———, "Black Mother Woman," Ibid., p. 52.
22. ———, "The Woman Thing," Ibid., pp. 14–15.
23. Hammond, "Interview with Audre Lorde," p. 18.
24. Lorde, *Zami*, p. 31.
25. ———, "Prologue," in *Chosen Poems*, p. 60.
26. ———, *Zami*, p. 255.
27. Ibid., p. 7.
28. Adrienne Rich, "Sibling Mysteries," in *The Dream of a Common Language: Poems, 1974–1977* (New York: Norton, 1978), pp. 47–52.
29. Lorde, "A Family Resemblance," in *Chosen Poems*, p. 29.
30. ———, "Harriet," in *The Black Unicorn*, p. 21.
31. Tate, "Black Women Writers," p. 109.
32. Lorde, "The Erotic as Power" (Brooklyn, N.Y.: Out and Out Books, 1978).
33. ———, "Love Poem," in *Chosen Poems*, p. 77.
34. ———, "Woman," in *The Black Unicorn*, p. 82.
35. ———, "Walking Our Boundaries," Ibid., p. 39.
36. ———, "Meet," Ibid., p. 33.
37. ———, "Recreation," Ibid., p. 81.
38. ———, "From the Greenhouse," Ibid., p. 101.
39. ———, "Letter for Jan," Ibid., p. 88.
40. Ibid., pp. 88–89.
41. For a discussion of Mawu's powers of creation, see Merlin Stone, *Ancient Mirrors of Womanhood: Our Goddess and Heroine Heritage*, vol. 1 (New York: New Sibylline Books, 1979), pp. 137–140. It is interesting to note that Mawu was sometimes known as Mawulisa, an androgynous blend of Mawu, the moon goddess-creator, and her son Lisa, the sun god. Also,

despite her associations with Dahomean Amazons, Mawu according to Stone was a peace-loving goddess who stressed human humility and taught that aggression and fighting are wrong.

42. Lorde, "Scar," in *The Black Unicorn*, p. 50.
43. Lorde describes *The Black Unicorn* in these words in her epigraph to *Chosen Poems*.
44. Lorde, "When the Saints Come Marching In," in *Chosen Poems*, p. 22.
45. ———, "The Winds of Orisha," Ibid., p. 48.
46. For an overview of Yoruba creation myths and the roles of Yemanja and Oshun, see Harold Courlander, *A Treasury of African Folklore: The Oral Literature, Traditions, Myths, Legends, Epics, Tales, Recollections, Wisdoms, Sayings, and Humor of Africa* (New York: Crown, 1975), pp. 184–238. Since Courlander's analysis is male-centered, one might also consult Merlin Stone, *When God Was a Woman* (New York: Harcourt Brace Jovanovich, 1978). Lorde provides a useful "glossary of African Names Used in the Poems" in *The Black Unicorn*, pp. 119–122.
47. Lorde, "The Winds of Orisha," in *Chosen Poems*, p. 48.
48. ———, "From the House of Yemanja," in *The Black Unicorn*, pp. 6–7.
49. ———, "Dahomey," Ibid., p. 10.
50. Lorde herself has had a mastectomy, a fact that may help explain her frequent invocation of Seboulisa, the one-breasted deity, as muse. See *The Cancer Journals*, 2nd ed. (San Francisco: Spinster's Ink, 1980), for Lorde's account of her surgery and recovery.
51. Lorde, "Dahomey," in *The Black Unicorn*, pp. 10–11.
52. Stone, *Ancient Mirrors*, pp. 137–138.
53. Lorde, "125th Street and Abomey," in *The Black Unicorn*, pp. 12–13.
54. ———, "Dear Toni Instead of a Letter," in *Chosen Poems*, p. 58; "Chorus" and "For Assata," in *The Black Unicorn*, pp. 44 and 28.
55. ———, "The Women of Dan Dance with Swords in Their Hands to Mark the Time When They Were Warriors," in *The Black Unicorn*, pp. 14–15.
56. ———, "The Black Unicorn," Ibid., p. 3.
57. ———, "A Woman Speaks," Ibid., p. 4.
58. ———, "Power," Ibid., pp. 108–109.
59. ———, "Solstice," Ibid., pp. 117–118.
60. Tate, *Black Women Writers*, p. 125.
61. Lorde, "A Litany for Survival," in *The Black Unicorn*, pp. 31–32.
62. ———, "Sequelae," in *The Black Unicorn*, pp. 25–27; "Change of Season," in *Chosen Poems*, p. 40.
63. Tate, *Black Women Writers*, p. 104.
64. ———, "Chain," in *The Black Unicorn*, pp. 22–24.
65. ———, "Afterimages," in *Chosen Poems*, pp. 102–105.
66. ———, "Need: A Choral of Black Women's Voices," Ibid., pp. 111–115.
67. Hammond, "Interview with Audre Lorde," p. 20.

68. Rich, "It Is the Lesbian in Us," in *On Lies*, p. 201.
69. Hammond, "Interview with Audre Lorde," p. 21.
70. Ibid.
71. Lorde, "October," in *Chosen Poems*, p. 108.

CHAPTER 7

1. The title quote is taken from a poem by Marge Piercy in *Circles on the Water: Selected Poems of Marge Piercy* (New York: Knopf, 1982), p. 97. Other quotes are from *The White Goddess: A Historical Grammar of Poetic Myth* (1948; reprint ed., New York: Farrar, Straus and Giroux, 1975), p. 447; "The Laugh of the Medusa," trans. Keith Cohen and Paula Cohen, in *Signs: Journal of Women in Culture and Society* 1 (Summer 1976): 881–882; "Speaking in Tongues: A Letter to Third World Women Writers," in *This Bridge Called My Back: Writings by Radical Women of Color*; ed. Cherrié Moraga and Gloria Anzaldúa (Watertown, Mass.: Persephone Press, 1983), p. 173.
2. For a discussion of Queen Elizabeth's poetry, see *The World Split Open: Four Centuries of Women Poets in England and America, 1552–1950*, ed. Louise Bernikow (New York: Vintage, 1974), pp. 51–52.
3. Graves, *The White Goddess*, pp. 303–315.
4. Harold Bloom, *The Anxiety of Influence: A Theory of Poetry* (New York: Oxford University Press, 1973), pp. 60–65.
5. ———, *A Map of Misreading* (New York: Oxford University Press, 1975), p. 33.
6. Denise Levertov, "Song for Ishtar," in *Poems, 1960–1967* (New York: New Directions, 1967), p. 75.
7. Margaret Homans, *Women Writers and Poetic Identity: Dorothy Wordsworth, Emily Brontë, and Emily Dickinson* (Princeton: Princeton University Press, 1980), pp. 215–236; Pamela DiPesa, "The Imperious Muse: Some Observations on Women, Nature, and the Poetic Tradition," in *Feminist Criticism: Essays on Theory, Poetry and Prose*, ed. Cheryl L. Brown and Karen Olsen (Metuchen, N.J.: Scarecrow Press, 1978), pp. 59–68.
8. Ruth Perry and Martine Watson Brownley, eds., *Mothering the Mind: Twelve Studies of Writers and Their Silent Partners* (New York and London: Holmes & Meier, 1984), pp. 3–11.
9. Quoted in Elizabeth Frank, *Louise Bogan: A Portrait* (New York: Knopf, 1985), p. 352.
10. Adrienne Rich, response to Susan Stanford Friedman's "Adrienne Rich and H.D.: An Intertextual Study," in *Signs: Journal of Women in Culture and Society* 9 (Summer 1984), 734. Hereafter cited as Rich to Friedman.
11. "The Transformation of Silence into Language and Action" was the title of a Modern Language Association panel on which Lorde and Rich appeared in 1977.

12. May Sarton, "Louise Bogan," in *A World of Light: Portraits and Celebrations* (New York: Norton, 1976), p. 215.
13. ———, *Mrs. Stevens Hears the Mermaids Singing* (New York: Norton, 1965), p. 154.
14. Bogan to Sarton, April 24, 1940, in *What the Woman Lived: Selected Letters to Louise Bogan, 1920–1970*, ed. Ruth Limmer (New York: Harcourt Brace Jovanovich, 1973), p. 207.
15. Sarton, *A World of Light*, pp. 217–218.
16. Bogan to Sarton, February 16, 1954; cited in *What the Woman Lived*, p. 285.
17. Sarton, *Journal of a Solitude* (New York: Norton, 1973), pp. 30–31.
18. The first quote is from a letter to May Sarton, September 6, 1962; cited in *What the Woman Lived*, p. 346. The second is from a letter quoted by Frank, *Louise Bogan*, p. 355. The verbs "march," "proceed," and "open out" are used in praise of Sarton in a letter from Bogan dated October 31, 1961; cited in *What the Woman Lived*, p. 333.
19. Sarton, *A World of Light*, pp. 224–225.
20. Frank, *Louise Bogan*, p. 353.
21. Ibid., p. 355.
22. Bogan to Sarton, January 28, 1954; cited in *What the Woman Lived*, p. 283.
23. Quoted in Sarton, *A World of Light*, p. 216.
24. Bogan, "The Sleeping Fury," in *The Blue Estuaries: Poems, 1923–1968* (New York: Ecco Press, 1977), pp. 78–79.
25. Sarton, "The Furies" and "The Angels and the Furies," in *Collected Poems, 1930–1973* (New York: Norton, 1974), pp. 162 and 379–380.
26. Bogan, "Medusa," in *Blue Estuaries*, p. 4.
27. Sarton, "The Muse as Medusa," in *Collected Poems*, p. 332.
28. Bogan, "Poem in Prose" and "Sonnet," in *Blue Estuaries*, pp. 72, 48.
29. Sarton, "A Divorce of Lovers," in *Collected Poems*, p. 207; "Letters from Maine," in *Letters from Maine* (New York: Norton, 1984), pp. 18–27.
30. "It is wonderful to know that my poems *spoke* to you: 'The Daemon,' especially, which was written (given!) one afternoon almost between one curb of a street and another." Bogan to Sarton, November 13, 1959; cited in *What the Woman Lived*, p. 317.
31. From a letter quoted in Frank, *Louise Bogan*, p. 355.
32. Bogan to Sarton, October 31, 1961; cited in *What the Woman Lived*, p. 333.
33. Quoted in Frank, *Louise Bogan*, p. 356.
34. Ibid., p. 353.
35. Bogan to Sarton, October 31, 1961; cited in *What the Woman Lived*, p. 333.
36. Bogan to Sarton, August 9, 1962; Ibid., p. 346.
37. Bogan to Sarton, January 28, 1954; Ibid., p. 282.

38. Bogan to Limmer, September 28, 1960; cited in *What the Woman Lived*, p. 325.
39. Bogan to Sarton, August 9, 1962; Ibid., p. 346.
40. Sarton, *Journal of a Solitude*, pp. 129–130.
41. ———, "Elegy for Louise Bogan," in *Collected Poems*, p. 399.
42. This essay first appeared in *Signs: Journal of Women in Culture and Society* 9 (Winter 1983). However, I have used the longer version from *Reading Adrienne Rich: Reviews and Revisions, 1951–81*, ed. Jane Roberta Cooper (Ann Arbor: University of Michigan, 1984), pp. 171–206.
43. Adrienne Rich, *The Dream of a Common Language: Poems, 1974–1977* (New York: Norton, 1978). The epigraph is taken from H.D.'s *The Flowering of the Rod.*
44. Friedman, "Adrienne Rich and H.D.," p. 171.
45. Ibid., p. 174.
46. From *The Walls Do Not Fall*. Both this and *The Flowering of the Rod* are published as part of *Trilogy*, in H.D., *Collected Poems, 1912–1944*, edited by Louis L. Martz (New York: New Directions, 1983).
47. Adrienne Rich, "Power and Danger: Works of a Common Woman," in *On Lies, Secrets, and Silence: Selected Prose, 1966–1978* (New York: Norton, 1979), pp. 256–257; quoted in Friedman, p. 176.
48. Friedman, "Adrienne Rich and H.D.," p. 182.
49. H.D., *Trilogy*, in *Collected Poems*, p. 552.
50. Rich, *Of Woman Born: Motherhood as Experience and Institution* (New York: Norton, 1976), p. 225; and "Sibling Mysteries," in *Dream*, p. 52.
51. ———, "Conditions for Work: The Common World of Women," in *On Lies*, pp. 208–209; cited in Friedman, p. 188.
52. H.D., *Tribute to Freud*; cited in Friedman, p. 188.
53. Rich to Friedman, p. 735.
54. Rich, *A Wild Patience Has Taken Me This Far: Poems, 1978–1981* (New York: Norton, 1981), pp. 52–59.
55. H.D., *Trilogy*, in *Collected Poems*, p. 566.
56. Ibid., pp. 571–572.
57. Ibid., p. 571.
58. Rich, "Self-hatred," in *Wild Patience*, p. 55.
59. ———, "Particularity," Ibid., p. 56.
60. Ibid., p. 57.
61. Rachel Blau DuPlessis, "The Critique of Consciousness in Levertov, Rich and Rukeyser," in *Shakespeare's Sisters: Feminist Essays on Women Poets*, ed. Sandra M. Gilbert and Susan Gubar (Bloomington: Indiana University Press, 1979), p. 299.
62. Rich to Friedman, p. 735.
63. Audre Lorde and Adrienne Rich, "An Interview with Audre Lorde," *Signs: Journal of Women in Culture and Society* 6 (Summer 1981): 731.

64. Karla Hammond, "An Interview with Audre Lorde," *The American Poetry Review*, March/April, 1980, pp. 18–21.
65. Lorde and Rich, "Interview with Audre Lorde," p. 714.
66. Rich, "When We Dead Awaken: Writing as Re-Vision," in *On Lies*, p. 35.
67. "Audre Lorde," in Claudia Tate, ed., *Black Women Writers at Work* (New York: Continuum, 1983), pp. 105, 116.
68. Rich, "When We Dead Awaken," in *On Lies*, p. 35.
69. ———, "Frame," in *Wild Patience*, p. 49.
70. Lorde, "A Song for Many Movements," in *The Black Unicorn: Poems* (New York: Norton, 1978), pp. 52–53.
71. From an essay in *Sinister Wisdom*, vol. 6; quoted in Hammond, "Interview with Audre Lorde," p. 18.
72. Cited in Hammond, "Interview with Audre Lorde," p. 18.
73. Rich, "Particularity," in *Wild Patience*, p. 56.
74. Tate, *Black Women Writers*, p. 109.
75. Rich, "Power," in *Dream*, p. 3. The first section of *Dream*, which consists of eight poems, is entitled "Power."
76. ———, "Disloyal to Civilization: Feminism, Racism, Gynephobia," in *On Lies*, pp. 278–279; and Rich and Lorde, "Interview with Audre Lorde," p. 734.
77. Lorde, "Power," in *The Black Unicorn*, pp. 108–109. For a discussion of the circumstances under which this poem was written, see Rich and Lorde, "Interview with Audre Lorde," pp. 734–735.
78. Rich, "Power and Danger," in *On Lies*, p. 247.
79. Lorde, *Zami: A New Spelling of My Name* (1982; reprint ed., Trumansburg, N.Y.: Crossing Press, 1983), Acknowledgments.
80. ———, "The Master's Tools Will Never Dismantle the Master's House," in *This Bridge*, pp. 98–101.
81. Rich and Lorde, "Interview with Audre Lorde," p. 735.
82. See *The Cancer Journals* (San Francisco: Spinsters Ink, 1980), for Lorde's expression of gratitude to Rich for her support.
83. Rich, "Hunger," in *Dream*, pp. 12–14.
84. Tate, *Black Women Writers*, p. 105.
85. Rich and Lorde, "Interview with Audre Lorde," pp. 731–732.
86. Ibid., p. 733.
87. Ibid., p. 732.
88. This quotation is taken from the book jacket of *Dream*.
89. The phrase "hearing each other into speech" is attributed to the feminist theologian Nelle Morton. Cited in Rich, *On Lies*, p. 185.
90. Maya Angelou, "Phenominal Woman," in *And Still I Rise* (New York: Random House, 1978), pp. 8–10.
91. Nikki Giovanni, "Ego Tripping," in *Re-Creation* (Detroit: Broadside Press, 1970), pp. 37–38.

92. Judy Grahn, "The good weef is both," in *The Queen of Wands* (Trumansburg, N.Y.: Crossing Press, 1982), p. 32.
93. Julia de Burgos, "To Julia de Burgos," trans. Grace Schulman, in *The Penguin Book of Women Poets*, ed. Carol Cosman, Joan Keefe, and Kathleen Weaver (Middlesex and New York: Penguin Books, 1979), p. 327.
94. Gloria Anzaldúa, "Speaking in Tongues: A Letter to Third World Women Writers," in *This Bridge*, pp. 169–170 (used with permission of Kitchen Table Women of Color Press).
95. Carol Gilligan, *In A Different Voice: Psychological Theory and Women's Development* (Cambridge, Mass.: Harvard University Press, 1982).
96. Ntozake Shange, *For Colored Girls Who Have Considered Suicide: When the Rainbow is Enuf* (New York: Bantam Books, 1975), p. 67.
97. Marge Piercy, "Unlearning to Not Speak," in *Circles on the Water*, p. 97.

Permissions

Reprinted by permission of Atheneum Publishers, Inc.:
James Merrill, excerpted from "From the Cupola" in *Nights and Days*. Copyright © 1966 James Merrill.

Reprinted by permission of Cleis Press:
Alexandra Grilikhes, *On Women Artists: Poems 1975–1980* (Minneapolis: Cleis Press, 1981). Copyright © 1981 by Alexandra Grilikhes.

Reprinted by permission of Collection of American Literature, Beinecke Rare Book and Manuscript Library, Yale University and Perdita Schaffner:
Excerpt from H.D. to Bryher, March 23, 1933 (unpublished letter); Excerpt from H.D., "Because One is Happy," in *The Gift* (previously unpublished); Excerpt from H.D. journal, March 10, 1933; Excerpt from H.D., *Pilate's Wife*.

Reprinted by permission of the Crossing Press:
Excerpt from "Muteness," by Bella Akhmadulina in *Three Russian Women Poets*, edited by Mary Maddock. Copyright © 1983 by Mary Maddock.

Excerpt from alta, "euridice," in *I Am Not a Practicing Angel*. Copyright © 1975 by alta.

Reprinted by permission of Rachel Blau DuPlessis:
"Eurydice," in *Wells*, by Rachel Blau DuPlessis. (Montemora, 1980). Copyright © 1980 Rachel Blau DuPlessis.

Reprinted by permission of Farrar, Straus and Giroux, Inc:
Excerpt from "In Dedication" from *The White Goddess* by Robert Graves. Copyright © 1948 by International Authors N. V. Copyright renewed © 1975 by Robert Graves.

Excerpt from *Homage to Mistress Bradstreet* by John Berryman. Copyright © 1956 by John Berryman. Copyright renewed © 1984 by Mrs. Kate Berryman.

Reprinted by permission of Farrar, Straus and Giroux, Inc., and Ruth Limmer, Literary Executor, Estate of Louise Bogan.
Louise Bogan, *The Blue Estuaries*. Copyright © 1923, 1929, 1930, 1931, 1933, 1934, 1935, 1936, 1937, 1938, 1941, 1949, 1951, 1952, 1954, 1957, 1958, 1962, 1964, 1965, 1966, 1967, 1968 by Louise Bogan.

Reprinted by permission of Grafton Books, a Division of the Collins Publishing Group:
Excerpts from "Demeter in Sicily" in *Early Light: The Collected Poems of Dorothy Wellesley*, by Dorothy Wellesley. (London: Rupert Hart Davis, 1955.)

Reprinted by permission of Harcourt Brace Jovanovich, Inc.:
Excerpt from "Women," in *Revolutionary Petunias & Other Poems* (as reprinted in *In Search of Our Mothers' Gardens*) by Alice Walker. Copyright 1984.

Reprinted by permission of Harcourt Brace Jovanovich, Inc. and Faber and Faber Ltd.:
"Ash Wednesday" in *Collected Poems 1909–1962* by T. S. Eliot. Copyright 1936 by Harcourt Brace Jovanovich, Inc.; Copyright © 1963, 1964 by T. S. Eliot.

Reprinted by permission of Harper & Row Publishers, Inc.:
"Kaddish," from *Collected Poems 1947–1980* by Allen Ginsberg. Copyright © 1959 by Allen Ginsberg.

Reprinted by permission of International Creative Management, Inc.:
"The Poem as Mask," in *The Speed of Darkness* by Muriel Rukesyer. Copyright 1968 by Muriel Rukesyer.

Reprinted by permission of Kitchen Table Women of Color Press:
"For the Color of My Mother", "From a Heart of Rice Straw"
From *This Bridge Called My Back: Writings by Radical Women of Color*, edited by Cherrie Moraga and Gloria Anzaldua. (Persephone Press, 1981, reprinted by the Crossing Press.)

Reprinted by permission of Carolyn Kizer:
Carolyn Kizer, "A Muse of Water," in *The Ungrateful Garden*. (Bloomington, Indiana: Indiana University Press, 1961.) Copyright © 1961 by Carolyn Kizer.

Reprinted by permission of Alfred A. Knopf, Inc.:
Sylvia Plath, "The Disquieting Muses," in *The Colossus and Other Poems*. Copyright © 1962 by Sylvia Plath.

Reprinted by permission of Martin Secker & Warburg Limited:
"Muse," in *Way of All The Earth* by Anna Ahkmatova, translated by D. M. Thomas. Copyright 1979.

Reprinted by permission of New Directions Publishing Corporation:
Denise Levertov, *Relearning the Alphabet*. Copyright © 1970 by Denise Levertov Goodman.

"Song for Ishtar", "The Wall", "In Mind":
Denise Levertov, *Poems 1960–1970*. Copyright © 1961, 1962, 1963 by Denise Levertov Goodman. "The Wall" and "In Mind" were first published in *Poetry*.

"The Wanderer: A Rococo Study" in William Carlos Williams, *Collected Earlier Poems*. Copyright 1938.

William Carlos Williams, *Paterson*. Copyright 1948, 1949, by William Carlos Williams.

"Praise of Ysolt", "The Summons", "N.Y.":
Ezra Pound, *Personae*. Copyright 1926 by Ezra Pound. Reprinted by permission of New Directions (New York) and Faber & Faber, Ltd. (London).

Reprinted by permission of New Directions Publishing Corporation and Perdita Schaffner:
"Pygmalion", "Triplex", "All Mountains", "Huntress", "Moonrise", "Amaranth", "Eurydice", "Chance Meeting":
H.D., *Collected Poems: 1912–1944*. Copyright © 1982 by the Estate of Hilda Doolittle.

"The Walls do not Fall", "Tribute to Angeles", "The Flowering Rods":
H.D., *Trilogy*. Copyright © 1972 by Norman Holmes Pearson.

H.D., *Helen in Egypt*. Copyright © 1961 by Norman Holmes Pearson.

H.D., *Hermetic Definitions*. Copyright © 1972 by Norman Holmes Pearson.

H.D., *The Gift*. Copyright © 1982 by the Estate of Hilda Doolittle.

H.D., *End to Torment*. Copyright © 1979.

H.D., *Vale Ave. New Directions, 44* (1982), pp. 18–166.

Reprinted by permission of W. W. Norton and Co.:
"Autumn Sonnets", "My Sisters, O My Sisters", "Poets and the Rain", "Journey Toward Poetry", "These Images Remain", "The Return of Aphrodite", "A Divorce of Lovers", "The Furies", "A Storm of Angels", "After the Tiger", "The Godhead as Lynx", "The Muse as Medusa", "She Shall Be Called Woman", "An Invocation to Kali" "An Observation", "The Angels and the Furies", "Elegy for Louise Bogan":
From *May Sarton Collected Poems, 1930–1973*, by May Sarton. Copyright 1974.

"Letters from Maine" in From *Letters from Maine: New Poems*, by May Sarton. Copyright 1980.

"Of the Muse", "Control":
From *Halfway to Silence: New Poems*, by May Sarton. Copyright 1984.

"Aunt Jennifer's Tigers", "Women", "The Loser", "The Roofwalkers", "Lucifer in the Train", "The Insomniacs", "Orion", "Planetarium", "Snapshots of a Daughter-in-Law", "Night-Pieces: For a Child", "I Dream I'm the Death of Orpheus", "Letters: March 1969", "The Mirror in Which Two are Seen as One":
From *Poems, Selected and New, 1950–1974*, by Adrienne Rich. Copyright 1975.

"The Stranger", "Diving into the Wreck":
From *Diving into the Wreck: Poems 1971–1972*, by Adrienne Rich. Copyright 1973.

"Mother-Right", "Natural Resources", "Splittings", "Cartographies of Silence", "Transcendental Etude", "Phantasia for Elvira Shatayev", "Sibling Mysteries", "Power", "Hunger", "Twenty-One Love Poems":
From *The Dream of a Common Language: Poems 1974–1977*, by Adrienne Rich. Copyright 1978.

"Integrity", "Grandmothers", "Heroines", "The Spirit of Place", "Burden Baskets", "Holokam", "Mary Jane Colter, 1904", "Turning the Wheel", "Self-Hatred", "Particularity", "Apparition":
From *A Wild Patience Has Taken Me This Far: Poems 1978–1981*, by Adrienne Rich. Copyright 1981.

"Harriet", "A Song for Many Movements", "Meet", "Outside", "Woman", "Walking Our Boundaries", "Recreation", "From the Greenhouse", "Letter from Jan", "Scar", "From the House of Yemanja", "Dahomey", "125th Street and Abomey", "The Women of Dan Dance", "The Black Unicorn", "A Woman Speaks", "Power", "Solstice", "A Litany for Survival", "Chain":
From *The Black Unicorn: Poems*, by Audre Lorde. Copyright 1978.

"Coal", "Story Books on a Kitchen Table", "The Woman Thing", "Black Mother Woman", "Prologue", "A Family Resemblance", "Love Poem", "When the Saints Come Marching In", "The Winds of Orisha", "Afterimages", "Need: A Choral of Black Women's Voices", "October":
From *Chosen Poems – Old and New*, by Audre Lorde. Copyright 1982.

Excerpts from "For the Muses," in *Emily's Bread: Poems*, by Sandra M. Gilbert. (New York: W. W. Norton, 1984).

Reprinted by permission of Random House, Inc.:
"Network of the Imaginary Mother," in *Lady of the Beasts* by Robin Morgan. Copyright 1976.

"Phenominal Woman," in *And Still I Rise* by Maya Angelou. Copyright 1978.

"Miss Rosie," in *Good Times: Poems* by Lucille Clifton. Copyright 1969.

Reprinted by permission of the University of California Press:
Robert Creeley, "Air: The Love of a Woman," in *The Collected Poems 1945–1975*. Copyright © 1983 The Regents of the University of California.

Reprinted by permission of University of Maine Press:
"'A Primary Intensity Between Women': H.D. and the Female Muse," in *H.D.: Woman and Poet* by M. K. DeShazer. Copyright 1986.

Reprinted by permission of Viking Penguin Inc.:
"Teach Me, Dear Sister" in *Teach Me, Dear Sister* by Irving Feldman. Copyright © 1982 by Irving Feldman.

Excerpts from *Journey Around My Room: The Autobiography of Louise Bogan, A Mosaic by Ruth Limmer*. Copyright © 1980 by Ruth Limmer, Library Executor, Estate of Louise Bogan.

Reprinted by permission of Yale University Press:
Excerpts from *Beginning with O* by Olga Broumas. Copyright © 1977.

Index

About the Author

Mary K. DeShazer is Assistant Professor of English and Women's Studies at Xavier University in Cincinnati, Ohio. She received her B.A. from Western Kentucky University in 1971 and her M.A. from the University of Louisville in 1972, studied at Oxford University in 1980, and completed her Ph.D. at the University of Oregon in 1982. The author of articles on Louise Bogan, H.D., May Sarton, and other women poets, she considers modern poetry and global feminism her primary research interests. In addition, she has published essays on writing and women's studies, sexism and language, and feminist educational reform.

At Xavier University she teaches courses in poetry, women and creativity, and feminist literary criticism. She currently serves on the Coordinating Council of the National Women's Studies Association and as Regional Coordinator for the North Central Women's Studies Association. During the summer she co-directs the North Carolina Writing Project at Wake Forest University.

THE ATHENE SERIES

An International Collection of Feminist Books

General Editors: Gloria Bowles and Renate D. Klein

Consulting Editor: Dale Spender

MEN'S STUDIES MODIFIED The Impact of Feminism on the Academic Disciplines
Dale Spender, editor

WOMAN'S NATURE Rationalizations of Inequality
Marian Lowe and *Ruth Hubbard*

MACHINA EX DEA Feminist Perspectives on Technology
Joan Rothschild, editor

SCIENCE AND GENDER A Critique of Biology and Its Theories on Women
Ruth Bleier

WOMAN IN THE MUSLIM UNCONSCIOUS
Fatna A. Sabbah

MEN'S IDEAS/WOMEN'S REALITIES
Louise Michele Newman, editor

BLACK FEMINIST CRITICISM Perspectives on Black Women Writers
Barbara Christian

THE SISTER BOND A Feminist View of a Timeless Connection
Toni A.H. McNaron, editor

EDUCATING FOR PEACE A Feminist Perspective
Birgit Brock-Utne

STOPPING RAPE Successful Survival Strategies
Pauline B. Bart and *Patricia H. O'Brien*

TEACHING SCIENCE AND HEALTH FROM A FEMINIST PERSPECTIVE
A Practical Guide
Sue V. Rosser

FEMINIST APPROACHES TO SCIENCE
Ruth Bleier, editor

INSPIRING WOMEN Reimagining the Muse
Mary K. DeShazer